Princess Lieven

Princess Lieven

Russian Intriguer

by

MADELEINE BINGHAM

HAMISH HAMILTON LONDON

First published in Great Britain 1982
by Hamish Hamilton Limited
Garden House, 57–59 Long Acre, London WC2E 9JZ

Copyright © 1982 by Madeleine Bingham

British Library Cataloguing in Publication Data

Bingham, Madeleine
    Princess Lieven.
    1. Lieven, Dorothea, *Princess* – Biography
    2. Russia – History – 19th century
    I. Title
    947'.07'0924   DK188.6.L/
    ISBN 0-241-10269-3

Photoset and printed in Great Britain by
Redwood Burn Limited
Trowbridge, Wiltshire

Contents

Illustrations   vi

Preface   vii

1 The Background – German with Russian Connections   1
2 Marriage and Murder   14
3 Bonsi is prudent   27
4 Darja – Chronicles of Court and Society   35
5 Diplomatic Overture   47
6 Successes and Civilities   63
7 Un bien joli petit congrès   80
8 'L'esprit est toujours la dupe du coeur'   97
9 'What a loss for us all ...'   114
10 'I will regret Verona'   134
11 When in Rome ...   150
12 To visit our beloved Emperor ...   167
13 La Chute   183
14 A return home – to exile   202
15 Vous n'êtes plus seule   214
16 Twenty years of love and happiness   229
     Select Bibliography   249
     Index   253

Illustrations

1 Alexander I (Mansell Collection)   32

2 Peterhof. Early nineteenth-century engraving after Shotoshnikov   39

3 Dorothea Lieven by Sir Thomas Lawrence (Tate Gallery, London)   78

4 Prince Metternich by Sir Thomas Lawrence (Mansell Collection)   82

5 Christopher Lieven by Sir Thomas Lawrence (from a portrait formerly in the possession of Prince Alexander Lieven)   111

6 Lord Castlereagh by Sir Thomas Lawrence (National Portrait Gallery, London)   120

7 The 'Cottage' at Windsor (reproduced by gracious permission of H.M. the Queen)   141

8 George IV by James Gillray (National Portrait Gallery, London)   144

9 Nicholas I (Mansell Collection)   176

10 François Guizot (Engraving of the portrait by Paul Delaroche in British Museum)   212

11 Princess Lieven by G. F. Watts (Private Collection)   234

Preface

There is a generally accepted idea that Russia is a 'new' country, reborn in 1917. This is not true. It is a very old and unchanging country. And its agents and patriots are as unchanging as the country which nurtured them.

If the story of Dorothea Benckendorff, later Princess Lieven, is set in the context of her intense, unswerving loyalty to Russia, right or wrong, she can be seen as a skilled operator whose emotions as a woman were always, in the end, subordinated to her country's good. The background to her life reveals the same Russian policies as Russia follows today: the Baltic States swallowed up, the Poles made vassals, the same push towards the Mediterranean as Turkish power crumbled, the same eyes cast on Afghanistan, and at the end of the Napoleonic wars, as at the end of the Second World War, the same inclination to take all the credit for the victory.

Consider two reports:

Russia at present occupies, in a very eminent degree, the attention of the rest of Europe. Hitherto Europe may be said to have communicated its light to that country, but by a singular chance, it now would seem as if we expected from it light for ourselves.

This may give rise to a double error. First in looking forward for greater efforts from that country than can possibly be accomplished, and in under-rating the real merit of what is actually performed, and secondly in misleading the Russian nation itself, by over-rating its degree of culture and political powers.

Russia, which has always engrossed in a high degree the attention of Europe, is now playing a part which has spread uneasiness on all sides, and is exciting a feeling of curiosity ... There exists with regard to this country a profound state of ignorance kept up by books written in a spirit of complaisance and in which fiction has almost invariably usurped the place of truth.

The national historians do not possess the power of writing to the dictates of their consciences: it is the *gold* of the Government that determines the conclusion at which they arrive.

As to foreign travellers they are watched with such strictness that in respect of the impression produced on them during their travels they can hardly be supposed to bring back with them any more than just so much as the Russian police is kindly pleased to allow.

These two pieces are not from a recent newspaper article. The first was written by a German traveller, G. Reinbeck, in 1807, when Darja, afterwards to become Princess Lieven was twenty-two years old, before she came to England; and the second in 1854, towards the end of her long life, by a Frenchman, Germain de Lagny. Today they could be printed again without alteration.

Russia has never changed either in climate of weather, climate of thought, or climate of ambition. America is a new country which started afresh, but Russia is built upon layers and layers of old thought and old history, and expects today, as it did in the day of Darja, unquestioning obedience and unquestioning loyalty from its subservient subjects. Should either of these two fail, Russia will still inflict, as it did in the past, great cruelties on its recalcitrant countrymen and women. For most Russians there is no moral conflict involved in the slogan *My Country Right or Wrong*, for Mother Russia is always right, and never wrong.

Although of German origin, Dorothea Benckendorff, known to her family as Darja, was Russian to the depths of her soul, and the Tsar was her earthly God. Each Tsar she served had for her a mystic halo. One was murdered, another connived at the murder, a third usurped the crown. But none of that mattered to her – any more than the eccentricities of a General Secretary of the Russian Communist party worry a true Russian Communist today.

Darja's husband, Prince Lieven, was sent to England and remained in London for twenty-two years as Russian Ambassador to the Court of St. James. He could be relied upon never to put a foot wrong, and never to embarrass the Tsar or the Embassy. He was the perfect 'front' behind which his sparkling wife could carry on the real work for the Tsar.

Metternich, the great Austrian Chancellor, was her lover at a critical period in international diplomacy. François Guizot, who played an important role in French politics, was devoted to her for twenty years. During her years as wife of the colourless Russian Ambassador in London she was constantly in the society of the Prince Regent, later George IV. The Duke of Wellington, Castlereagh, Canning, Earl Grey, Palmerston – all the outstanding men of the period – were among her intimates.

In London society, most people accepted her because of her social position, her charm, vivacity and elegance. Others did not. They regarded her as a spy, and also what in modern Intelligence parlance would be called an agent of influence working to keep England's policy in line with the Tsar's wishes. She was undoubtedly both.

It could be argued that all embassies harbour spies and agents of influence from the ambassador downwards. But Darja sometimes went too far in her machinations. She has indeed always been portrayed as the classic archetypal intriguer who sought not only to influence, but to overthrow governments for personal satisfaction and the enjoyment of secret power. It is an over-simplification of the simple fact that she was a Russian patriot, an iron butterfly whom the Tsar was able to use.

Butterfly she was, endlessly fluttering among the most useful flowers in the social garden, scheming, influencing and gathering information that she faithfully sent back to St. Petersburg via the diplomatic bag. Iron she was because – whether well or badly treated by whichever Tsar happened to be reigning – her devotion to her country never wavered. She was Russian and a patriot to the depths of her being.

No great social occasion was considered complete without this charming and witty Russian guest. It was on these occasions that her uncanny talent-spotting ability was of such great use to the distant Tsar and his Foreign Office. A born collector of gossip as well as hard facts, she was able to predict the rise, or impending fall of everybody on the political and diplomatic scene, where this one was strong, and that one weak.

Small wonder that she was in such frequent communication with her brother Alexander. For services rendered to the Tsar Nicholas, Alexander was well rewarded and became head of the Tsar's Secret Police. Though not such a finely tempered instrument as its successor, it was in its day, an embryonic K.G.B. No wonder it was said in London that there were two Ambassadors – Prince Lieven and his wife. It was the second Ambassador whom the Tsar, the Secret Police, and the Russian policy makers all needed. For ironically it was thanks to his maritally unfaithful wife that the dull and uninspired Russian Prince kept his job for so long.

Did he know of his wife's affaire with Metternich, or was he the

Tsar-encouraged *mari complaisant*? While 'Bonsi', as Darja called him, nodded and smiled, Darja diligently wrote to her favourite brother. If Alexander was her favourite brother, Darja must have been his best-placed and favourite agent.

If Russia has not changed, her agents have not changed either – they have the same inbuilt unswerving patriotism, and the same acceptance of the blows and cruelties used against them.

Darja had both the patriotism, and the acceptance of cruelty.

CHAPTER ONE

The Background – German with Russian Connections

Dorothea von Benckendorff, afterwards Princess de Lieven, was descended from an old German family said to have been 'long settled in Livonia'. Her husband, Christopher Lieven, stemmed from the same race. The impression given is of benevolent landowners living on their estates surrounded by happy, rosy cheeked peasants. The reality was more sombre.

Dorothea and her husband were part of the German ruling class in the Baltic, the same race as the Teutonic Knights who had conquered those provinces in the thirteenth century. The unhappy land of Livonia was made up of part of modern Estonia and part of Latvia. This was the country laid waste and conquered by the Knights. For 200 years the Germans were masters of the country. Any attempt by the inhabitants to free themselves from the foreign yoke was answered by death and slavery. By the middle of the sixteenth century Livonia became the battleground of warring foreign armies. Ivan the Terrible invaded it in 1558. The Swedes and Poles marched in to redress the balance, and the Russians were beaten back. Livonia became first a Polish province and subsequently fell under Swedish rule. But at the beginning of the eighteenth century, the Russians and the Poles had decided to sink their differences. The way was clear for the Great Northern war against the Swedes.

It has been the custom for many modern historians to dismiss eighteenth-century wars as mere gentlemanly affairs, like stately, princely manoeuvrings or military minuets. The war in the Baltic provinces was not like that. All the towns in Estonia were destroyed, most of the inhabitants murdered, some who survived were herded into slavery in Central Russia. Such few peasants who remained on the land had their ears and noses cut off. Savage Bashkirs and Kalmuks burned and looted the countryside. This

1

war, known as the Great Wrath in Livonia, left the countryside a desert. The Russians took a more optimistic view of the outcome – Peter the Great received a triumphant message from his General, Cheremetiev: 'There is nothing left to destroy – not a cock crows from Lake Peipus and the Gulf of Riga.'

Ironically, the barbarities of the war had left the path clear for Peter the Great to found his great and civilised capital of Petersburg, and to give Russia a window into Europe.

The families of the Benckendorffs and the Lievens were part of the ruling class, the Germans who survived to administer the conquered lands. The Russians had no trained Civil Service, and, having effectively laid the country waste, they were forced to rely on the local landowners for administering what remained. The German ruling class had welcomed the Russian conquerors and they also welcomed the security which the Russian armies and Navy gave to them. All they wanted was to remain masters of their estates – and their serfs. Sensibly, they became part of the Russian ruling class, as had Catherine the Great, also a German. And like the great Empress they regarded themselves as Russians.

Dorothea's father was Baron Christopher Benckendorff. He had served in the Russian Army and risen to the rank of General and, at the time of Dorothea's birth in 1785, he was Military Governor of Riga. Darja was born in the Castle of Riga, well protected from the sights and sounds of the governed serfs, mere slaves who lived in appalling misery. This was reflected in the local newspaper – for three years after her birth the *Rigascher Anzeiger* was advertising: 'Four families of serfs are to be sold cheap. Buyers should apply to the Government Officer, 51 Schloss strasse.' A little earlier in 1777, Pastor Upel had written: 'These men go cheaper than niggers in the American Colonies. A man servant can be bought for 30 to 50 roubles, an artisan, cook, or weaver for anything up to one hundred roubles. The same price is asked for a whole family; a maidservant rarely costs more than 10 roubles, and children can be bought for 4 roubles each. Agricultural workers and their children are sold or bartered for horses, dogs, – and even tobacco pipes.'

Once the Russians had defeated the Swedish Empire, and were about to dispose of the Polish threat, the German ruling classes, with their passion for order, were only too happy to please the conquering Russians, and they made the Baltic lands the best governed provinces in the Russian Empire. It could have been said of these countries, as it was said of Poland, it was heaven for the nobility, paradise for the clergy, a source of gold for the adventurer, and hell for the peasants.

Fortunately for Darja Benckendorff she belonged to the nobility from whom were drawn empresses, governors and administrators of the vast Russian lands.

Darja's mother, Baroness Charlotte Schilling, had been brought to Russia as maid of honour to Sophia Dorothea of Württemberg, niece of Frederick the Great, who married the Grand Duke Paul, son of Catherine II. She was the Grand Duke's second wife, the first having died in childbirth. Because of these connections, from her early childhood Darja was never far from the throne and the levers of power in Russia. When it came to her education the Grand Duchess took a personal interest in the progress of the Benckendorff family. Darja and her sister were sent to the Smolny Institute. The Empress Elizabeth had founded the Smolny Convent originally as a school for orphans. The Empress Catherine, herself well and deeply self-educated, had little regard for the idea of creating what she sarcastically called '300 brides of Christ'. The Empress was anxious that girls of Russian aristocratic families should follow in her footsteps.

There was, as the Empress realised, a crying need for female education. The model she had chosen was that of the Convent of St. Cyr which had been founded by Madame de Maintenon. But Catherine, child of an enlightened century, did not wish to staff her college with nuns. She only wished to emulate the idea, without bringing in the piety and narrow instruction she felt might be the result of allowing nuns to teach in her *Maison d'education de demoiselles nobles*. Her *demoiselles nobles* must have wider and better instruction than mere pious practices. Catherine gave new statutes to the Convent, and gradually managed to ease the nuns and novices out. The Smolny Convent became the Smolny Institute. Catherine always took a deep interest in her *jeunes filles nobles*. She wrote to Voltaire: 'You know – for nothing escapes you – that five hundred young ladies are being educated in a house which was formerly designed for three hundred brides of heaven. The young ladies, I confess, far surpass our expectations. They make astonishing progress and everyone admits that they are as lovable as they are knowledgeable. Their conduct is justly regarded as blameless without having at the same time that strict and stern manner of the cloister.'

Other commentators noted that the officers of the nearby barracks kept a sharp eye on the young ladies, and were inclined to marry the prettiest ones, on their emerging from the chrysalis of their educational institute.

The building itself was designed by Rastrelli, the cupolas of the central church dominating the building, which was described as being lighter and more charming than the Winter Palace itself, with white columns and pilasters with bronzed capitals contrasting against a tender turquoise blue. The Smolny Institute stood out starkly against the winter ice of the frozen Neva.

It was here that Darja began her education, an education which looked outwards towards Europe rather than inwards towards Russia. She learned to speak and write in French, German and English. Even her religion was different from that of her Russian homeland, belonging as she did to the Baltic German ascendancy, her family was Protestant and she had been baptised in the Lutheran faith. At the time of her birth this does not seem to have been a disadvantage as so many of the dominating personalities in and around the Russian court were of German origin and Russia was governed by a German empress. But everything which Darja learned at the Smolny Institute, from her knowledge of several foreign languages, from her instinctively graceful and good manners, to her love and practice of music, was to prove useful to her in the course to which fate, and her future husband's career were to lead her. Here, protected from the outside world the *jeunes filles nobles* were tended and trained like the delicate hothouse plants they were to become.

A Frenchman, Louis Réau, wrote that it was in winter that the Polar Venice should be seen. Then, under a sky the colour of steel, the trees powdered with hoar frost stood stiffly and strangely, like a fabulous white coral forest. The snow stretched across Petersburg, a huge mantle of ermine which blended perfectly with its cold beauty, a beauty which became iridescent with nuances of colour from a milky whiteness to the delicacy of a rainbow opalescence, to a pearl grey or blue the colour of flax.

It is to be wondered whether the young girls studying and giggling under the strict supervision of their governesses were as enamoured of a winter which kept them locked in their seminary. Did Darja not dream of the unlocking of the great river when the spring came; when April sent the huge blocks of ice drifting out towards the Gulf of Finland and the lands beyond? In some senses this was to be a symbol of her life. For she was destined early to be detached from her Russian background.

While the *jeunes filles nobles* were carefully tended in their polite academy, the realities of the Russian struggles for power which beset the throne were less polite.

Catherine II had been implicated in the plot which ended in the murder of her husband, and now, as Darja was growing up, further plots were casting shadows around the throne. Catherine, aware of the growing instability of her son, had told his German wife, Maria Feodorovna, that he must be passed over in favour of his son

Alexander. But Maria, perhaps still hoping to win the affections of her husband back, or perhaps fearing his future power over her, had refused to sign the letter sanctioning this. It had been the custom for the Tsars to appoint their successors, a system lending itself readily to plotting and to murders. Catherine herself had no claim to the throne of Russia over which she had ruled so successfully for more than thirty years. Now old and approaching her end, she had no longer the energy to enforce her will. Or perhaps, like Queen Elizabeth I, she felt that by not facing the fact of her own death, it could be pushed aside.

Catherine II died in 1796, when Darja was ten, and Paul I came to the throne of all the Russias. He was forty-two and had been at odds with his mother Catherine for most of his life. She had taken his sons, Alexander and Constantine, away from him and educated them under her own supervision. Deprived of power, he had become more and more eccentric, devoting himself to Prussian military ceremonies and the niceties of intricate methods of drilling.

But as soon as his mother died the flood-tide of his resentment was unleashed. While the young girls of the Smolny Institute applied themselves to their lessons, their beloved and noble Tsar was having his alleged father's body dug up in order to place a crown on its rotting skull and to have it carried into church to be more greatly honoured than the remains of his mother who had reigned with such distinction over Russia for so long. But these were not Darja's recollections of her future Tsar. She remembered him coming to the Institute. He had amused himself and joined in their childish games. She remembered him playing Blind Man's Buff. Others joined in the game – the last King of Poland, the Prince de Condé and Marshall Souvaroff. Even Blind Man's Buff was played on a high aristocratic level at the Smolny Institute. The future Tsar was in cheerful mood and as Darja put it: 'fit mille folies très gaies et toujours convenables'. It would never have done to shock the *jeunes filles nobles*.

Even in jolly games Darja had always been surrounded by the highest in the land. Perhaps the strange split in the character of the Tsar was not made apparent under the circumstances in which the young girl first saw him. There was always an admiring, almost religious attitude amongst Russians, even adopted Russians like the Benckendorffs, for the person of the Tsar. It was, perhaps, an admiration compounded of fear for the absolute power which the Tsar wielded, and a certain self-interest and regard for the hands from which all benefits were likely to flow.

A year after the death of the Empress Catherine, Charlotte,

5

Darja's mother, followed her to the grave. The Empress Maria Feodorovna, wife of the Tsar Paul, took as acute an interest in the Smolny Institute as had its founder. She was devoted to Charlotte Benckendorff, who had been one of her favourite Court ladies, and whom she had brought with her from Germany at the time of her marriage to the future Tsar. Darja's mother had stayed at Court with the Empress even after her own marriage to Baron Benckendorff, but the increasing instability, not to say madness, of Paul, and the intrigues of his mistress Mlle. Nelidova had caused the Grand Duke to dismiss Madame Benckendorff from Court. Maria Feodorovna had complained to the ageing Empress Catherine before her death. But the Empress had already given up her son as a human being whose actions could be regarded as sane or predictable. She is alleged to have taken her daughter-in-law to the looking-glass and said: 'Look at yourself, and then think of the little monster's face.' But the little monster had his way, and Baroness von Benckendorff was banished. In 1797 the news reached Maria Feodorovna, now Tsarina, that her darling 'Lilli' was dangerously ill in Berne.

Maria Feodorovna by this time had become reconciled to her husband's now deposed mistress, Mlle. Nelidova, and wrote to her saying that her poor Lilli was causing the greatest alarm to her doctors. The Tsarina was afflicted to the depths of her soul. If God should take Lilli from this world she would lose the friend of her childhood, and the most virtuous of women. Forgetting perhaps that it was through the intrigues of Nelidova that Lilli had been driven abroad the Tsarina wished that 'you had known her better as I did, and you would have loved her as I do'. In the absence of news the Tsarina still hoped and prayed. It was all in vain, Lilli died leaving the two girls and their brothers motherless. The Tsarina immediately took the girls under her wing, and acted as their adopted mother. Charlotte had died at the end of May, and by early June they had been brought to the palace, to visit her so that she could concern herself with their welfare and their progress. The girls were not content with a visit to the Palace, they were anxious to be out in the great world and complained at not yet having been officially received at Court.

The Tsarina sent a message through their father that at their tender age 'retreat was essential, especially as the girls had been deprived of a mother to guide and counsel them in the great world'. She was quite prepared to bring them every fortnight to the theatre performances at the Hermitage, but they were not to go to Court before the correct age. Count Benckendorff was entirely satisfied with the arrangements which the Tsarina was making for his

6

daughters. Even Mlle. Nelidova who, having lost her power over the Tsar, had retreated to apartments at the Smolny Institute, was also keeping a watch on the girls. Nelidova wrote that she had heard from Madame de Calemberg (presumably one of their *institutrices*) that she was very pleased with them, and she herself found 'les petites Benckendorffs' very interesting as did 'their august protectress'.

Darja's progress whether from the point of view of birth, education, or patronage began under auspicious stars. She was the eldest of the two girls, and was considered to be educated by the time she had reached the age of fourteen. She spoke and wrote four languages, Russian, French, English and German. But like many educated Russians of the period, French was the medium in which she thought best, and in which she wrote and conversed most easily. Her other accomplishment was music.

At fourteen Darja was held to be quite ready for marriage, and the Tsarina looked around her court for suitable partners for her protégée.

Reinbeck, a German inhabitant of St. Petersburg, writing on the subject of marriage in Russia stated quite baldly: 'Happy marriages among persons of fashion and high rank are a great rarity in all countries, but nowhere more so than in Russia. Interest or subserviency to family arrangements is the universal principle on which matches are formed ... Youth is indispensable in every case. For a girl of 18 in Russia is almost past the desirable age.'

Darja was therefore considered ripe for marriage, and perhaps she was judged by the Tsarina to be overripe, for at the age of eleven she had already fallen in love. Years later she wrote of the passion she had at that age. 'I had already been asked in marriage by a young man, very handsome and intelligent. He was an extremely suitable husband, as regards both birth and fortune, and my mother, who was still alive at that time, encouraged his suit.'

But the Tsarina had other plans for the girl, and one day she came into Darja's room and took possession of all her letters including the love letters from Count Elmpt, her beloved. Darja remarked that even the love affairs of little girls were treated with military strictness. She was handed over to a stricter governess, and the sentimental *gouvernante*, who had acted as go-between, was handed over to two police dragoons and escorted – with great promptitude – over the frontier. The Tsarina's word was law even when it came to a love match.

Maria Feodorovna's choice for Dorothea was Count Arakcheiev, at that time a favourite of the Tsar. The Tsarina was already feeling the insecurity of her position, and the Tsar's increasingly clouded mind had turned against his wife. Everyone was suspected of plotting against him. Count Arakcheiev may have seemed a suitable choice to help the Tsarina, but he was a man whom the young Darja held in horror. He was instrumental in carrying out many of the brutal and savage orders of the Tsar, and, it was said, lent himself happily to the trade of executioner. Like the Tsar, the Count was a stickler for military etiquette and was said to have torn off a soldier's ear with his teeth when in a fit of military rage. Fortunately for Darja and the Empress, in the general atmosphere of suspicion, the Count fell from favour, and the marriage negotiations were dropped.

It was then that the Tsarina fixed on Count Lieven as a second choice. He was the son of the Baroness Lieven, a woman of high influence and power at the Russian Court. Her story was curious.

She had been left a widow by Baron Lieven, an artillery general of uxorious propensities, by whom she had fourteen children. Without fortune she had been forced to leave Kiev when he died, and went back to Riga in Livonia, the country from which she had originally come. Not only was she without fortune, but her husband had left what little money he had to found a Lutheran church at Kiev. Livonia was a poor country owing to the wars and oppressions which it had suffered. The serfs, held in tight slavery by the ruling classes, saw no reason to produce food for their masters, and so governed and governors were reduced to the same state of miserable poverty. Having sold some of her goods, the Baroness Lieven established herself with her large family in a house in Riga where she lived in penury and obscurity. But she was not so obscure that her name had not been mentioned to the great Catherine, who was seeking a woman of character to direct the education of her grandsons. The moulding of the characters of these two splendid boys was not to be left to their father.

One morning the Governor-General of the Province, Count Broron-Camus, came to the Baroness's house. He was the direct messenger of the Empress and arrived with a call to the widow to come directly to court to take over the education of the Empress's grandchildren.

From the imperial level at which the appeal was made it had more the appearance of a royal *ukase*, a command which could not be denied, than an offer of advancement. But, in spite of this, and the perils which a denial of the Tsarina's wishes could entail, the widow refused. It was possible that she had already heard of the dissensions which existed between the Tsarina and her son, and did not want to get drawn into the cat's cradle of imperial differences. It was also possible that she was repelled by all that she had heard of the morals of the Empress and did not wish to get involved in Court and sexual intrigues. The Baroness sternly rejected the offer, giving no reasons for her refusal, except that she had daughters growing up and did not want to live in St. Petersburg. The Count persisted in his negotiations, but the widow held her ground. He then pointed out to the lady that three of her small sons were running about the room barefoot.

'You would at least have the wherewithal to buy shoes for your sons,' he said.

She blushed, and, after a brief hesitation, finally said: 'Very well. It will be for *them* that I shall try.'

The Baroness was received at the Imperial Palace by Countess Branicka who asked: 'Why did you not want to take on the education of the Tsarina's grandchildren?'

The widow did not disguise her reasons but baldly stated that it was the Tsarina's disorderly life in which she did not want to involve herself, or her family. It was a courageous statement which could have brought death to herself, and dire consequences to her fourteen fatherless children. Although a German by birth, Catherine had become the classic Russian despot. Like the Fates, she held the threads of the life and death of her subjects in her hands. Like the Fates she could snap those threads at any moment at her will.

There was a sudden noise during the interview between the courtier Countess and the poor Baroness, and from behind a screen came Catherine herself. She appeared unruffled, and not in the least angry at the references to her mode of life. She looked at the Baroness and spoke at last: 'You will see nothing of that.'

The great autocrat, the dictator, the woman of unbridled appetites, took the young woman by the arm and leading her into the park, sat beside her on a bench. For more than an hour the Tsarina cross-questioned Baroness Lieven – her acute mind probed into the widow's ideas, and from them she assessed the young woman's moral stature. No doubt, like many libertines, she could value moral worth – in others. The conversation ended with the Tsarina's words: 'The more I listen to you, the more you inspire me with confidence. You are absolutely the woman I need.'

It was not possible to refuse. The Baroness accepted the task which had been imposed on her. But whatever the difficulties of the role assigned to her, which she was to fulfil with firmness and solicitude, one thing she did retain: her independence. The grandmother Tsarina could pass on her ideas as to the general tenor of the boys' education, but, in the view of the Imperial Governess, the parents had a role which could not be left out of account. The widowed Madame Lieven never flinched at crossing swords with the Tsarina, and often declared that, rather than allow anything which was injurious to the parents' authority, she would leave her post. It was a threat which allowed the Imperial Governess to govern. Her features, as she began to age, showed a woman with some physical attractions, strong willed and capable, but with an understanding heart. All her life she was held in high esteem by her pupils, and by their father, the Tsar Paul I, and by his successor, Alexander I, who always paid tribute to her influence in forming his intellect.

From living in poverty in Riga with her fourteen children, the Baroness, by the sheer strength of her will, had become one of the great servants of the State. Her situation at Court was unique. From the beginning of her devoted service, the Baroness Lieven was the trusted friend and confidante of the powerful Catherine, she was loved by her pupils, and looked up to by her inferiors and envied by her equals. No courtier dared to criticise her words or actions. Any move against her would have been a perilous mistake.

The children of the Imperial Governess were naturally in a position to benefit from the rewards which their mother had won by her services. Her three elder sons joined the Imperial army and were quickly promoted to positions of power and influence. Charles became Major-General and ADC to Souvaroff. Jean was also promoted to General.

Christopher, the youngest of Baroness Lieven's sons, had a more malleable character than those of his two brothers. At the time when Maria Feodorovna's eye fell on him as a suitable match for Darja Benckendorff, he was already twenty-seven, and for three years had been ADC to the Tsar Paul I, and had been given the portfolio of Minister of War. He was in daily consultation with the Tsar and under his direct authority.

From the swift rise of his career and the important posts which he subsequently filled, it might be thought that Christopher Lieven shared the brilliance of his brothers, but this is proved to be an erroneous view. He was regarded by many people as sharing his mother's rigid views, but lacking her strength of character – or her courage. But all that was for the future. At the age of fourteen Darja was to be married to a handsome young man with a brilliant career before him.

The Tsar himself had approved the marriage, and both the Benckendorff and Lieven families were agreed on the terms of the settlements. Madame Lieven was happy to have found a *jeune fille noble* who had the additional advantage of bringing a suitable dowry to the union. General Benckendorff was equally happy to have found a husband for his daughter who was so well-placed as to assure to him, and to his family, the patronage of the Tsar. Under so capricious a ruler as Paul I, it was as well for his family to be under the care of one so well-loved – and well-placed – as the Imperial Governess. There was only one thing lacking, it was for the young people to fall in love, and this they seem obediently to have done.

At the moment of her marriage – she was two months from her fifteenth birthday – Darja was a slim girl, too slim for early nineteenth-century taste, very tall, and she was still likely to grow taller, with a flat bosom and a long ungraceful neck. But all her imperfections were redeemed by her grace of movement, swift like that of a dancer, and the sparkle of her demeanour and attitudes. Her large dark eyes reflected her vivacious intelligence. But now, at the beginning of her life, she had a frivolous nature, which was hardly surprising in a girl of fourteen just out of school.

She was never to be a woman of great learning, or to probe into the depths of the philosophical content and meaning of life. Brought up from a young age in courts, and with courtiers, her tastes always inclined to the social, and eventually to the political. She was always to interest herself in people and their actions, or their projected actions, rather than in intellectual pursuits.

But now at the beginning of her life, she was to be presented with a handsome husband, and the opening of a door into the great world beyond her *pension de jeunes filles*.

She was married in St. Petersburg on 24 February 1800. Many years later she wrote of how delighted she was with her beautiful clothes, and how well her wedding dress suited her. The Tsarina had lent Darja her diamonds for the occasion and ushered her into the presence of the Tsar Paul. 'He led me into his drawing room to show me to his Court. I should have liked to get married every day, and I thought of everything – except that I was taking a husband.'

They were presumably married according to their Lutheran rites, in spite of their Court connections. This was possibly just as well, for Reinbeck has some harsh words to say about Russian marriages. Having remarked on the formality and self-interest on which they were founded, he wrote, 'But as divorces according to the Greek church are very rarely granted, they endeavour to lighten the burden for themselves as much as possible by making all the separation which lies in their power. . . . The most powerful chain which nature has formed for the restraint of female desires, namely bashful modesty is almost unknown among the fair sex of Russia, and even should something like it exist in the virgin state, the nuptial ceremony is well-fitted for its complete removal; it being

11

customary for every marriage rite to be consummated previously to the departure of the company who on being apprised of it by the display of certain signs return their congratulations to the new-married pair.'

The Court into which Dorothea Benckendorff was to be introduced was a curious mixture of splendour, culture, and immense riches. Yet the ostensible civilisation was wafer thin.

Reinbeck described a ball supper which he had attended at the end of Catherine's reign. While Catherine watched her charming grandchildren dancing, the future Tsar Paul stood by clad in red velvet, looking puffy and uninterested in the proceedings. The Grand Marshal announced that supper was ready.

The Tsarina rose and the dancing and the music immediately ceased ... the Processions were preceded by a great number of pages carrying silver sconces. All followed her in crowds into the hall where the table was extended in the form of a horse-shoe and everything was united that taste and splendour could produce in order to excite sensuality. The effect of the whole, of the gold and silver vessels, of the rich liveries about the table, and of the splendid circle that was admitted to it, surpasses all description.

The Tsarina left the table, smiling and gracious followed by her grandchildren.

Suddenly the whole scene changed and presented an image of primitive chaos. I saw the fruits and blossoms, the ribands and flowers torn off; I saw pockets filled with the remaining fruit and confectionery, and the servants, apprehensive of going away quite empty, mixed among the high nobility, and availed themselves of their house-right; so that all depended on who could grasp the most. Several pieces of plate are said to have disappeared on that evening. I stood in the crowd like one who was petrified, and exerted my utmost endeavour to avoid the kicks and blows; but to escape was impossible; indeed this was not the conclusion which I ever could have expected of such a fête.

It was that brooding figure in dark red velvet, the man who had played so cheerfully with Darja at Blind Man's Buff in her *pension de jeunes filles* who was to involve the young Lievens in his own dark destiny.

Like the banquet, which was one minute a source of pleasure to the eye with its bright blossoms, its sparkling gold and silver, and the band playing softly in the background, the next, total chaos, Christopher Lieven was to discover that from being a trusted employee and servitor of the Tsar, he was suddenly to be confronted with an abyss.

CHAPTER TWO

Marriage and Murder

The young couple set up their home in the centre of St. Petersburg not far from the Winter Palace, for Lieven's duties as War Minister and aide-de-camp to the Tsar meant that he was in constant attendance at the Court. When he was away, his young wife missed him, and was frequently at pains to express her love for him in her letters to her favourite brother Alexander. When General Benckendorff married off his daughter, he had left his two sons, Alexander and Constantine, in St. Petersburg to finish their education. His other daughter, Maria, who was also in Petersburg, had been promoted to lady-in-waiting and was living at Court. In spite of their motherless state the Benckendorffs were excellently placed to succeed in life.

Some few weeks after her marriage Darja wrote to Alexander: 'Believe me, my dearest Alexander, I suffer as much as you in being deprived of seeing you. I need your presence to complete my happiness. It is impossible for me to describe this happiness to you. You know my husband (with what pleasure I am able to call him by this name), you will be able to understand how I love him, and how completely happy I am. Come and see me soon.'

Her love for her husband and her brother spilled over in effusions of girlish sentiment which were a sincere expression of the happiness, the fulfilment and the expansion of her life as a married woman. Everything pleased her. Everyone smiled on her. It was hard not to see a whole lifetime of pleasure and amusement stretching in front of her. Her days were spent in the duties attendant upon her husband's position, whether at Court, or *en ville* as she put it, she attended all the social functions, and basked in the reflected glory of her husband, who in his turn owed all his eminence to the power and stern character of his mother, the Baroness.

But behind this glittering façade the clouds were gathering. The strange capriciousness of the Tsar was now verging on madness, favourites rose and fell like bright comets and were as speedily extinguished. The Turkish ex-barber Kutaissov – a valet risen to rank and riches – had ousted Nelidova, the mistress. He had been elevated to the rank of Chief Master of the Wardrobe, and rewarded with huge sums of money and estates. But this was not enough to satisfy his ambitions. His avarice sated, he had set his eyes on further elevation. He demanded the glittering Star of St. Anne. The Tsar listened, the smile left his face and he struck the ex-barber across the face, and called for him to be thrown out of the room. But Kutaissov threw himself on the mercy of the Tsarina, and the ex-mistress Nelidova. The two women, who were by now allies in an increasingly hostile sea of uncertainties, decided that Kutaissov with his passion for intrigue was best enlisted on their side. They interceded for him with the Tsar – and the favourite was restored.

Although Kutaissov had a huge palace of his own in the capital, he made it his business to be at the Winter Palace day and night. Like some soothsayer he felt he would be able to gauge and interpret his master's fitful moods and pander to his every passing whim. When the Tsar banished faithful servants to torture and exile, called home his victorious general, and turned the Russian defeat of Prussia into a Prussian victory, the soft voice of the ex-valet told the Tsar that his swift decisions had turned dark December into spring. It was Easter all the year round, and jewelled gifts of eggs were in order on every day of the year, under the happy aegis of the beloved Tsar.

Among the caprices of his master which the ex-barber had encouraged was the building of the St. Michael's Palace. Kutaissov had often heard his master express his hatred of the Winter Palace. Why should he not build himself a better and more splendid palace which did not bear the imprint of the mother he had loathed? By one of those happy coincidences which so often guide the actions of rulers, the favourite heard that one of the sentries on guard at the Winter Palace had received a brief visit from the Archangel St. Michael. The ex-barber was well aware that the clouded mind of the Emperor could be governed by signs and visions. Was this vision of the sentry not a bright omen to guide his beloved Tsar? Paul decided that the favourite had reflected his very own thoughts. St. Michael would give him special protection from the enemies by whom he now felt himself to be surrounded.

The castle was commenced and proved to be a vast and ugly conglomeration of buildings and styles. For his protection the Tsar insisted on a deep moat whose waters were diverted from the

15

Fontanka Canal. There were five drawbridges, and several gateways destined to be manned day and night by soldiers specially chosen by Paul. There were courtyards and colonnades surrounding an enormous building of three storeys which was granite below and red marble above, with a roof painted a vicious green. The inside was painted in brilliant red, but no ingenuities of the engineers could keep out the terrible damp which seeped into the building from the waters of the canal. Some of the important state rooms had ice clinging to the cornices. Through the window frames the fog seeped in. Fungi sprouted from the satin-panelled walls of the bedrooms, and the Grand Duchess Anne's rooms were invaded by slugs.

The Tsar Paul surveyed the monstrous edifice which he had created, and finding it good, said: 'Here I was born and here I shall die!'

It was to prove one of the few truths which he ever uttered.

During the year 1800, while Darja was settling down to married life, being bored while visiting various Imperial Highnesses (to whom her husband insisted she should be polite and attentive), the plots around the Tsar grew. While perfectly innocent officers were sent to exile, or condemned to be flayed alive by the 'knout', the black thoughts of the courtiers around the mad Tsar were being translated into action.

It has been suggested that Darja knew nothing of these tortures or of the plots. But the dark despairs of the people at Court could not have failed to penetrate to the young couple. Bacon said: 'Suspicions amongst thoughts are like bats among birds – they ever fly by twilight.' Whatever suspicions the young Lievens might have had, it was wise to know nothing, to see nothing, to hear nothing – and to remember nothing.

Later in her life Dorothea recalled, with some truth, her feelings at the time. She wrote: 'The dark and confused character of the Tsar had in the last year (1800) taken on a terrifying aspect. In his eyes the most trivial actions assumed the proportion of a plot. He would arbitrarily condemn men and women to destitution and exile. The Fortress was ever ready to receive his numberless victims. It only needed a waistcoat which was too long, or a jacket too short. In the Tsar's mind they had been one of the causes of the French Revolution; if he saw anyone wearing one in the street the man was immediately taken into custody.'

The French Revolution had undoubtedly been a great shock to Paul I, and from the moment of the downfall of the Bourbons, he saw Jacobins everywhere. Jacobins wore round hats, so the first act of the new reign was an attack *à l'outrance* against round hats,

16

waistcoats, and dress coats. As soon as Catherine II was dead, over two hundred police were out combing the streets. They had their orders – to snatch round hats from the heads of all found wearing them and destroy them. Frock coats were to have their collars cut away, and although waistcoats were totally proscribed their disposition could be left to the lower ranks of sub-officers and corporals.

Darja heard the news of what was happening in the city. 'In the last six weeks more than a hundred officers of the Imperial Guard were thrown into prison. My husband had the misfortune to be the person to carry out these iniquitous orders. Everyone trembled before the Tsar.' She went on to explain that the simple soldiers loved their Tsar, for, in spite of the excessive drilling and disciplines with which he loaded them, largesse followed which consoled them. 'His cruelties towards the officers were always compensated by huge sums of money scattered to the soldiers.'

Then, as if to excuse her husband's lack of action during the events which followed, Darja added, 'in spite of his violence and his extravagances the Tsar had real and true qualities which could be admired. He was great and noble, a generous enemy, a magnificent friend, knowing how to pardon with generosity, or to right a wrong or an injustice with overflowing kindness.' Her explanation was that because the Tsar had absolute power, power (that creator of monsters) had overtaken the good in his character.

Fortunately for Darja, her husband had not suffered from the cruelties of his master; discreet, and possibly lacking the character which is needed to destroy tyrants, Christopher Lieven had managed to walk the tightrope of courtier to the Tsar without offending. There had been one difficult moment. The Tsar had sent one of his aides-de-camp to his War Minister to tell him – quite simply – that he was an idiot. It was not an easy assignment for a colonel to hurl this insult in the face of the Minister of War, but Christopher Lieven stood his ground – he passed over the insult. 'It was', wrote Darja, 'the only bad moment which my husband had to suffer at the hands of the Tsar.' That statement says much for the tact of the lady's husband, and does much to explain his absence in the moments of crisis.

But even for the young Lievens, the hours were ticking away. At the beginning of March 1801 the Count was ill. He had been ill for some days. It is difficult not to suspect that his illness was overlaid with the suspicion that his days as one of the trusted colleagues of the Tsar were numbered.

Paul must have suspected something, for he sent the Count a letter to his sick-bed. 'Your illness has been too prolonged, and as

17

public business can hardly be altered to suit your blisterings and the disposition of your blood, you must give the Portfolio of Minister of War to Prince Gagarine.'

Then there was another change of mood. Count Lieven heard the news that the Tsar, on the insistence of Gagarine himself, and in order to mitigate the harshness of his loss, had promoted him – on the day of his dismissal – to the rank of Lieutenant-General. In spite of this sop, Lieven went to bed in an uneasy state of mind, and fell asleep.

There was no doubt that he must have known of the black shadows which were increasingly surrounding the Tsar. If no-one had told him specifically what was planned, he could hardly have been unaware that the fate of Paul hung in the balance. There are many things which hover in the back of the mind, but can never be admitted to the light of day.

Count Panin had originally devised the plot.

Many had murmured against the horrors and injustices of Paul's rule, but Nikita Panin was the sole person who had summoned the courage to act against the Tsar. The Vice-Chancellor was aware of the tortures, murders and banishments, but these did not force him into action. It was his strong feelings as a Russian patriot which thrust him forward. The Tsar had never listened to his advice. He preferred to heed the valet-barber Kutaissov who flattered and cosseted him. Count Panin had seen the victories and achievements of the great Catherine thrown away. It was too much for his patriotism, and his sense of honour as a Russian and a distinguished soldier.

Everyone was now convinced that the Tsar was mad. Torture and death awaited those who raised their voices. The living flesh could be torn from their bones and it was necessary to move with caution.

Panin was well placed to instigate the deposing of the Tsar for it was only a person who was on terms of close friendship with the Imperial family who could set such a plan *en train*. He spoke openly to the Grand Duke Alexander, saying that the nation and Empire demanded that he, Alexander should take over the reins as co-regent with his father. Although Panin spoke words which the Grand Duke wished to hear, Alexander shied away from the implications. What if the plan should fail?

Admittedly in England the Prince Regent had taken over from his mad father, but Russia was not England. And the shadows of unguessed punishments hovered over the Imperial family itself. Rumours abounded. Alexander's mother, Maria Feodorovna, was

18

to be sent to a convent in Kholmogory, near Archangel not far from the Arctic circle, Alexander's brother Constantine was destined for the Citadel in St. Petersburg, and he himself was to be banished to the fortress of Schlusselberg. His father's words: 'Very shortly I shall be compelled to cut down heads that once were dear to me' had been relayed to him. No one was safe. The Fortress, like a drawn sword, menaced Alexander as it did so many others. He was aware of the morass into which Russia had sunk during the four years of his father's reign. But to express one's feelings had become more and more dangerous during those four years, when banishment, floggings and violent punishments had become everyday occurrences. Censorship was the rule. Foreign books were forbidden, even the printing of books in Russia had become difficult. Everyone knew that correspondence was opened. It was the day of secret ink, and requests for the burning of letters became a usual postscript.

But in spite of the dangers of writing letters, and even more deadly of writing letters to Switzerland, Grand Duke Alexander in his distress wrote to his old liberal Republican tutor, La Harpe: 'My unhappy country is now in a state of chaos which cannot be described... Security is well-nigh destroyed... Trade is almost at a standstill... If and when my turn comes I shall have to dedicate myself to my country, and not let it become a toy in a madman's hands.'

Count Woronzov, the Russian Ambassador to England, had been recalled by the Emperor, but he prudently took the view that he was wiser to stay where he was. He wrote to a fellow Russian, Novozylskov, who happened to be in England, and to whom he could write freely: 'Try all I can I am unable to find any comfort in the thought of the future. It is as if you and I were on a vessel of which the crew spoke a language that was unintelligible to us. I am seasick and cannot rise from my berth. You tell me that a storm has risen and that there is no hope for the ship and that the Captain has gone mad and is showering blows on the crew.'

It was against this background that the plots were spreading like the fungi sprouting on the walls of the St. Michael's Palace. At first the Grand Duke pushed aside Panin's suggestions that he could be the saviour of his country. But he did this in such a way that the subject was not considered to be tabu, and could be repeated. Little by little, like the soft drip of spring rains on a parched earth, Alexander's mind was prepared, and he began to give a sympathetic ear to the suggestions. The plots advanced slowly. The Tsar was to be deprived of power, forced to give up the crown, the Grand Duke was to act as Regent. But as the body of conspirators grew in

19

numbers the plots became more difficult to control.

Count Panin had the confidence of Alexander but was not close to the Tsar. It was necessary to win over Count Pahlen, who was in the confidence of Paul – and trusted by him. Pahlen was Governor of St. Petersburg, head of the Police, and in daily consultation at the Winter Palace. As part of his official duties he had access to the Tsar's private apartments, and the ruler's safety was in his hands. Panin needed Pahlen's closeness to the Tsar as Pahlen needed Panin's friendship with the Grand Duke Alexander. Together they formed gunpowder and fuse.

Darja draws a good picture of Pahlen, the man who took it on himself to change the course of Russian history. 'He was a tall man, with heavy shoulders, an open countenance, with a high forehead, and yet most honest and cheerful, full of wit, originality, finesse and joviality in his manner of speaking. He had a nature which was wild but strong, full of good sense, firm, brave, taking life lightly. He was the picture of absolute honesty, and joy – without a care in the world. I always saw him arriving at our house with the greatest pleasure. He never failed to make me laugh – and to amuse me.' An engraving of Pahlen does indeed show him in a careless pose, looking out on the world with a humorous eye. 'I was always put out when I was sent out of the room when the conversation took on a more serious turn, and he needed to tell my husband the incidents of the day. I was *de trop* at those moments, but I was always intrigued and often heard from my husband confidences which I had not been allowed to hear at first hand.'

It was a talent which Darja was to retain all her life, for confidences were to become the very breath of existence to her. In this roundabout way she learned that the Tsar had now included his own sons in his suspicions of conspiracy. He had decided unexpectedly to have supper in the apartments of the Grand Duke. 'He wished to catch him out,' wrote Darja. 'He found on his table amongst other books, the tragedy of the Death of Caesar. This seemed to him to be decisive.'

It was in the course of his secret conferences with Lieven that Pahlen told him that he was only waiting from one moment to the next to see the Tsarina locked up in a convent and the Grand Dukes sent to prison. But Darja, in her account, written long after the events, added tactfully: 'Count Pahlen never pushed his confidences to the limit. Seeing his young colleague so ill and unable to help, he refrained from telling him about the projected plot.' So while Count Lieven languished in bed, the conspirators perfected their plans.

To the easy, outgoing Pahlen fell the task of convincing

Alexander that it was only his father's abdication which was being planned. There was no thought of endangering the Tsar's life – the open countenance of Pahlen could vouch for that.

'It must be an unconditional pledge', stated Alexander.

'Of course', said Pahlen reassuringly.

He had the idea in the back of his mind that if their plans were frustrated and the Tsar called on his army to help him, the lives of the conspirators would be held in the balance against that of the Tsar. Events would solve that problem.

The preliminaries were ingenious. Paul had condemned to banishment many hundreds of high-ranking officers in the Army. Pahlen begged the Tsar to mitigate their lot. Amongst them were the three brothers Zubov and General Bennigsen. It was necessary to choose a day when the Tsar was in a sunny mood, and to work on the sentimental side of his nature. Imagine all those officers, devoted to the cause of the Tsar, men who had spent their lives in the defence of their country against foreign enemies, now languishing in poverty and exile perhaps through wrong information. Yet the all-powerful Tsar had only to raise his hand in order to remedy their ills.

Tears came into Paul's eyes, and within hours horsemen were riding out of St. Petersburg. The officers were to be pardoned and allowed to return to their homes. This was a clever move, because Pahlen, in daily conference with Paul knew the unpredictable nature of the man. Once he had signed the pardons, he would do nothing more for the men who had been so unjustly punished, and the capital would be full of disaffected military with no money to keep body and soul together. They would have no means of livelihood – except stealing. Pahlen, wearing his hat as Police Chief, gave orders that their small scale thefts were to be totally ignored. On the other hand, the sad state to which so many loyal officers had been reduced was made only too apparent to many in the city, and underlined the injustices perpetrated by the Tsar.

The conspiracy grew and grew, but always with the ostensible idea that the Tsar's abdication was the end in view. As the conspiracy grew so the rumours became current, and eventually, and inevitably, they reached the Winter Palace – and the ears of the Tsar. When Pahlen appeared for one of his daily conferences with the Tsar, he was met with a blunt and dangerous question.

'Where were you during the Palace Revolution of 1762?'

1762 was the year in which the Tsar Peter had been killed with the connivance of Paul's mother, Catherine II.

Even Pahlen, easy and confident as he always was, was taken aback.

21

'I was merely a simple ensign in the Army, there was nothing important for an ensign to do.'

But Paul, roused to one of his ungovernable rages shouted: 'There are some who wish to see the events of 1762 repeated in 1801.'

The nature which Darja called 'wild but strong and brave' came to Pahlen's rescue.

'That is perfectly true your Majesty, and *I* belong to their number. How else could I protect Your Majesty's sacred person unless I *joined* the conspiracy?'

In his turn, the Tsar was taken aback, but he still stared at Pahlen and demanded the list of the names of the conspirators. The nervous suspicious nature of Paul was gaining the upper hand. His worst fears were being confirmed. Pahlen continued to be reassuring. The Tsar should have the list the moment the plans were ripe. 'When?' rapped out the Tsar.

It was the end of January 1801, and Pahlen gave it as his firm pledge that he would present the Tsar the list 'at an early date'. At the back of his mind the Count was calculating that the plot would take six weeks to ripen.

But the Tsar kept on muttering to himself, '1762 – they murdered my father in 1762.'

Much later Count Pahlen recounted some of the close shaves with death which the conspirators had had. 'Someone had awakened the Tsar's suspicions concerning my intimacy with the Grand Duke Alexander.' Although their Court duties brought them together they did not dare to be seen together or even to speak to one another for more than a moment or two. Pahlen explained that as a consequence, they had to write notes to each other, although admittedly this was nearly as dangerous. The plan was that Count Panin carried the notes from one to the other. Panin and Pahlen read the Grand Duke's replies, answered them, and burned them immediately. 'One day, while I was waiting in the Tsar's ante-room, Panin thrust a note into my hand. I was on the point of entering the Tsar's room, and thought I had time to read the note, answer it and – burn it. Suddenly and unexpectedly Paul came out of his bedroom and seeing me, called me to follow him into his boudoir.'

The Tsar closed the door behind Pahlen who scarcely had time to push the note into his right-hand coat pocket. For once the Tsar was in jovial mood, and then, 'quite in a joking way tried to thrust his hands into my pockets: the Tsar said: "I'm going to see what you have there – perhaps a billet doux?"'

When he told this story Pahlen was speaking to a Frenchman

Langeron and said: 'Well, dear Langeron, you know me, I am not timid, nor easily put out of countenance, but I confess that if at that moment any one had opened my veins, they would not have found a drop of blood in them.'

'How did you save yourself?' asked Langeron.

'Quite easily, I said to the Emperor "Sire, what are you doing? Leave my pockets alone! You hate snuff, and I am a great snuff taker; my handkerchief is full of it. You will soil your hands, and make them smell in a way you do not like." He took his hands away, and exclaimed, "Phew, how disgusting! You are right!" And so I got out of the fix I was in.'

But events were overtaking the guiding hand of Pahlen. The plotters wanted to see the end of the rule of Paul I, and Paul in his turn was becoming even more impatient to have in his hands the list of the names of the plotters. Panin had been banished from St. Petersburg, but his fellow conspirators, the Princes Zubov, had managed to return with their sister Olga Zubova (Mme Gerebzova), who was mistress to the English Ambassador Sir Charles Whitworth. Everyone knew that something was in the air.

The Tsar continued to demand the names of the conspirators. 'Arrest them all! Put them in chains, send them to fortresses, to casemates, to Siberia, to the mines!'

Pahlen said, 'Sire, that is impossible. There is a list of the conspirators. Your Majesty will see that the Tsarina and the two Grand Dukes are among them. I cannot arrest these august personages without a special *ukase*.'

Paul signed the *ukase*, ordering the arrest of the Imperial family. The Tsarina and the Grand Duchesses were to be sent to a convent. Alexander and Constantine to be imprisoned in a fortress, and floggings and banishments meted out indiscriminately to the other conspirators. Pahlen still managed to delay the Tsar's orders saying that he must move at the right and propitious moment. He managed to quieten the Tsar's fears by his reassuring attitude, but Paul was not entirely free of his suspicions. He now recalled from exile Count Alexsei Aracheiev and Count Rostopshin, favourites he had previously banished in a fit of rage. They were to arrive too late.

The night of 11 March (old style) 1801 was the chosen date. The shadows were closing in, and the Tsar was aware of them. Four or five days before he died, Paul, when out riding, had suddenly reined in his horse and turned to his Master of the Horse in great alarm saying: 'I feel quite suffocated. I feel as if I were going die! Will they strangle me?'

The very evening of his death, when he had dined with General

23

Koutousov, the Tsar looked into a flawed mirror and suddenly said: 'What a strange mirror, my neck looks as if it were twisted.'

While the conspirators hurried about plotting and counter-plotting, Christopher Lieven was prudently keeping to his bed, and Darja carried on her trivial social round, visiting Grand Duchesses, and worrying about her *toilettes*. But the young couple felt the tensions in the very air. February was a dead season in St. Petersburg, the cold purity of the snow, lyrically described by Louis Réau, had by then turned into muddy drifts. The thaw would not come till April or May when the thick crust of ice would begin to break and the river be filled with floating icebergs which would bang violently against the sides of the embankments and the stone pillars supporting the bridges. It was the custom to announce the opening of the river to navigation with a cannon shot from the Fortress – a celebration of the return and liberation of the spring.

There was to be no cannon shot for the deliverance of Russia from the rule of Paul I.

The Tsar had not yet managed to get a list of the conspirators from Pahlen, but he decided to act and to force Pahlen to carry out his orders. A wave of terror began. There were executions. Men and women vanished without trace. Torture was the lot of others. Torture such as the knout, a flaying alive of a man – or a woman – where the flesh, muscles, and sinews were torn down to the bone. The victim was stretched out like a skin to be dried in the sun and the executioner cut the flesh into shreds with a hundred strokes of the knout from the shoulders to the lower portion of the loins.

There was good reason to fear the all-powerful Tsar. It was no wonder that Count Lieven kept prudently to his bed.

There were many *petits soupers fins* at the house of Olga Zubova, mistress of the British Ambassador, hurried conferences and even more hurried secret notes, just as secretly burned. The horror was augmenting daily. Something had to be done. Count Pahlen took a different view. The terror and horror of the executions and tortures were playing into the hands of the men who wished to depose – or dispose of the Tsar. But delay was becoming dangerous. The conspirators decided to act. The blow was to be struck.

On the evening of 11 March Platon Zubov gave a supper and invited all the conspirators, generals and officers. In an atmosphere of fervid excitement, large quantities of champagne were drunk. Just before midnight Pahlen came to Zubov's house.

'Is all prepared?'

'Yes!'

At midnight the conspirators set out. They were divided into two groups. The first headed by the two Zubov brothers and General Bennigsen, and the second under the command of Count Pahlen. He had chosen that particular night because the Commandant of the Semenovsky Guards was one of the company of conspirators. Pahlen had given precise instructions as to the plan of procedure. But this was impeded by the drunken state of some of the conspirators, who had to be left behind at the first drawbridge. But Bennigsen and one of the Zubov brothers had taken care to moderate their drinking and were met by the ADC Argamakov who took them quietly to the secret spiral staircase which led to the Emperor's private rooms.

The ADC left them. Arrived at the private door, Bennigsen knocked. The two soldiers and the valet guarding the entrance were asleep. The valet woke first – lit the candles – and alerted the hussars. A swift scuffle followed, Zubov brought down one of the men with the flat of his sword. The other two escaped down the staircase. 'It does not matter', said Bennigsen, 'our men are on guard!'

He and Zubov made for the Tsar's bedroom, quietly crossing the library, with only the flickering candles shining obliquely into his inner room to guide them. In the bedroom itself the lamp on the night table shone. The bed was empty.

'He's got away!' shouted Zubov. He wanted to rush back to call the other conspirators. But General Bennigsen stood his ground. The screen had been moved, and searching the room he found Paul in the chimney space.

On hearing the scuffle in the ante-room the Tsar had made for the secret door which led into the Tsarina's apartments. Frantically tugging at it, he realised that, on his own orders, it had been locked, and the key hidden. Now he stood shivering in his night clothes clutching a little jacket around him miserably.

'You are my prisoner,' said Bennigsen, 'Sign at once! A deed of abdication in favour of your son Alexander.'

'What have I done?' Paul asked, trembling with cold and fear.

'What have you done?' said Zubov. 'Haven't you tortured the whole country since you came to the throne?'

The fracas and the noise grew. The five drunken men who had been left on the drawbridge rushed in. Other soldiers from the Semenovsky Regiment were hammering at the door. Paul was shouting for help. The conspirators maddened equally by their hatred of the tyrant and their fear of his possible rescue were struggling to hold him back. Zubov struck Paul with a tobacco box, others threw themselves at him, and one of them knotted his scarf round Paul's neck.

'Gentlemen in heaven's name – give me time to say my prayers.'

The officers were taking their revenge and deaf to his frantic cries, they merely tightened the silken noose round his neck with a malachite paperweight taken from the Tsar's own desk. He struggled for a while, and then there was a final gasp.

Bennigsen who had left the bedroom in the struggle, came back into the room and heard the words: 'Il est achévé!' It was indeed finished – the life and the reign of Paul I.

Christopher Lieven's mother was curtly told to break the news to the Tsarina that her husband was dead of a fatal stroke.

Maria Feodorovna looked at her and cried out disbelievingly: 'No, no – they have murdered him!'

She began to scream and to demand to see the body but was prevented. The embalmer must exercise his delicate artistry before the body could be seen by anyone. The Tsarina's sorrow was changed to furious anger when soldiers barred the entrance to her husband's apartments. She shouted that if her husband was indeed dead, then she was sole Empress and Tsarina. For some time she had cherished the illusion that she could reign, as the great Catherine II had reigned after the murder of her husband. And indeed the Tsarina, fearful of her fate, had in fact started a small conspiracy of her own to depose her husband. But this notion of the Tsar's widow was speedily brushed aside by the conspirators.

Pahlen hurried off to inform the Grand Duke Alexander that he was now Tsar and ruler of all the Russians. He found the new Tsar sunk in the depths of dejection. It was some time before he could persuade him even to appear before the troops and to be honoured and acclaimed as their new Emperor, to whom they should be true till death: an oath they had taken to his murdered father.

CHAPTER THREE

Bonsi is prudent

While the aftermath of bloody murder was leading to confusions, recriminations and shuddering repentance on the part of the conspirators and the Tsar, the young Lievens slept. The luxurious bedroom of Bonsi and Darja faced what was called La Grand Millionne, near the barracks of the 1st Regiment of the Preobrajensky Imperial Guard, and this road abutted on the Winter Palace.

On the February night when Paul had choked his last breath, there was a loud knocking on the young couple's bedroom door. The Count was woken by a valet announcing the arrival of a *feldjäger*. These were fast messengers who in troika or sledge so often brought evil news to one time favourites. *Feldjägers* were generally thought to form part of the spy network of the Tsar.

There was silence in the room.

Finally the Count said: 'Let the officer in.'

It was two-thirty in the morning.

The young wife opened startled eyes.

'It is the Fortress!' said the Count.

He feared for his life, but when the messenger entered the room he merely announced that the Count was summoned to the Winter Palace where his Imperial Majesty awaited him. Count Lieven knew that the Tsar lived at the Michael Palace where he had recently moved. In his anger and fear, Bonsi turned on the officer, 'You're drunk!'

But the officer standing in the half-dark at the side of the bed replied equally angrily that he had just left his Imperial Majesty and was repeating the Tsar's own words. The Count found it hard to believe that the Tsar, however unstable, would have changed his residence in the middle of the night.

Then seeing the Count's puzzled expression, the messenger explained.

27

'The Tsar Paul is very ill, and it is the Grand Duke Alexander – I mean the Tsar – who has sent me.'

Bonsi, who did not share the easy bravery of Count Pahlen, turned to the officer and motioned to him to go away. His surprise had turned to terror. He sat down on the bed, and looked at his young wife. Could this be a trap, he asked her? Had the messenger been telling the truth?

In Russia, a land of sudden murders and palace coups, favour and even life itself hung by the frailest thread. It seemed pointless to try to solve the enigma. It was time to take action. The young Countess looked at her husband. She knew it was a moment of great danger. Bonsi went to the bell and rang for his servants and ordered his sledge to be made ready.

Darja wrote: 'My husband made me get up and pushed me to the window telling me to observe everything which happened in the street – and to warn him.'

He himself went into his dressing-room which faced on to the inner courtyard of the house.

Darja took her duties lightly, in spite of the danger:

'Here I was on sentry-go. I was fifteen years old, of a cheerful disposition, liking any excitement and taking everything lightly, even the odd catastrophe, always provided that it led to a change of routine from the day before. I had nothing in my head except what tomorrow would bring. What would I do? Should I visit my mother-in-law and the Grand Duchesses as I did every day? Those were the only worries in my mind. There was only a small night-light in the room. I pulled up the curtain from the window and stayed there with my eyes fixed on the street. Nothing to be seen except the whiteness of the snow and the dark glitter of the ice. Not a passer-by. The sentry had retired huddled in his sentry box, a refugee from the intense cold. Not a light from a single window of the barracks, nor the slightest movement or sound. My husband called softly to me from the dressing-room. "Can you see anything?"
'I said: "Nothing at all."'

Bonsi was not hurrying with his dressing, for he was hesitant to go out. The time wore on and Darja grew bored with looking at nothing. She was weary and longing to go back to her warm bed to sleep. At last she heard a noise, very faint at first but she recognised it as the sound of a carriage. She shouted the news to Bonsi: 'A carriage is coming, a carriage is coming!'

But before her husband had time to run to the window, the

carriage had already passed. It was a coupé with two horses. Darja, who was always acutely aware of the status of various grades of carriage, wrote: 'This was unusual because at that time anyone with any pretensions to grandeur always drove in a four- or six-horse carriage.'

Consequently the carriage seemed to the young girl to have a wretched appearance, but the perceptive eyes of Darja had noticed in the light thrown up by the snow that one of the passengers seemed to be Monsieur Ouvarov, aide-de-camp of the Tsar. On hearing this her husband hesitated no longer. He went downstairs and, throwing himself into his sledge, set off immediately for the Winter Palace. Delay could mean disaster.

What the young Countess did not know was that in the dark shadows of the carriage which she described as of *chetive* (miserable) appearance, were also the new Tsar, Alexander, and his brother, the Grand Duke Constantine. They were speeding over the snow to take into their hands the inheritance released by the strangling of their father.

This outcome had been achieved by the shedding of blood and had left an aftermath. For while the drunken officers who had taken part in the murder staggered round the Michael Palace celebrating, the heir to the murdered man had been lying on his bed awaiting with dread and hope the news that his father had agreed to abdicate. Perhaps to the last Alexander shut out from his thoughts the logical conclusion that army officers, in fear of their lives and jealous of their country's honour, would not be content with a piece of paper as a guarantee of their safety.

There was a knock on his door. One of the Zubov brothers stood there and repeated words which mirrored a murder.

'Il est achévé.'

'What is over?'

'Your father is dead. You are the Tsar Alexander.'

He was the successor chosen by Catherine II, but it had taken a murder to achieve the result she so desired, and already his conscience was working within him. 'I will not accept a crown stained with the blood of my father!'

Many writers and historians have endeavoured patiently to wash the blood from the reputation of Alexander indicating that he had never actually approved of the assassination. Count Adam Czartorsky wrote: 'His grief and the remorse which he was continually reviving in his heart were inexpressibly deep and touching. He continually saw in his imagination the mutilated body of his father and his mental tortures never ceased.'

'Sire, it is time to put away childish things. Come – show

yourself to the Guards.'

The new Tsar of all the Russias was then half-carried into the presence of his soldiers who swore fealty to this new autocrat.

Meanwhile Platon Zubov woke the Grand Duke Constantine and bluntly told him that the Tsar was dead, and that he was summoned to the presence of the new ruler.

'I dressed quickly', said Constantine, 'and followed the Count into the presence of my brother, whom I found crying bitterly.'

It was then the new Tsar and his brother left for the Winter Palace in the closed carriage which the young Countess Lieven had watched disappearing along the frozen street.

Maria Feodorovna chose to ignore the facts. Further complications and confusions ensued. The dangers of her imprisonment by her late husband forgotten, the widow accused Bennigsen and Pahlen: 'As your Tsar has died – a victim of treason, then *I* am your Empress.'

But Alexander's wife, the new Tsarina Elizabeth, kept her head. She tried to pacify her mother-in-law. Looking at the now Dowager Empress, the new Empress said sternly: 'You must go to the Winter Palace and acclaim your son as Tsar!'

'Who calls Alexander – Tsar?'

'The voice of the nation', said his wife.

'Tell him that I shall never acknowledge him for my sovereign until he has given me an account of his conduct in the affair.'

Although her daughter-in-law continued to try to calm her down, Maria Feodorovna still passionately held her ground.

'It is not for me to obey. You can obey – if you wish.'

On which thought she seized the arm of Bennigsen and commanded him to bend his knee to her as sole Empress. Bennigsen, after the events of the night, was in no mood to be intimidated. He said curtly: 'Madame, on ne joue pas la comédie!'

When Alexander heard of his mother's reactions he groaned aloud. 'Mon Dieu! Encore ce surcroit d'embarras!'

Embarras would seem to be an understatement in the murderous circumstances.

All dangers and fears forgotten, the young Countess Lieven wrote of the universal joy at the beginning of the reign of Alexander. 'We have lacked historians and poets to describe this enthusiasm, the heady excitement which swept over the people. Four years of despotism, sometimes bordering on madness, often on cruelty, had been ended. The catastrophe was forgotten, or even lauded. This thought dominated all others. We had been starved of happiness and now we were free. A life of happiness stretched before us.'

The same cult of happiness and joy enveloped the future of the young Tsarina. 'She was so beautiful', Darja wrote, 'beautiful and charming, full of gracious dignity, dressed in a simple robe of white muslin, her head without ornaments, nothing around her neck, her beautiful blonde curls which fell to her shoulders her sole adornment. Her figure was beautiful, and nothing was to be compared with the way she carried herself, or the dignity with which she walked. The Tsar was equally handsome. He shone with youth and with that serenity which was the distinctive trait of his face, and of his character. The whole aspect of the Imperial couple was striking. One bowed before them, and surrounded them with a love which bordered on passion.'

Darja was only voicing the universal feelings of the country. A new era of freedom and happiness had dawned. Its dark beginnings could be forgotten.

The young Emperor immediately issued a manifesto to his people. It had, it seemed, pleased the Almighty God to cut short the life of his beloved father the Tsar Paul Petrovich, who had died of an apoplectic stroke. Calling all the glory of the great Catherine to his aid, he hoped that he would rule according to her wise intention. 'We hope to be able to carry Russia to the summit of Glory, to procure peace, and uninterrupted happiness for all our faithful subjects.'

Alexander, Tsar of all the Russias, was twenty-four years old and of liberal training and ideas. On the morning after the murder of Paul, it was reported that the sun had come out when Alexander was proclaimed Tsar. The sun shone after so many weeks of darkness. All seemed set fair as the young Tsar and Tsarina were applauded and acclaimed.

Many knew the truth behind the rejoicing, but officially it was buried with the corpse of the Emperor. Princess Lieven, writing many years later did not reveal the facts. The official story that Paul had died of a sudden apoplexy was kept up for more than a hundred years. No book, pamphlet or newspaper could be published unless this fiction was continued. N. K. Shilder wrote the biography of Paul I, but although he knew the true facts he was not allowed to mention them even in the year 1900. The truth, although universally and tacitly acknowledged, was never openly admitted. The Tsar, whoever he was, must remain a holy and cherished object, an icon for the people.

Darja participated in the universal fiction. Loss of memory was rife when it came to the accession of Alexander. About her husband Bonsi's illness Darja wrote that it was one of the best pieces of good

31

1 Alexander I: 'he shone with youth and was surrounded with a love which bordered on passion'

fortune of his whole career. She had often heard him debating the question of the events of that evening. What would he have done about the dangerous secrets of the conspiracy? Save the Tsar – that was his duty. But think of the other side – to deliver to his vengeance, to his harshness all the best and noblest in Russia. Where would the proscriptions end, when the numbers of those implicated were so great? The scaffold, or exile, or prison for everyone? And afterwards? A regime more horrible than that under which Russia had already suffered. 'If Pahlen had spoken to Bonsi, there was only one course to take, it was to blow one's brains out.'

It sounds very much as if the young Countess was aware of the truth. But at fifteen it was natural to prefer to dwell on the sun shining on the Tsarina's golden curls.

Alexander was crowned on the 27 September 1801 (new style) in Moscow by the Metropolitan Platon.

'Monarch of Russia', he exhorted the young man, 'a struggle awaits you. Gird on your sword for the contest. Draw it with valour, young hero. Fight, conquer and govern; the omnipotent arm of the Almighty will protect you. And though the decree of the Eternal Being has appointed for you an exalted rank among men, you are nevertheless a man like any one of us.'

Metaphorical shining swords laid aside, Alexander was to live to prove only too well that he was as frail in character as any of his subservient subjects. Little by little he fell under the influence of his mother's hatred of the conspirators. The easy-going brave Pahlen was banished to his estates in Courland, for he came from the same Baltic Provinces as the Lievens and the Benckendorffs. Count Panin, already banished by the Tsar Paul, was briefly recalled to St. Petersburg, but the Dowager Empress was pursuing him too. She was determined on vengeance against all the murderers of her husband. No doubt it would have been a less necessary task if the bloodstained crown had fallen into her hands, rather than those of her son. Gradually Panin and many of the other conspirators were sent away from St. Petersburg. The fury of the Dowager was fuelled by the weakness and bad conscience of the young Tsar himself.

Only the prudent Count Lieven and his family survived the general upheaval. His mother, the formidable Imperial Governess, remained at Court, still carrying out the same functions, closely attached to the Dowager Empress, and honoured with all her confidences. Count Lieven himself, although no longer Minister of War, was aide-de-camp to the new Tsar. He had lost none of his credit, nor was his total loyalty to Alexander ever in doubt. Bonsi was one of those fortunate few who had that shining attribute of

33

being able to transfer total loyalty from father to son without a backward glance.

Count Lieven remained in military affairs right up to 1809 when he transferred his somewhat mediocre talents to a diplomatic career. The soul of prudence, the acme of devoted subservience, he may not have inherited his mother's strength of character, but he had inherited in full measure her ability to survive in the treacherous waters of Court life.

CHAPTER FOUR

Darja – Chronicles of Court and Society

During the period of eight years when Darja was bearing and bringing up her children, there was no indication in her attitudes of the great role she was to play on the public and international stage of the future. She was a wife and mother, frivolous, worldly and feminine, and simply recorded the small happenings of her life in the world of Court and Society, as if she were writing for some early nineteenth-century version of a modern gossip column.

Some two years after the unfortunate demise of the Tsar, Darja's eldest brother Alexander went into the Army. He was naturally – as a general's son – marked out for rapid promotion. But in the meantime had to serve an apprenticeship like any other soldier, far away from home. The sister and brother, devoted to one another, promised to write to each other as often as they could when they were apart.

'I had much pleasure, my dear Alexander in receiving your note of yesterday.' She was impatient to have news of his journey and had been thinking of the fatigues he must have endured. Her husband had just left her, and the mornings seemed to her to be boringly long, and interminably tedious. But there was some gossip. Count Flinsky was going to get a divorce and marry the Princess Lubomirska. Countess Flinska had found another husband, but his name was uncertain. The weather was bad. The streets very dirty, 'but this does not stop the beautiful ladies trailing their long trains – and their charms on the quays.'

At the German masquerade there was an amusing joke played. Five masks went up to the buffet and were served, gulping down a hundred roubles worth of wines etc. Four of them went out, and the fifth remained sitting at the buffet. As it was already late the host went up to the seated mask and demanded the payment which was due to him. The mask did not reply. The host

35

reproached the man, and continued to demand to be paid. He threatened him with the police. Still silence. Finally a police officer was sent for, marched up to the man and shook him by the shoulders. Then suddenly the whole thing crumbled and fell to the ground, it was a man made of straw!

She ended her letter by wishing Alexander a happy journey, and hoped that he would think from time to time of his friends – when it came to friends she would put herself first for no one was more sincerely attached to him than she, Darja. But in spite of the fervent assurances of her sentiments for her brother, she uses the formal and aristocratic 'vous' when writing to him, and never the familiar and bourgeois 'tu'.

The letters which Darja wrote to Alexander reveal her as an inveterate chatterer, a retailer of small pieces of history, those tiny details which bring the people of the past into startling life. Births, deaths, elopements and fashion notes follow one another in her letters like a river of cheerful scandals. Count Valerien Zubov, former lover of Catherine II had had an apoplectic stroke. Darja remarked that if his death should unfortunately ensue, his widow would certainly soon console herself. The Russian Ambassador in Paris had made a fool of himself. Princess G, the fifteen-year-old daughter of the former Minister of Finance, had disappeared from her home. It would seem, indeed it was rumoured, that she may have eloped with someone not of her class. A postscript stated that this was indeed the case, the misguided girl had fled with a clerk of her father's. What a ridiculous business! The French Ambassador Jedouville had arrived. Darja, being fashion-conscious, did not approve of his way of dressing – very old-fashioned with a great deal of powdered hair, buckles and his forehead totally bare!

Her hurriedly scribbled letters underline how her husband managed to keep always close to the Court – and to the Tsar. 'The Tsar will go to live at Kameni-Ostrov, and we have already rented a house very close to the Palace. It is *vast*. But Costa [her brother Constantine] will be living with us.'

One thing she had forgotten to tell her brother was that she had been forbidden to walk in front of her house. This order had come from 'very high up'. She had a shrewd idea of the cause. Probably it was because a man friend had met her there, spoken to her and 'this has been the result – it has been dubbed scandalous.' Bonsi was very annoyed about it. But 'one must submit...'

Reading between the lines it is possible that it was Bonsi himself who objected to Darja's chatting and laughing with another man so openly – and in the street.

Then the French Ambassador's ladies arrived. Darja had heard that they were quite ugly – 'General Ouvarov, a great admirer of the fair sex, confirmed it to me. Not only are they ugly, but badly turned out'. Their reputation for chic and charm was totally undeserved. But, in spite of that, everyone was running after them. Costa had been to Court, and as the result of this he 'will probably be sent to Ratisbon, and after that employed on some mission abroad'.

The sons of General Benckendorff were always well-placed to take advantage of Imperial favours.

There were others who were not so lucky. General Talisin had been banished. The reason was that he wanted to be Commandant of the Semenovsky Regiment. In order to achieve this desirable end he had suborned two valets of the Tsar, who had discovered the plot. Talisin was ordered to leave Petersburg. The two valets were sent away with the *feldjägers* – those much feared messengers of summary justice.

The next phrase gives the impression that Darja, for all her loyalty to Mother Russia and her much loved ruler, had a shrewd idea that letters could be opened. 'Everyone blesses the justice of our dear sovereign who every day more and more merits the love of his people.' Except, presumably, people who were despatched to unspecified punishments.

Having paid due homage to her dear and much loved sovereign, the source of all favours and graces, Darja passed on to more amusing matters. 'The Tsarina has settled in at Pavlovsk. On Saturday there was a ball to celebrate the feast day of the Grand Duchess Catherine.' She and Bonsi had both been invited, and, as there were only to be ten dancers, 'Bonsi will be forced to display his graces on the dance floor.'

The ball at the house of Countess Schouvaloff was really grand – a delicious entertainment – '*A gouter* in the Viennese manner. They had made a charming garden in the *salle du thé*. All the rooms were lighted with transparencies, and it was really like fairyland.' Both Tsar and Tsarina graciously condescended to be present.

It was May and the Tsar was about to set out on his travels, and where the Tsar went Bonsi went because of his appointment as aide-de-camp. The first town they visited was Memel as the guest of the King of Prussia. Bonsi had decided that, in his absence, it was prudent that his wife should live at the Palace with her mother-in-law. This was not at all to Darja's taste.

The Palace etiquette, she had decided, was excessively boring, and Bonsi's absence made it even more insupportable. Darja, although all her life she had many women friends, preferred male company, and the presence of so many grass widows of other aides-de-camp was no consolation for the lack of husband – and brothers. She awaited news of the Imperial progress with impatience, and reported it at second hand to Alexander. 'Everywhere the Tsar has been acclaimed. At Riga – at the gates of the suburbs – the crowd took his horses out of the shafts, and pulled his carriage to the castle. The guards, who had the order not to come out to meet him, ran out enthusiastically, receiving him with cries of joy – these were echoed by all the inhabitants. The sailors of all the nations who were at Riga seemed at this *wonderful* moment to form one nation with Russia. The Tsar was moved to tears – and with good reason. He stayed at Riga for three days, and during that time there was nothing but balls and fêtes. Bonsi danced from morning till night.'

What the aristocratic and Court-orientated Darja did not know was that the oppressed peasants and *le peuple* of Riga were greeting the man whom they hoped would deliver them from the slavery of serfdom and the oppressive and evil taxes which were weighing them down.

In the springtime of his reign Alexander was hailed as a liberator and a liberal, a man who was going to change everything for the better. As the ice melted on the Neva and the royal party progressed along the margins of the Baltic Sea all seemed to be sunshine, and the dawn of a new age with the new Tsar. In effect, nothing was to change, and the peasants, as always, were cheering a chimera, a liberal and liberating Emperor who did not exist.

While Bonsi was dancing the night away, Darja was bored to tears. 'You have no idea, the etiquette which holds sway here!' But she had found a solution. She had decided to avoid all social gatherings on the pretext that she was taking a cure, and so she was free and felt much better.

News of the trivial and the disastrous follow in swift succession. The Chevalier de Saxe, pursued by the vengeance of Prince Scherbatov, had fallen in a duel. The Prince had been given a pistol with a faulty aim. But he had found this out beforehand, and knew that the shot went wide by three paces to the right. He had so arranged it that his first shot had gone straight through the Chevalier's body. The Chevalier cried 'I die!' and fired one last shot. The dying man was out of luck, because this last salvo only made a hole in Scherbatov's hat. The Chevalier had, of course, died on the spot. Darja announced the facts casually, and went on to relate that she rode every day and had a splendid new horse which was being especially trained for her.

In July the Court moved again to Peterhof, a palace much loved

38

by the Dowager Empress. Since the murder of her husband, she had kept to a strict and gloomy way of life, and never showed herself in public – neither at Mass nor at any of the public gatherings. In fact, she was prepared to do anything to spoil the joy of the new reign.

But Darja approved of the Palace itself – it was quite charming.

2 Peterhof: the Grand Cascade and the Samson fountain

In front of the great Samson fountain before the Palace, there are two beautiful pavilions from which a superb colonnade is crossed by a pathway. The cupolas of the pavilions are gilded. A fountain sheds its crystal drops on the cupolas and runs down the Venetian windows. The effect is one of great beauty. When you are in front of the pavilions, it is as if a heavy rain were falling. On the terrace, which falls away from the Palace on descending levels, there are huge vases of gilded bronze in the antique style. And all the statues in the gardens are gilded.

Every prospect pleased except the Empress Dowager and the etiquette. But there had been some foreign visitors. The Prince of Baden had arrived, and the Duke of Gloucester, nephew of the King of England. 'He appeared at Peterhof the day of the fête when there had been a masquerade and fireworks. He is about the same height as the Tsar, but thinner with a handsome face and figure.' Her good opinion of the Duke lasted no longer than the fireworks. She had met him at the ball and found him to be 'of a stupidity which is very rare'. In spite of that, Madame Bagration was mad about him – there seemed to be no accounting for the taste of some women.

But even entertainments on the highest level had their disadvantages. Her sister Masha came with Princess Alexander of Württemberg especially to see the ascent of the air balloon. Two days running everyone, including the Tsar and his family, were eager to see this phenomenon. The assembled company waited with bated breath. The balloon did not go up. It stayed on the ground. The populace, baulked of the ascending balloon, took it out on the police. It was rumoured that the head of the St. Petersburg police had been injured. Truly the police can be blamed for everything.

Even after the return of Bonsi, attending on Imperial Highnesses, and humbly awaiting royal favours were not agreeable duties, as Darja was not slow to point out. She had to wait about for Bonsi to get back, forced to dine as late as four o'clock, and sometimes even later. 'This does not suit me in the least,' wrote Darja crossly, 'and some days I never see Bonsi at all, which leads to disputes between us. He goes to the Palace every morning, sometimes finishing at three o'clock. He dines there and after dinner – more work!'

Lack of occupation and the diligent attention of her husband towards the Tsar made life boring. The following year – 1803 – she decided to go on a holiday when her husband was away. In any case she was quite determined not to go back to the total boredom of staying at Pavlovsk where she had had nothing but disagreements. She thought that, rather than be bored at Court, she would go to Marienbad, to stay with her sister-in-law, and from there to Kurland to sample either the sea water, or possibly some other spring water of which she had heard very good reports. Darja's health was to continue to be useful from time to time all through her life.

She had little other news for Alexander except that Scheremitov had married 'one of his slaves' and declared her to be his legitimate spouse when she was brought to bed of a son. 'She died recently, and was buried with all the pomp imaginable. Her son is now called Count Dmitri and has become the sole heir of the vast estates of his father, the Count.'

From her letters and comments, the sharp differences between aristocrats, the bourgeoisie, and those she calls the 'slaves', – more properly serfs, become clear. She was to live most of her life amongst kings and aristocrats, and made few concessions to the rise of egalitarian feelings.

The letters of the young Countess in the first years of her marriage hardly foreshadowed her future passionate interest in politics and world events. The rise of Napoleon passed her by. When the French defeated the Austrians at Hohenlinden, she was occupied with thoughts of her *toilettes* for her approaching marriage. When Nelson destroyed the Danish fleet at Copenhagen, she complained of the boredom at Court; when Prussia occupied Hanover and Bremen, she wrote disgustedly of the dirt in the street; and while Russia and France agreed on redistributing Germany, she wrote ecstatically of her new and charming riding horse. While the French armies swarmed over Germany and occupied Hanover, she wrote of the arrest of an aide-de-camp for wearing a black jacket on parade.

In 1804 the Duke of Enghien was executed and Napoleon crowned Emperor. But Darja was more interested in the fact that her mother-in-law had been given lands in Poland, and the Tsarina had graciously added to this gift a large quantity of diamonds as a *bonne bouche*. Her father had been made Privy Councillor, her brother Alexander, who was fighting in Georgia, had been made a lieutenant and aide-de-camp to the Tsar. Costa was named as secretary to the Russian Embassy in Berlin. And the crown of her year was that she was expecting her first child.

She had kept up her social life, in spite of her pregnancy and what she called her 'ungraceful figure'. But what did it matter so long as she was amused. 'Three weeks from now, I hope to be able, my dear Alexander, to tell you of my deliverance. I am very impatient that all should be over, and happily over.' Then, with the natural fear of a woman expecting her first child she added: 'I am a little nervous of that moment.'

In the middle of February Count Lieven was able to write to his brother-in-law. 'My dear friend, I am at last a father. My wife was happily brought to bed of a little girl, and I am delivered of a great cloud of worries. She is already almost entirely in the full bloom of health, in spite of the fact that it is hardly four weeks since she was delivered of the darling little baby to which I am more attached than to most babies.'

Alexander was kept informed of all the little complications of motherhood by Darja. 'I pass most of my time with my little one when I am not interrupted by society ... my little one was vaccinated last week, and that is one great worry the less for me.

41

She is going on well, and I hope to be able to show her in public in a few days.'

Her child made it easier for her to escape the crushing boredom of Court life.

The Tsarina wanted me to go to Pavlovsk as I have done in past years. But I managed to get out of it – because of my little one. It was too much trouble to take her there, and perhaps to have been put in damp apartments. So I have stayed here alone with her, and my time passes much faster than I would ever have believed. She begins to be very charming and very pretty. What would I not give for you to see her, dear Alexander! You would love her I am sure. I wish you could see Bonsi with his child, he spends every spare minute with her. You have no idea how he loves her. It has to be admitted that she *is* charming, a beautiful little creature, formed to give pleasure. She already has so much spirit and understanding. How I wish she could already speak!

It could be said that these were the sentimental outpourings of a woman with her first child, but Darja remained a devoted mother for the rest of her life. On the stage of politics, diplomacy and worldly affairs which she would occupy in later life, this care for her children was one of the mainsprings of her character. She may have seemed disdainful of her duties as a mother, and perhaps tried not to show in public how she felt about her children, but her passionate feelings for them dominated her thoughts.

Between 1805 and 1807 she bore three boys, Alexander, Constantine and Paul. But in the latter year the charming, well-formed, so welcomed and so much loved little girl died. The young mother never referred to her death, she preferred to write of the growing good looks of her three boys. 'My three boys are all well. Constantine will be very handsome in time, he will certainly be better looking than the two eldest, although I don't think he will be able to alter my affection for Paul . . .'

Unlike her gossipy letters about births, marriages, deaths, divorces, duels and demotions, her letters about her children were full of solicitude and good sense.

It is not difficult to form the impression that, after the first excitement of being a wife instead of a schoolgirl had worn off, dear Bonsi's preoccupation with his duties about Tsar and Court had begun to pall. One of her lovers was supposed to have been Prince Petrovic Dolgoruki, for she later confessed to Metternich that Dolgoruki had 'blundered' in his diplomatic career. Metternich agreed and added approvingly that her past love for the man had obviously not blinded her to his indiscretions.

Darja, once she had decided against a man – or a woman – was not slow to discard the person in question. Prince Dolgoruki appears to have been a classic Russian aristocrat who could have stepped out of the pages of Tolstoy. At a ball he had picked a quarrel with one of the *chevalier gardes*, the lover of Zubova. Dolgoruki, presumably in his cups, tried to get Borodin to repeat the insult to the lady in question. Borodin refused, and told Prince Dolgoruki to carry out his own quarrels.

'After further angry words', wrote Darja, 'they gave one another a rendez-vous for yesterday – a duel with pistols. Dolgoruki was shot in the knee – the bullet is still there. I ought to be upset about this, but in truth it gives me great pleasure.' She added that the whole town was laughing at Dolgoruki. Her heartless comment was, 'Comme il est bête cet homme d'esprit.'

But a week later, in spite of her protestations of indifference, she sent news of the injured man. He was still in the same state, for the bullet was lodged too near to the main artery to be taken out. 'La Zubova is leaving for Poland – the rumour is that her husband is sending her away.'

The story of anger and stupidity finished tragically. 'This post brings news which you, dear Alexander, will not have expected – the death of Dolgoruki. A day or two ago he fell into a malignant fever, and after three days became near to death. From this time to the day of his death which was a week after his illness, he was so enfeebled that he was only conscious for brief periods. He died, or rather fell asleep, without any suffering. He had always refused communion. My husband went to see him at every moment he could spare from his duties with the Tsar.'

The last sentence either indicates a very kind heart on the part of Count Lieven, a lack of knowledge of his wife's attachment, or perhaps an underlining of the fact that Darja's relations with Prince Dolgoruki were more innocent than she was later to indicate.

But there were other rumours – that she had cast her eyes upwards towards the Imperial family itself, and that her lover was the Grand Duke Constantine. He had recently abandoned his German wife, and was leading the kind of dissolute life which could also stem from the writings of Tolstoy, drinking, gambling, and carrying out absurd and cruel practical jokes, usually on underlings who could not refuse, such as forcing a terrified French actor called Froger to jump out of the window, without letting on that there was a mattress to break his fall. Darja related his exploits as amusing eccentricities. If these two men were indeed her lovers, they do not seem to have been more than amusements to cure ennui.

During the time between 1805 and 1807 when she was occupied in bearing her children, flirting, and being bored at Court, the greater arena of war and politics was gradually changing her little world. The French army had smashed its way into Poland, and Napoleon's epic victories of Austerlitz, Eylau and Friedland were only stages in the march which would eventually bring Darja's beloved Tsar into conflict with the usurping Emperor Napoleon. But there was no mention of these terrible events in Darja's letters. This seems astonishing in view of the fact that her patriotism was intense, and that her husband was aide-de-camp to the Tsar, who had joined his armies in the field, and that her brother was attached to General Bennigsen. No doubt the latter's part in the murder of Paul I had been overlooked in the general emergency. The only references that Darja makes to war, are wishes for her brother's success, and complaints about her separation from her husband.

'You have no idea, dear Alexander, how this separation is upsetting me, especially as I am in the dark about when I shall see him again, and it seems as if their absence will be for a long time. But at least I have the advantage over the other wives. I am told that a strong French army is near you, and I must say that this makes me very worried and increases my desire for letters from you.'

She preferred to gloss over the dangers of war, as she had refused to dwell on the death of her little daughter. Yet her husband had fought not only at the battle of Austerlitz but also at Eylau. But like Jane Austen who preferred that the pens of others should dwell on shame and misery, so did Darja prefer to send news of gossip and scandal, and to ignore the real dangers of the bloody battlefields so far away from her own world, while remaining concerned with what she euphemistically called the 'success' of her brother, and the absence of her husband. Hers was a personal war.

Bonsi's attitude was more patriotic, professional and practical. 'Do not neglect, my dear Alexander', he wrote, 'to keep me posted of everything which is interesting to know, adding your own thoughts. I will know how to draw from these something for the general good. You told me that Bennigsen had need to be encouraged. I have not forgotten to send a flattering note to him by the present messenger. I cannot conceal from you, my dear friend, the anxiety which I feel on the destiny of our army.' He writes of his fear of a second defeat. 'There must be great events going on near you. I am basing these suppositions on the news which we have of the march of the French army ... But if Bennigsen has the good sense to fall back on the main body of our army, when he sees the enemy forces are superior to his – perhaps the danger will not be

44

so great. But I fear that he may not wish to fall back – so he will be too exposed.'

Count Lieven goes on to record the departure of friends and relations. All the young men are going. Everything is being done for the needs of the Army, and he hoped that in view of their exertions the Russians will be able to endure – at least until the spring – without great and tragic losses, because by then 'we shall have the help of the great masses in the interior of Russia which will make us superior to the enemy'.

The dangers which Count Lieven had foreseen were at first avoided. Bennigsen was able to elude the French and to avoid closing with them. But finally, hard pressed by Napoleon, he had to give battle at Eylau. This encounter was indecisive in spite of bloody losses. But it prepared the way for the crushing of the Russian forces at Friedland. A few days after that battle the Tsar and Napoleon signed the treaty of Tilsit which made peace between Russia and France. But the way was being prepared for 1812.

The deadly blows and humiliating disasters which had fallen on Russia had their effect in making Darja aware of the evil abroad in the world. She was no longer the happy lover and bride whose laughter had filled the house. She had seen her beloved and adored Tsar treating with an upstart, a soldier of fortune who had come from nowhere to beat down countries and kings by the power of his armies and the skill of his military strategy.

Darja was twenty-two years old, but, although she expressed herself in simple and homely terms, the underlying bitterness of her affront at the defeat of Russia and its consequences ran like a dark thread under her naive description of her feelings.

I have neglected to write to you, my dear Alexander, for the same reason that you have given me for your silence. I have a mentality which takes ill to these events. I am in an abominable humour. I am in conflict with everyone and everybody I meet, from morning to night, and particularly with my husband – without of course that this makes any difference to conjugal love. It is the need to dispute, to give full rein to my bad humour which I cannot conquer.

Everything and everyone flows back to Peterhof for the festivities. I am staying alone at home because my feelings make me ill disposed to take part in the pleasures of society. Although my husband has arrived, I have remained at Tsarskoe Selo, and I content myself with seeing him for a few hours once a week. I have a double interest in staying here. First of all – for my health and that of my children who are benefiting so much, and secondly because I would be ashamed to see anyone. I cannot tell you the deep humiliation which I feel at what has passed.

Soon after Darja had written this letter, Alexander was made a captain in the Army, and returned to St. Petersburg to carry on his duties as aide-de-camp to the Tsar, and there were no more letters. The brother and sister saw one another every day.

In 1808 Count Lieven resigned from the Army and took up his Court appointments again. No doubt Darja resumed her routine and her boredom. There were undoubted disadvantages in a husband who was so conscientiously attached to the minutiae of Court life. There must be something more interesting that he could do . . . It has been suggested that it was the young Countess's idea that her husband should leave the Army and try for a post in Russia's diplomatic service. It is well possible that her feelings towards the total tedium of life at the Russian Court, impelled her to make this suggestion.

Outside in the wider world there could be more amusement, and possibly more opportunities.

CHAPTER FIVE

Diplomatic Overture

In April of 1810 Count Lieven was appointed Russian Ambassador to the Prussian Court at Berlin. Bonsi had changed careers.

The Lievens' stay in Berlin opened in unfortunate circumstances. King Frederick William of Prussia was hardly in high humour to welcome the Russians who had made peace with the victorious Napoleon. He had lost that part of his kingdom west of the Elbe, and had watched Europe falling vassal to the all-conquering French armies.

It need hardly be said that the mission of Count Lieven to Berlin was without distinction, nor could any diplomatic plums be pulled out of a pie which had been cooked and baked by others. Frederick William, presiding over his dismembered kingdom, was merely playing for time; the role of the Russian Ambassador was somewhat ambiguous. It was to keep the Prussian King's hope high in rather depressing circumstances. On the other hand, Bonsi could not commit his Tsar to any form of action, or even express his beloved ruler's fears of a further outbreak of hostilities.

Whatever the feelings of Count Lieven himself, the Prussian Court had even less appeal for Darja than Court life at home. She was not yet aware of her talents in the realm of social diplomacy. She still saw herself as helpmeet and mother, and savoured the joy of having her children with her, while enjoying the privileges of her husband's rank and status. A letter to her sister Masha indicates more interest in frills, and finery than high policy. She had been presented to Queen Louise and the picture she paints of her visit gives the impression that for all their rank they were just two young women gossiping and comparing *toilettes*.

She received me most amiably and kept me with her for over two hours, asking thousands of questions about Petersburg, about you and in general only speaking about Russia and the Russians

47

whom she seems to like very much. She showed me her apartments which are quite pretty, especially her bedroom which is arranged rather after the taste of Petersburg, draperies, alabaster columns and a great incense burner smoking in the middle of the room – in one word, it is very pretty.

She herself was even prettier. She wore a short jacket which was open in the front, poppy-red, embroidered in gold, embroideries like the uniforms of the Cossacks, matching cossack sleeves, and underneath a robe of white satin with embroideries in gold.

The cap the Queen was wearing seems to have been a political compromise, and possibly a sartorial disaster, for Darja described it as half-Cossack and half-Uhlan: 'very wide at the top, and narrow at the base. It was also poppy-coloured and embroidered in gold like her jacket. The whole ensemble was charming and suited her to perfection. Her collar was high on her neck like those of the Cossacks. I found it odd, but pretty. She has not changed since Petersburg – but the King has got much fatter. Today is the Queen's feast-day, and there is to be a huge ball at the Palace. I am going, and intend to make myself as beautiful as possible.'

But her brief interest in Berlin soon faded, and her boredom returned.

The receptions here are wearisome in the extreme, the women far from amiable; the men only cheerful so long as they are eating. As my house is not yet in a state to receive many people, I do not know what effect the cuisine of my cook will have on the men's humour. At the moment I am simply seeing a few foreigners, amongst whom are the Ministers of France and Austria. They are the most distinguished as far as I can hear. . . . Bonsi goes out much more than I do. I walk in the Park with my children, then I eat and sleep. These are the pleasures of Berlin.

Time did not change her opinion. 'These are the most extraordinary people. The King is nothing at all, and as obstinate as a mule. It had been suggested to him that it was as well not to be too friendly with us, and he followed this advice exactly. On the other hand I have been told that he travelled thirty miles to see a few Russian sailors who happened to be passing through. His son is dressed like a Cossack and appears like this both in the streets – and even at balls.'

It would seem that the wretched King of Prussia was uncertain how to proceed. Should Napoleon attack him again, he might need the Tsar. On the other hand it was no good provoking the tyrant, better perhaps to give the Russians the cold shoulder – at least in public.

'I am looking after my health while I am in Germany, and I hope it will not be for long.' It was to be longer than she thought – nearly two years. Meanwhile she devoted herself to her children, and did as little as she could in the diplomatic and social field. Her husband could attend to this, it was part of a man's work, and a man's world. But she did seize the opportunity once she was away from the Russian Court restrictions to travel with her children. She went to the sea, to the spas to take the waters, and stayed away as long as she could without upsetting her husband, or jeopardising his mission. Unless something grand and violent happened soon, she felt they would wither away in Berlin. She had not long to wait.

In the spring of 1811 she wrote: 'The district around here is filling up with French troops. You will soon have laurels to cut. These laurels will no doubt make me take the road to Russia, and I will be very easy with the thought. My health is not good, my looks have gone to the devil, and my temper is not of the best, in any case there is nothing here to make me kind or gentle.'

At the end of 1811 the Lievens were back in Russia – recalled by the Tsar. The following spring Darja was still hanging about in Russia, and impatiently waiting to know what was to become of them. What post was her husband to be given? It seemed it all depended on the progress of the war. But Darja was anxious to be abroad again. Her health was not good, and the Russian climate had adversely affected her well-being, she wrote. In retrospect, Berlin took on the air of a spa. It is natural to pine for home, and when one arrives there to find it not quite as it was imagined in retrospect.

There was a good deal to complain about when it came to the climate in Russia. Lady Londonderry, who visited Russia in the 1830s described the climate very vividly.

The cold is not to be imagined, but is fearful when felt. Light furs feel like cold linen. The eyelashes are painful, the breath freezes, the windows become opaque, and a sickening feeling pervades the whole frame as of a knife cutting to one's very marrow.

I had a little room with a fireplace. Here I have sat on the fender and lain on the rug without feeling warm and have gone from that to the next room to glue myself against the stove and then back again in despair to look at the fire.

How the coachmen and horses stand the cold I know not. They wait for hours. Their beards are as white as snow with the frost. Nor can I conceive how the women contrive to bear it. It is very true that only one instant suffices to jump into the carriage. But in full *toilette* these Russian ladies rush from a heat of 25 degrees to a cold of 25 below zero, a transition of 50 degrees in a moment.

Frances Anne, Lady Londonderry, was totally uninterested in the state of the serfs or the despotism under which even her aristocratic friends were forced to live. What interested her was the luxury. In the great houses orange trees bloomed all the year round and the air was scented with their blossoms, while the fountains played. The dresses of the Court ladies were trimmed not with frills or embroideries but diamonds from shoulder to hem.

And then there were the furs – she had inspected the fine sables of Madame Stroganov, but she had been warned by experts. Black fox was more esteemed than sable. Lady Londonderry was undecided, fox seemed to her to be too long a fur for use in England. She had a fancy perhaps to have black fox as a cloak lining. 'But I found the finest fox linings cost fifty or sixty thousand roubles, and that their beauty consisted in the black of the raven, and the lightness of the eiderdown.' To collect enough to form one cloak lining was quite an undertaking; it took five or six years and two thousand dead foxes – for in order to achieve the requisite colour and lightness, only one small piece near the tail was fine enough to be used.

Diamonds, sables and black fox – all was richness and luxury. Yet squalor lurked near. When Lady Londonderry went to a Court ball her chest was so flea bitten that the Tsarina remarked on it. On being informed of the true reason for the lady's rash, the Tsarina remarked succinctly: 'Quelle honte!'

Lady Londonderry did not explain whether the Tsarina meant that it was shaming for a lady to be bitten, or shaming that it had been made patently plain that Russian houses contained so many fleas.

While the Countess Lieven was in Berlin she had presumably forgotten the sharp contrast between the soft cloaks of the finest sable, and the fleas in the vestibules where they had to be left. When abroad it was comfortable to remember the warmth of the houses where the living vines trailed round the marble statues, and the orange blossoms perfumed the air; to recall the swift sledges gliding across the snow, and the glitter of jewels in the Imperial ballrooms. But now some of the realities were rammed home. It was not as she remembered it. Like some restive horse, Darja was eager to be off, the stable had become too confining. 'The uncertainty of my lot means that I cannot settle down happily ... I have no idea from one moment to the next when or where I am going to see my husband.'

One thing she had settled in her mind. She was not going to see the ice on the Neva, and if her husband did not get another diplomatic appointment, she had decided to travel south. 'Crimea appeals to me, and Constantine is absolutely decided to accompany me if I go there.'

She was annoyed about her situation. But the whole of Europe was in as great a state of turmoil as the young Countess Lieven. Darja, like many women, was inclined to see wars as affronts deliberately fostered for her personal inconvenience. Men can view a war as a moment for adventure, and an escape from domesticity, but women, except in rare cases, seldom do, and Darja was a very feminine woman.

The background to her uncertainties was that the French and Russian Emperors were engaged in a diplomatic dance in which each hoped to deceive the other, while gaining some political benefit without war. But now the cards were on the table.

Up to that moment the Tsar Alexander had hoped to avoid further battles with the French, but already it was becoming too late for feints. He decided to become reconciled with the English, and part of that reconciliation was the appointment of Count Lieven as Ambassador to London. The previous Russian Ambassador, the prudent Simon Romanovich Woronzow had stayed *en poste* from the reign of Louis XVI, through the upheavals of the French revolution, and the Terror, until 1806, the climax of Napoleon's power when he dominated Europe, and filled its thrones with his family and friends. It was *then* that the Russians, always eager to be on the right side, withdrew Count Woronzow. A pro-English ambassador seemed to them to be a diplomatic blunder. But the Count pleading his delicate health, warily stayed on in London as a private gentleman until his death nearly thirty years later. Woronzow Road N.W. still commemorates the prudent Ambassador who decided not to return to his native country. The rise and fall of favourites under the Tsars was too risky a business, and the Count elected to remain in England as a simple gentleman of delicate health living quietly in healthful St. John's Wood. Prudence is ever the better part of valour.

From the time the prudent Count retired into private life until the invasion of Russia in 1812, there had been no Russian ambassador to the Court of St. James. The lack of an ambassador in London had been all part of Alexander's policy of pleasing and placating Napoleon after the Treaty of Tilsit. But now even Alexander could see that war could not be avoided, and in war one

51

needs allies, however belatedly chosen. For the appointment of Count Lieven as Ambassador to London was decided in September of 1812 when the French had already defeated the Russians at Borodino. By 14 September Napoleon was in Moscow, but Darja was much more concerned with her imminent departure for London than with the burning of the Russian capital.

'I am very impatient to leave here, but there are always new obstacles at the last minute. Now that everything is fixed for our departure, my husband has a very bad chill with fever, and as in the case with most men he is always in bed. This is really upsetting me because of the season.'

Bonsi's illnesses in the past, as with the murder of the Tsar Paul I, had sometimes turned out for the best, but in this case Darja could see no advantage in it. There is a lack of sympathy and immense irritation in the way she wrote of dear Bonsi's fever. Here was this amazingly lucky opportunity for a new and brilliant life, and he managed to catch a most inconvenient chill. For the young Countess knew that the later the season, the worse the journey was going to be. St. Petersburg was built on a bog and a westerly blowing wind could easily flood the town. Lady Londonderry wrote graphically about a winter journey: 'It will be a fearful journey, hundreds of versts through howling wilderness. I am getting chilblains like a housemaid … they say wolves attack single travellers only, and when they do they leave nothing but the boots with the toes in them.'

The terrors of winter travelling, even if the danger of wolves was eliminated, were the snowdrifts, the bad roads, the fear of bandits, the accidents to the heavily laden coaches, and the squalor and dirt of the roadside rest houses. It was small wonder that Darja was anxious to be off before the Neva froze over. Their journey had been carefully planned to avoid all the horrors of travelling overland in winter.

'We are still waiting for news of the Grande Armée. The last bulletins announced that the forces of Napoleon were bearing down on our army. I am not really upset at being here in order to hear the results of this great event.' As always, Darja tempered patriotism with a liking to be *au fait* with the latest events.

Count Lieven took a different, if equally self-absorbed point of view, when writing to his brother-in-law:

I am hoping to leave here in six or eight days. I would have been on the eve of leaving if a slight indisposition had not delayed me.

I have been given the most brilliant, the most important, and the most agreeable post to which I could possibly have aspired.

The present moment gives it not only importance, but the greatest relief.... My happiness overflows, as does the thankfulness which I feel towards the Tsar at this outstanding demonstration of his goodness and of the extent of his confidence in me. My wife, as you can imagine, joins with a full heart in my happiness – how could she possibly wish for anything better?

The letter said everything. Darja was as overjoyed as her husband. Although she purported to be bored with the tedium of life in Berlin, she had at least been free to come and go. All her close relatives were under the sway and the whims of the Tsar, whether it was the madman Paul I, or the more vacillating Alexander. She had felt the pleasure of a lighter rein, and tasted the amusement of being able to travel without asking permission. Being at the Russian Court was restrictive – restrictive in etiquette, restrictive in movement, and restrictive in thought. Until the day when a Tsar was murdered or died in his bed, and was carried off to the tombs of his ancestors, he was there to be flattered and deferred to as the All-Powerful. St. Petersburg may have been a window on to the world, but it was not the wider world itself.

The Lievens finally sailed for England in late October of 1812 and disembarked at Harwich in early December.

No letters or diaries of Darja describe her feelings on leaving Russia, nor her first impressions of England. No doubt the physical energy needed to transport her family, those retainers whom she needed to bring with her, and the immense number of chattels with which the rich of that time needed to impress both themselves – and foreigners – was enough to sap the energy of even the most energetic of wives.

It was not until the following spring when she was already installed in the Russian Embassy at 36 Harley Street that she again began to write to her brother Alexander, who was at the front. 'I read this morning some extracts from the *Moniteur* that we have had a brush with the French Army on the Elbe ... one acquires a certain facility in being able to comment on the French newspapers. It is only necessary to substitute the word *defeat* for the word *victory...*'

For now her best hopes were beginning to be realised. The forward march of the Allies was again changing the face of Europe. The British victories in Spain had added to Napoleon's difficulties, and the disastrous retreat from Moscow in the winter of 1812/1813 had gradually induced wavering countries like Austria and Prussia to change sides, albeit slowly, and with backward glances and conditions.

Darja had no qualms about the ultimate end of the wars. Alexander's accommodations with Napoleon were all forgotten in the glow of victory. Forgotten also was the fact that the Tsar had not taken up arms against the tyrant of his own volition but rather had been forced into renewed battles. The nobility, the grandeur and the gigantic scale of the Russians' victories swept over Darja with a wave of enthusiasm and patriotism. The Russians had swept the invading hordes of French from Moscow to the Elbe. Even more wonderful was it that after such a series of victories and triumphs her beloved Tsar was acting with such *moderation*. This placed him above everyone, and how happy it was for Europe that her destiny was in the hands of such a ruler as Alexander!

'How the world has been turned upside down since we saw one another. What a brilliant year you have seen!' She rejoiced in the fact that her own brother was in the victorious army which was smashing its way through to the final defeat of Napoleon. As for their Tsar, he was not only admirable and noble, but admired by everyone, everywhere. It is undeniable that loyalty goes to the powerful, and on this head the Tsar's glory stood firm and, to the Lievens, holy.

But in England the Lievens found a less reverent attitude towards royalty. It must have astonished them to see the coarse cartoons of Cruikshank. The Regent (with his overflowing stomach), reclining beside his mistresses (with their equally overflowing bosoms). This was hardly the way a future king could be depicted in Russia. Nor were the lampoons in the newspapers about the relations of the Regent with his wife flattering, or decorous. Whatever happened in Russia was hidden. The attitude of the English towards their rulers must have come as a profound shock.

After a few months the Lievens decided to have another home outside London, and rented a house in the adjoining countryside – in Streatham. This was the residence of Mrs. Piozzi, the friend of Dr. Johnson, formerly Mrs. Thrale. It was an opulent and well-appointed house, for Henry Thrale had made his large fortune in brewing. Mrs. Piozzi, while admitting that the Lievens paid her well, took the usual jaundiced view of tenants. 'His dependents smoke their tobacco in my nice new beds and play a thousand tricks that keep my Stewards, whom I have left there, in perpetual agony.' From these remarks it sounds as if the Lievens had brought some of their servants from Russia; and if they had brought their Russian ways of behaving into the decorous house of Mrs. Piozzi, it was not surprising if their Slav disorder did not please the stewards. In Russia servants, and sometimes indeed the family, had no bedrooms. The servants threw rugs or odd mattresses down anywhere they pleased; they slept in passages, on staircases, or outside the bedroom doors of their masters. The masters and mistresses themselves did not have sleeping chambers, but some sort of combination room. In the case of a lady it could be a boudoir drawing-room with a bed behind a screen.

The Lievens had chosen this rural Streatham retreat for the sake of their three sons, away from the fog and smoke of the centre of London, and yet a mere short carriage drive from the receptions and dinners necessary for carrying out the delicate diplomatic mission on which dear Bonsi was engaged – to make plain to the English that the Russians were at last to be part of the peace-making force in Europe.

In 1813 the Prince Regent was seven years away from becoming King in form, although he was acting as King in fact. The Lievens were well received in London society, for they were a novelty. But it took them, and particularly Darja, some time to get the measure of the English character. After ten months she wrote to her brother:

This beautiful England is always the same. It is a long chain of perfections, but they are perfections which strike your mind, and not your imagination. I will admit that there are two months of infatuation, because everything here is beautiful – and extraordinary, so that your curiosity and your imagination are always in play. But once you have seen everything, you are fatigued with admiration. You wish to *feel* and this is not a country of emotions.

Personally I find myself well-looked after, and under such splendid auspices that I have been received as no other foreigner has been received. Personally I feel that I have succeeded, but I would not like to die in this country. I am always astonished at the Anglomania which seems to overtake my countrymen. There are many good reasons for shaking off this passion when one lives amongst the English.

Time was to correct her first view of the English, and the cultured aristocrats amongst whom she moved were gradually to draw her into their circle. But in the first months of her life in England, she was a spectator and not a participant in the social game. She was still in her own soul a part of Russia feeling intensely, although from the other side of the ocean, the agonies, anxieties and vicissitudes of her country, and its Tsar. She was not only excited, but impatient, and in many senses, felt isolated being so far away from the events which followed one another in such swift succession.

Nor was the weather conducive to a happy frame of mind. The year 1814 began with one of the coldest winters for centuries. The Thames between London Bridge and Blackfriars, according to Lord William Pitt Lennox, was frozen solid. All the fun of the Fair, usually seen at St. Bartholomew's Tide, moved on to the ice. There were fortune tellers, hawkers of everything from ribbons and laces, to ballads celebrating the Great Frost, ballads which were printed on presses set up on what was called the Great Mall. Countess Lieven had left St. Petersburg before the ice had closed in, and now it seemed to have followed her to London. Although it had to be admitted the Cockneys enjoyed the unusual sight of their frozen river in a jollier way than her compatriots.

After the Great Frost, snow fell continuously for six weeks. But on the other side of the Channel the empire of Napoleon was crumbling. The Grande Armée had been destroyed, and now both the Austrians and the Prussians had marched into Paris, while Wellington had defeated Soult at Toulouse.

The defeats of Napoleon and his abdication, and exile to Elba filled Darja with triumphant joy. Like many Russians since her day, she attributed the defeat of Europe's enemies entirely to the force of Russian arms. The sea power of Britain, the decisive battle of Trafalgar, the long slog of Wellington through Spain into France might never have happened as far as Countess Lieven was concerned. To Russia alone were awarded the laurels of victory.

The spring had come, the snows had melted. The war seemed to be over, and London was *en fête*.

At Carlton House, the Prince Regent celebrated the return of the Bourbons with a rash of *fleurs de lys*. *The Times* seemed to be as besotted as the rest of the world at the ending of the Napoleonic threat and announced: 'The Prince Regent and Louis XVIII have each in his sphere done their duty before God and man.' Neither King nor Regent had been noticeable in the field of battle, nor concerned overmuch in the peace negotiations which followed, except as pawns to be used by politicians. But no doubt reading these hymns of praise gave the whole nation a warm feeling that happiness was spilling over, and the unpopular Regent might as well enjoy the applause.

The aristocratic English, having been deprived of Continental travel and the Grand Tour for so long, all set off for Paris, the women to search for new fashions, and the men for a change of women. Caricatures of English and French women emphasised the dowdiness into which English dress had fallen as a result of being cut off from French designers, and the taste and fashion of Paris. The gap from the Peace of Amiens in 1802 until the abdication of Napoleon had led to a strange dichotomy between London and Paris. English fashion plates show corsetted ladies with dowdy flat bonnets and dresses with no particular elegance of line. When the elegant Englishwoman arrived in Paris she found that she was not elegant at all. As a consequence she quickly abandoned her stuffy clothes, and with them her natural waistline and her restricting corsets. It is possible that the Countess Lieven included the dowdy local fashions in her strictures on English society.

But there were other ennuis for the Russian Ambassadress in the spring and summer of 1814. If the English were flocking to Paris, the Russians had decided that London was the place to visit. Already, at the end of March, the Tsar's sister, the widowed Grand Duchess Catherine of Oldenburg, had sailed into Sheerness with a large suite of attendants and four carriages to keep up the dignity of her State and status in London. The Grand Duchess appears to have embodied in her person and manners all the worst traits of her race. She was overbearing in her person and manners, and liked to be the centre of attention. Darja noted her as being seductive in glance and manners. It could have been dangerous to criticise the Tsar's sister adversely. Others, less politically or diplomatically involved with the Duchess, remarked on her flat Slav face, small black eyes and crinkled black hair.

She and her entourage took over the whole of Pulteney's Hotel in Piccadilly, the Grand Duchess termed the hotel 'a furnished mansion'. For this she paid a mere 210 guineas a week, and, not feeling herself subject to the laws which usually pertain between host and guests, she stayed there for a disastrous three months, during which time she did everything she could to upset the Regent, and irritate those with whom she came into contact, including the Countess Lieven.

The visit had begun badly because the Prince Regent had turned up at Pulteney's Hotel before the lady had donned her finery, or put on her war paint. As a result of this contretemps the Prince and the Grand Duchess, put out by the stupidities which ensued as a result of this encounter, took an immediate dislike to one another. Opinion varies as to the aims of the mission of the Grand Duchess to London. Some alleged that she was concerned to prevent the Princess Charlotte marrying the Prince of Orange, a match which the Regent himself was anxious to promote. The idea of a marriage alliance cementing the British and Dutch fleets was seen by St. Petersburg as a direct threat, and a threat which could be stopped by the Grand Duchess *en mission* to London. Others thought that the Grand Duchess, being a widow, was setting her personal cap at the Regent. If this was the original intention, the *premier rencontre* at Pulteney's Hotel had sadly altered the case.

The Regent had been disposed to be expansive to the Russians. They were victorious allies and, almost immediately after the arrival of the Grand Duchess, the Prince decided to give one of his splendid and elegant entertainments at Carlton House. The carefully chosen foods, the long French menus, the masses of hothouse flowers, and the musicians – everything was designed to give pleasure to the Russian Grand Duchess. The Regent, being a great lover of music, commanded the best musicians he had to play quietly as a background to the feast.

The first remark which the Grand Duchess made was that music 'made her vomit', and that the musicians must be silenced at once. The Prince angrily gave the order for the music to cease, and the crestfallen musicians beat a hasty retreat, no doubt much to the annoyance of music-loving guests accustomed to enjoy that part of the Prince's entertainments. Even the Countess Lieven, with her patriotic Russian feelings, remarked that during the silence which followed 'we no longer knew what to do'.

But as far as the Count Lieven's ambassadorship in London was concerned he had begun with everything in his favour. Owing to the exigencies of the long wars, there were only four ambassadors in the capital. Because of the war, the cost of living in London was very high, but the Russian Ambassador was well provided with funds. Only the previous year the Austrian Chargé d'Affaires had been forced to sell his silver plate from the Embassy in order to pay his tradesmen. He could not raise the £17,000 necessary to keep up his status in any other way. Even £17,000 was barely sufficient to keep an ambassador in the manner to give *éclat* to the entertainments he must give to reflect the grandeur of his country. The Lievens were in the happy position of being able to dispose of twice that sum. The result was that the Russians were able to make their Embassy, and their Embassy receptions and *ridottos* the most sought after and fashionable in London. A little foreign gold is ever able to oil the wheels of social commerce.

But in spite of their money and lavish entertainments, Darja does not at first seem to have made a success of her husband's mission. In the spring of 1814 the Russian Foreign Minister Nesselrode wrote: 'Lieven continues to succeed as well as his wife continues to fail.' Darja's lack of social success had been noted. The watchful eyes of the Russian Court were on their emissaries abroad as on their ministers at home.

It has ever been the fault of the English to be overpolite to foreigners, to conceal their feelings about the criticisms passed by foreigners on English manners and customs, and to make no reply to carping remarks made at the expense of their country. It is possible that when she came to London Darja had made the mistake of being too openly critical. But no doubt the even more monstrous mistakes being deliberately perpetrated by her compatriot, the Grand Duchess, must have inclined the Countess to see things from the English point of view. The Tsar's sister found the Regent licentious and obscene, while the Regent had been angered by references made by the Grand Duchess to his treatment of his wife and daughter, both subjects which were tabu in his intimate circle. Why was the Princess Charlotte not at the dinner, asked the Grand Duchess? The Regent remarked that his daughter was too young to be seen in the great world. 'Not too young,' remarked the Grand Duchess tartly, 'for you to have chosen a husband for her.'

'When she is married, madam, she will do as her husband pleases; for the present she does as *I* wish.'

The Grand Duchess made an even sharper reply that between husband and wife there could be only one will. She had emphasised this point by dressing in deep mourning, as a sign of respect for her late husband, and a lack of respect for the Regent's dinner party.

'The Regent', said Countess Lieven, 'turned sharply to me and observed loudly, "This is intolerable."'

From that moment onwards the relations between the Regent and the representative of his Russian ally went from bad to worse. The Regent himself was hardly the most popular figure in the land, and very often he had been hissed in the streets because of his bad relations with his wife, his debts, and his cold attitude towards his only child, the Princess Charlotte. Like many fathers he felt he could not risk the growing popularity of his young fresh-faced daughter. But while he, in his own country, was often unable to drive about the streets, the Grand Duchess bowled happily about London to the plaudits of the crowd. Her next blow to the Regent was to announce that she would visit his wife. This was too much, even for the cautious Count Lieven. He was *en poste* in London, and if the Tsar's sister insisted on flouting etiquette in this way – he would resign. At this juncture the Grand Duchess gave way, but she had not given up the idea of fishing in troubled waters, and went to visit the Princess Charlotte. If she could not insult the Regent by visiting his wife, she could at least annoy him by visiting his daughter.

With the wrangles between the Prince Regent and his wife delighting the town and causing much gossip, backbiting, and letter-writing, and the upsets caused by the Russian Grand Duchess, the atmosphere was hardly as calm or as conducive to joy and happiness as the victories of Britain and Russia should have merited. By the time the Tsar Alexander arrived things were already sadly awry.

The Tsar and King Frederick of Prussia landed at Dover on 6 June. Alexander, his character of 'liberal' Tsar well to the fore, made the appropriate remark: 'God be praised! I have set foot in the land that saved us all.'

But, forewarned, possibly in letters from his sister, of the Regent's unpopularity, he flatly refused to join in the triumphal procession which had been planned. The Prince, always delighted to plan some showy celebration, had arranged that he should meet the Tsar on Shooter's Hill and then make a triumphal entry into London – driving through the City, as the Regent saw it in his mind's eye, to the happy plaudits of the waiting crowds. The Tsar managed to disrupt this cheerful plan, by jumping immediately into Count Lieven's carriage, and driving through the streets of London, totally unrecognised. The Regent, baulked of cheering crowds, went sulkily back to Carlton House. The Tsar had also refused an apartment which had been specially and splendidly arranged for him in St. James's Palace, and went off to the 'furnished mansion', Pulteney's Hotel. This was another blow to the Regent, but doggedly he announced his intention of welcoming the Tsar by coming to his hotel, an unprecedented and gracious step. This was immediately marred by the fact that the Regent could not get there. The Tsar and his 'platter-faced sister', as Lord Clancarty called her, waited two hours. A message arrived: 'His Royal Highness has been threatened with annoyance in the street if he shows himself; it is therefore impossible for him to come and see the Emperor.'

It has to be admitted that the Russians had hardly behaved with tact. The Grand Duchess had been flirting with the Whigs, having gone to inspect Whitbread's Brewery, and been personally shown the brewing processes by Mr. Samuel Whitbread himself. As Mr. Whitbread was one of the most radical of Whigs and had constantly spoken against the Allies waging war against Napoleon, this again hardly endeared her to the Regent, who had long ago deserted his Whig friends. Even Sheridan was a voice from the past, and only two years from his sad death.

Worse was to follow – the Regent's banquet for the evening of the Tsar's arrival was ignored. He stayed in his hotel and dined privately with his sister, leaving the splendour of the Carlton House dinner severely alone. The Tsar, no doubt prompted by his sister, took every advantage of the cheering crowds, happy no doubt in the knowledge that the Regent himself could not drive about the streets of his own capital without being hissed.

The autocratic Tsar, with his millions of slaves, who had gained his throne by a murder which still haunted his conscience, now posed in London as the champion of liberalism. The Hon. Mrs. Robinson wrote: 'The Tsar is, I am told, rather flippant in his conversation sometimes and lectured the Regent the other day on toleration; the Regent replied that it might be very well in his Imperial Majesty's dominions to admit people of all degrees into offices and power, but that if he was thoroughly acquainted with our Constitution and habits he would know that it could not be.' It does not sound as if the Regent himself were well acquainted with the real conditions of horror and squalor in Russia or he might have made a much tarter reply.

The Tsar then proceeded to send for the Whig leaders, Lord Grey, Lord Granville and Lord Holland. Another insult.

The physical appearance of the two sovereigns gave the Russian the advantage. The difference between the fat Regent with his assorted coloured wigs and the elegant and noble-seeming Tsar was great. 'The contrast between his natural manner and the artificial manufactured appearance of our Regent is most striking', wrote one commentator.

The arrogant behaviour of the Russian Royal family and their deliberate attempts to upset the poor Regent in his attempts to do what he so enjoyed doing – planning festivities, firework displays, and banquets – turned out badly for the Lievens who were caught in the centre of the various fracas and social disasters.

By the autumn the fireworks were forgotten, the Emperors and the Kings had departed, and Vienna had become the centre of Europe. The Regent contented himself by staying at home, his representatives being Castlereagh and Wellington. It was not surprising if by this time he should have had enough of visiting celebrities and was happy to sink back into domesticity at Brighton, or at the Cottage at Windsor.

The Congress of Vienna, which was dancing rather than working, was rudely shaken out of its convoluted deliberations by the escape of Napoleon from Elba.

The Countess Lieven's spirits, like those of many others, plummeted from the triumphant joy of victory into despair, and the return of the war to Europe filled her with renewed apprehensions. In April of 1816 she wrote:

My Dear Alexander, what happenings in the last weeks, and how

61

a little foresight could have prevented so many calamities falling once again on Europe. At least the energy and the forces which the Allies can deploy will put an end to this new crisis. I do earnestly hope that you will be able to profit by the peace and – in England. Finish the task, and I will give you a rendezvous at Brighton for next August. Here there are some carpers who call for peace, but everyone with any common sense understands that it is only bayonets and bullets which can do justice to that man, and preserve Europe from his domination. Meanwhile he is not in a happy position in Paris. It is in the hands of the Jacobins whose party is very strong in France, and while waiting to get the advantage, this most despotic of men is forced to don the livery of republicanism.

She could easily have made the same remarks about her own beloved, but despotic Tsar, donning the mantle of liberalism once he was away from his own country, but to Darja, the Tsar was not only the holy and revered father of his country, he was the liberator of Europe.

Darja went on to rejoice in the fact that Napoleon was totally without money. 'His words may be of honey, but, like the bees which adorn his coat of arms, he had his venom ready. The French are the most despised and the most despicable of men. At this moment they are awaiting another peaceful revolution which will bring back the Bourbons, and they will receive them with the same indifference with which they saw them go. It is the triumph of blackguardism.... I have been much out and about this year, and my health has benefited. Staying up late does not agree with me at all, and yet the *need* for distraction pushes me to go everywhere.'

Her character had hardly changed since she left the Smolny Institute at the age of fourteen. There were the same heights of excitement and the same depths of despair, and the same frantic search after pleasure, the same ensuing ennui, and the same lack of solid thought or of study. Darja was never to become a woman who delighted in reading or in reflection. She was a participator, a keenly observing participator: this was to remain her strength – and her weakness.

CHAPTER SIX

Successes and Civilities

Suddenly, from finding the English cold and stand-offish, the Countess began to change her mind. She changed her mind because she herself was beginning to blossom in the warm balm of appreciation. 'She is becoming known for her politeness and her courtesy to everyone. Her manner is admired, and as far as one can judge a great change has taken place', wrote Lady Granville. 'She takes account of our manners, and towards her husband she is loving, *seeming* to have the greatest regard for him.'

The beau monde smiled on her, and she felt at peace with herself.

Lady Granville was to become one of Darja's greatest friends, and a very useful friend, for she was at the heart of the great Whig aristocratic circle. Her mother was the unfortunate Duchess of Devonshire, Georgiana, and her aunt Lady Bessborough. This older generation of Whig ladies had been the intimate friends of Sheridan and Fox and now the next generation were becoming the focus of social attention. In the letters of Lady Granville, as she recounts the daily amusements of her worldly friends and relations, one can hear the echoes of the amusing cynical conversation which so fascinated Sheridan.

Harriet Granville accepted Countess Lieven as an intimate, in so far as women of that stamp ever allow outsiders to penetrate their innermost circles. The impression given on reading the references to Darja in Lady Granville's correspondence is that, although a foreigner, she had succeeded by being amusing, scandalous, and amused by turns. It was perhaps not surprising that she had found a way to fit herself into this background. Her upbringing had never inclined her to mix in circles where birth and breeding were not a passport leading to every social advantage. But the impression is given that the young Countess had managed the transition from the stiff and formal Court of St. Petersburg to the easier, yet equally formal, life of Regency England with consummate skill. She seems

63

to have had that chameleon ability, which she always retained, to change to the colours of her background.

A little dinner at Devonshire House shortly after the victory of Waterloo gives a picture of Darja amusing Lady Granville and her friends, and even succeeding in drawing a smile or two from Lord Granville himself. 'Monsieur de Lieven', wrote Lady Granville, 'never uttered.' Nor was Darja put out of countenance by the rudeness or grandeur of the Duke of Devonshire. She said, 'But we are throwing him into despair. I have never seen a man so desolated at having *women* in his house. Let us go away – he can put up with it no more!'

Her letters to her brother reflect her change of heart. 'Poor little brother, I am sorry for you, and for myself! I had hoped to see you here; I had even calculated the time of your coming to coincide with my visits to the country where we could go together, and where you would be as amused as I have been. We would admire together this beautiful country, these magnificent establishments; and we would laugh together at the gaucherie of their owners; but we would find, as I have found, that one would consent to seem gauche at the price of the happiness which these people have, and which they give to others.'

Sometimes she felt that there was such a fund of goodwill, cordiality and high spirits on the part of the English that she had perhaps made some errors in the judgements she had made. Everything was changing for her, and she was received everywhere. Her summer was occupied with a round of country house visits. She had stayed with the Duke of Devonshire, and voted Chatsworth 'worthy of an Emperor'. The Countess had arrived in England at a time when its aristocracy was at the height of its power and riches, when the countryside was at its most perfect, when the spreading of industrialisation had scarcely laid its dirty hands on fields and woods.

Her social success was made more certain because she had been drawn into the entourage of the Prince Regent. He liked to receive ladies of the Diplomatic Corps, both at the 'Cottage' at Windsor, and at Brighton. Like some monstrous bird putting its head into the sand, the Regent felt that if he received some respectable ladies, it would provide suitable cover for his relations with his various elderly mistresses. It had to be admitted that the ladies of the Diplomatic Corps could hardly refuse invitations from the powerful Regent.

'My husband and I are going this week to Brighton, on the invitation of the Prince Regent to meet the Queen Dowager, who is coming there for a short time. I am delighted at this opportunity of again getting some sea bathing... I shall see Brighton again where I passed such a pleasant time with you, dear Alexander, and I leave you to guess what regrets this recollection will evoke.' The Countess was excessively pleased with her social progress and wrote – with some complacence: 'My life in England is very different from when you knew it ... I am literally fought for. It is not fashionable where I am not, and I have even arrived at amusing the English, and amusing myself at the same time.'

She had never enjoyed England so much, she wrote to her brother. She made the round of all the country seats of the kingdom and now was settled back in London. At last she felt herself at home, was received everywhere and conscious of her success. One of her successes was the introduction of the waltz to London. During the season of 1816 it was danced for the first time at Almack's – the first two couples to dance it being Lord Palmerston and the Countess Lieven, and Baron de Neumann and the Princess Esterhazy.

Countess Lieven had now become one of the formidable ladies who disposed of cards to the famous Almack's in King Street, St. James's. Though women were barred from the men's drinking and gambling clubs they had set up their own exclusive venue given over to suppers, dancing, gossip, diplomacy and politics. 'Many diplomatic arts, much finesse and a host of intrigues were set in motion to get an invitation to Almack's.' The fearsome quintette who controlled the social destinies of the beau monde were Lady Castlereagh, Lady Jersey, Lady Cowper, the Princess Esterhazy (wife of the Austrian Ambassador), and, of course, the Countess Lieven.

At Almack's gentlemen or ladies connected with trade were beyond the pale. Male guests had to be able to dance with skill, to wear knee breeches, white cravats and the correct form of coat. Once a week a ball and supper were given at Almack's, and the social status of unfortunates not issued with invitations was doomed. Henry Luttrell wrote a verse on the subject:

> All on that magic list depends;
> Fame, fortune, fashion, lovers, friends:
> 'Tis that which gratifies or vexes
> All ranks, all ages – and both sexes.
> If once to Almack's you belong,
> Like monarchs you can do no wrong;
> But banished thence on Wednesday night,
> By Jove, you can do nothing right.

The dragon ladies of Almack's barred even the Duke of Wellington for wearing an offending pair of trousers. He is not on record as saying 'Debag me and be damned!', but it is doubtless true that he must have been very irritated. The victor of Salamanca and Waterloo barred by social butterflies for wearing a mere pair of trousers!

Countess Lieven was not only accepted, but, by steering a careful and tactful course amongst the shoals of the Royal Marriage squalls, she had managed to remain friends with the Regent, while becoming an intimate of his daughter, now safely married to Prince Leopold and living at Claremont.

We have been having festivities of all kinds lately. Princess Charlotte is happy and contented; they are both of them prodigiously in love – he with his wife, and she with her husband and her freedom. I have my own part in the latter; for I can see her just as often as formerly, and she is always charming. London society is very gay and brilliant this season. I amuse myself like the rest; I keep late hours, I dance, but I do not walk, and I find the exchange excellent for my pleasure – and not even bad for my health. I see a number of people at home on fixed days, and without vanity I may say that my soirées and those of Lady Jersey, are the most agreeable, and the most brilliant.

Alexander, her favourite brother was about to be married, or there was a rumour to that effect. 'Will you announce it to me yourself shortly? Is there beauty, wit – and a fortune? The union of these three qualities is delightful – find it, or don't marry!'

Wit in the sense in which people of the time used the word seems to have been a combination of high spirits, quick repartee and the ability to bring enjoyment and those graces which can make any social occasion sparkle. The *bons mots* of Madame Lieven which have been preserved strike the reader as sharply observant, and even verging on the cruel, especially as she became older and more experienced in the ways of men – and women. But now, at the beginning of her brilliant social career in England, she was full of high spirits, enjoying her success, and while some of her remarks verged on the tart they were not malicious.

In the autumn of 1816 another influx of Russians drove in to London expecting to be entertained. Their arrival does not seem to have pleased the Countess who was just about to set out on her round of autumn visits to various grand and princely homes about the countryside. 'The arrival of a number of our countrymen has detained us in town just as we were setting off to pay visits, and take a holiday in the country, so we were unable to go anywhere. However we had the satisfaction of not feeling these disappointments so acutely as we might have done had any other Russians fallen upon our hands. All this autumn's gathering has been agreeable, and accommodating, and has given us far more pleasure than trouble.'

Darja was distancing herself from her countrymen and seeing them through different eyes. In spite of her early strictures on the anglicisation of her countrymen, she had become infected with the same disease. She now tolerated the Russians rather than welcomed them. The Prince Gortschakov and Count Wittgenstein were tolerable. Colonel Pancratieff, the bearer of gifts for the Regent, seemed well-mannered 'without that swagger so common to our young officers'. The Grand Duke Nicholas had announced his arrival and Darja hoped that his stay would turn out more satisfactory than that of the Grand Duchess.

The young Countess had obviously not recovered from the constant harassment and difficulties produced by that unfortunate visit, and there remained the feeling that she was keeping her fingers crossed for better behaviour on the part of the Grand Duke. There was also the additional worry at the back of her mind that any Russian misbehaviour might militate against the advance of her social career. That could not be jeopardised.

'I see a good deal of the Coburgs, and as a matter of fact I claim to be the most intimate friend of the Princess Charlotte; at the same time showing enough prudence and reserve to prevent her father taking offence, for the family relations are the same as in your time. Her husband is behaving very well; she is greatly attached to him, and very submissive. I will not answer for the duration of their conjugal happiness, but it is certainly to be hoped that it may be lasting.' The last sentence has a melancholy and ironic ring when the swift end of the marriage story of Princess Charlotte is recalled.

In spite of her busy social life Darja remained as devoted to her children as when they were born. 'My children are growing apace, learning a few things, and are as thorough little scamps as you wish. Paul is at a different school to his brothers; he boxes in a ring, he makes as much noise as a regular John Bull, and, as I should scarcely have hoped, has become very courageous.'

Bonsi was in good health, much esteemed, and sent his regards and good wishes to his brother-in-law Alexander.

By December the Grand Duke Nicholas (afterwards to be the Tsar Nicholas I) had arrived. Darja noted that he seemed to be generally well liked and charming, although he had a mania for uniforms. 'His relations with the Prince Regent are excellent, and his manners most captivating. With women he is very timid, but his taste is good, and he pays his Court with deference. He has been generally successful, and I am very proud of the fact.' There was obviously a tinge of relief in the Countess's tone. No one had put a foot wrong, and she could congratulate herself on introducing the Grand Duke to the right people, and in the right atmosphere. A commentator writing some years later added a footnote to the visit. 'You may remember the Tsar Nicholas fourteen years ago in London, when he lived in a large house at the end of Stratford Place. He was then one of the Grand Dukes of Russia, travelling for his amusement. A fine-looking youth, making a conspicuous figure at Almack's in the waltz, whirling our English beauties round the circle to a quicker movement than they had previously learned to practise.'

Not all the social relationships between the Russians and the English turned out so well. The Duke of Devonshire had come back from Russia. He had been delighted by his reception from the Imperial family, who had behaved with the utmost correctness. But the other Russians he had met had not pleased him. Darja wrote tartly to her brother on this head. 'I can understand what has happened. They amused themselves at his expense, and altogether wrongly, for in spite of his dull manner, he is full of cleverness and wit, and his reception will give people *here* a bad idea of Russian courtesy.'

Out of the fund of her extensive knowledge of the English she told her brother that she wished 'you would not send Russians abroad who do far worse than make other people laugh at them' – they make themselves rightly despised. She had met Russians like this in Paris and they made her really angry. 'It was quite a patriotic pleasure when I met Michael Woronzow': he was so different. But then he had been much in England, and knew how to behave. Prince Michael Semenovitch Woronzow, although born in St. Petersburg, had been educated in London where his Anglophile father had been ambassador for so long.

With her social success secured, Darja's interest in politics was awakening. In December of 1816 there were riots. A mob had assembled with banners, and armed themselves, deciding to march through the City and seize the Tower of London. Darja recounted the day's doings: 'We have had trouble in London; mobs assembled, became excited and set about pillaging the town. This was all the more amusing as nothing came of it all. One man injured and some gunsmiths shops sacked.... There must be fresh outbreaks from time to time, the misery among the poor is extreme, and the English are not submissive. Nevertheless they are so accustomed to popular outbreaks in this country that this prospect causes no anxiety.'

It is curious that the Russians, even Tsar Alexander himself, could parade their liberal sympathies abroad, while totally ignoring their application in their own country, or like Darja, could comment on the misery of the English poor, while accepting slavery on their own territory.

The Russian mind, whether in its nineteenth-century guise or in the modern context, has the ability totally to detach itself from criticism, while reserving the right to point out the monstrous injustices suffered by peasants and workers in other countries less happy than its own.

A visit to Paris enlivened her after London and she spent three weeks in a whirl of pleasure and novelty. 'After five years of serious habits the ways of Paris diverted me a good deal, but I cannot say that they pleased me, and I believe one would tire of this constant frivolity sooner than of anything else.'

But on her return from the Continent there was more sombre news. The Princess Charlotte had died in childbirth.

That charming Princess Charlotte, so richly endowed with happiness, beauty and splendid hopes cut off from the love of a whole people. It is impossible to find in the history of nations or families, an event which provoked such heartfelt mourning. One met in the streets people of every class – in tears. The churches were full at all hours, the shops shut for a fortnight (an eloquent testimony from a shop-keeping community), and everyone, from the highest to the lowest in a state of despair which it is impossible to describe. I have personally suffered more than most, for we were very intimate and she had shown me more actual friendship than to any other woman, and it was impossible not to feel the attraction of her charming qualities. Poor Prince Leopold is in a most distressing state, and the Prince Regent also feels the blow acutely.

Those who live in the social scene have short memories, and the waters soon closed over thoughts of the unfortunate Princess Charlotte. By the following month, having given a graphic account of the Princess's melancholy and untimely death, Lady Granville was already voicing the speculations on the possibility of the Prince Regent 'bringing forward a divorce. If he does, he will move heaven and earth to do it. It will be, to be sure, the most tremendous piece of work.'

Over the years Lady Granville and others drew quick vignettes of the social life led by the Lieven circle. There were amateur theatricals, Darja playing the piano *à merveille* at Wherstead, while Count Nicholas Pahlen, and Neumann, the Austrian Chargé d'Affaires, sang to the airs she played, and the Duke of Wellington looked on in benevolent mood.

This Count Nicholas Pahlen was the son of the man who had been one of the instigators of the plot which led to the murder of Paul I. He did not accept his father's guilt in the killing, and as a consequence spent most of his life away from Russia. He was one of those expatriates who were received with pleasure in all the capitals of Europe, who spoke many languages and could sparkle on any worldly scene. It was into this frame that Darja, the Countess Lieven was slipping so easily and with such grace and aplomb. She was the favoured guest of Lady Granville. 'We played at whist last night – Lord Stafford, Fagel, Madame de Lieven and I, and we were so noisy and merry that the room rang with our little effusions.' When on long country-house visits, apart from whist, music, and amateur theatricals, charades and practical jokes passed the days and the evenings. Darja was the star of all of these home entertainments.

Harriet Granville describes a party of charades in the greatest detail, giving all the clues and how they were portrayed, which seems to suggest that they were a new thing. There was Madame de Lieven in hat and pélisse being helped over an imaginary ford, the Duke of Wellington, staggering under the weight of Lady Worcester gallantly reaching the shore, and Neumann, pretending to have fallen in, and being fished out by Lord Worcester who wrung out his wet clothes. Then Madame de Lieven again reclining on a couch being given pills and a draught, getting up and dancing about – the solution: *guéris*! (The charade having been played in French.) French seems, literally, to have been the lingua franca of the beau monde at this time, because on one occasion Darja complained about the boredom of a dinner party where everyone was talking English. English! It seemed to her an outrage that people could not exert themselves to talk in a more civilised way.

Long and complicated practical jokes were organised. Paul Lieven dressed up as a veiled *belle inconnue* in order to lure Lord Clanwilliam into making advances. From the context of this contrived comedy it would appear that it was considered to be a social solecism to give a rendezvous to a lady in someone else's garden. Eventually the beautiful *inconnue* was led into the drawing-room leaning on Countess Lieven's arm. 'Lord Clanwilliam looks up, he sees *la demoiselle* – still veiled – she says his look was *impayable*. He did not know whether to apologise, to laugh, to speak, or to run out of the room.' At last the lady modestly raised her veil and Paul Lieven bowed to the bewildered Earl.

Princess Esterhazy, the Austrian Ambassadress, was also having some social success, but Darja always writes of her in a denigratory way. No doubt she felt that her own success might be threatened by other foreigners taking the centre of the stage. When she had arrived in England there were few diplomatic rivals, but now, with the outbreak of the peace, more countries were sending their representatives to London. Occasionally Darja showed her displeasure and this was recorded by Harriet Granville. 'Madame de Lieven was furious at being obliged to amuse herself ... she had the ends of her mouth drawn down; something had discomposed her. I do not believe they have as yet got the Tsar's permission to go to Paris.'

Even abroad the silken thread of their dependence on the pleasure of the Tsar held them in thrall. They were not free to come and go.

The little pictures which Lady Granville draws of her society life and that of her friend Darja – give one the feeling of watching a film. We see the ladies in morning *déshabille* (scarcely even proper for receiving), with gossiping gentlemen and ladies calling on them while they still had their hair in curl papers, covered with a fetching cap. Harriet wrote: 'In my bedgown, Mr. Wilmot having dropped in like a bomb into our early breakfast – on his *knees* for news till eleven. Mrs. Wyatt tapping at the door with caps and bodices ... and now see me when my destined day is half done still in my bedgown, with the carriage harnessed for Chiswick.'

Darja seems to have been one of the number of Harriet's early morning callers. Yet she was so amusing she came only too seldom – Lady Granville could see more of her, and was always prepared to hear more of the gossip which she purveyed so agreeably, so volubly, and with such perception. Occasionally Harriet Granville had her qualms of conscience at appreciating gossip and scandal so much, but there could be little doubt that Darja was both agreeable and amusing. Although some people reserved their judgement....

On a visit to Paris Harriet called on Maréchale Moreau, who seems to have been a shrewd and detached woman who had a good knowledge of Countess Lieven. Lady Granville described her visit in some detail to her sister.

'Madame Moreau is not agreeable, but very good and sensible. She knows Madame de Lieven thoroughly and puzzled me by asking how it was possible that *une si grande amitié* could exist between two persons so different as Madame de Lieven and myself between whom there was not one common interest, one sympathy of opinion, whose principles and opinions she was certain differed as wide as day and night on every essential point. I talked of my gratitude for her affection, and admiration of her understanding.'

It appears that Madame Moreau looked at Harriet for a moment and then said: 'Eh bien, Miladi, let us say that as Madame de Lieven is agreeable, you *must* like her.' And she added that, if this were not so, Harriet's liking for Darja could be censured. (The word used was *condamnée*.) Harriet Granville went on to say that the Maréchale had certainly hit the right nail on the head. It was to her worldly side that Darja appealed. It had to be admitted, and presumably was admitted by Harriet Granville, that there was a great deal of boredom in the worldly life, and it was this that Darja succeeded in dispelling. The amusing things she said were often to the point, and if not always kind, the ability to amuse, even at the expense of one's friends was a priceless asset in the constant whirl of nodding, smiling, and being agreeable to which the grand ladies and gentlemen of the period were so constantly subjected.

Darja made no bones of the fact that she was easily bored, and there are constant references to this built-in *ennui* from which she suffered from herself and from observers. It was possibly because she was so easily bored that she felt herself impelled to be amusing at all costs. Sometimes she went a little far in offending people's susceptibilities. Writing to Harriet Granville she added: 'Your sister had the great kindness to come to see me. She seems to have become as *thin* as her daughters have become *fat*.' And on another occasion she remarked to Harriet herself: 'How well you look, dear. I am so happy to have a friend *qui a de l'embonpoint*!' Even the most tolerant friend does not like to be designated fat, not even when the remark is made in French.

The Countess herself always, until much later in life, remained very thin, over-thin. Possibly she was sensitive about her lack of figure. In an age when ample bosoms and rounded shoulders were admired, to be thin might indicate a tendency to tuberculosis and a speedy decline. English caricatures of the period depict Darja as a thin gaunt haglike creature, waltzing at Almack's with a fat rounded partner.

Between Lady Granville and her best friend Darja, there was much correspondence in fervent, almost girlish French, and small asides in less fervent English on the part of Harriet when she wrote to her relations. Apart from her excessive leanness, Darja is described as rushing forward, as if out of her body. Everything written of her gives the impression of an excess of activity in talking, travelling, writing, and commenting. She could not have been a restful woman to live with.

The Count Lieven on the other hand comes in for very little comment. Either he says nothing, or is merely recorded as being present, like some alter ego of his wife. His nickname was 'Vraiment' Lieven. It is easy to perceive why this label was put on him. He sat at dinner parties or *routs*, contributing little to the conversation, and then would suddenly interject the word 'Vraiment?' 'Really' was a useful word, indicating either surprise, astonishment, or even total lack of interest. 'Really' did not commit one to anything, one way or the other.

Apart from contributing little to the general gaiety of society 'Vraiment', as the years went on, appeared to be mediocre in other ways. The euphoria of the early years when he had been appointed to his brilliant post in London was gradually ebbing away. The reins of power were falling into the capable hands of his wife. Darja was here, there, and everywhere, picking up all the crumbs of political, diplomatic, sexual and international gossip. She knew everyone, she heard everything, and she was in the confidence of everyone who mattered. She had an unerring instinct for spotting those who were on the way to power, and those whose power was ebbing. She was the intimate friend of ministers, ministers' wives, the Prince Regent, and the Prince Regent's current mistress. When Lady Hertford was succeeded by Lady Conyngham, it was quite simple for Darja to change allegiances. She travelled on jaunts with the Regent. She was at the 'Cottage' at Windsor, she was at Brighton. The boredom of Brighton, the rich food, the music, and the tedium of royal personages about which Harriet Granville complained, did not tire Darja. This was the breath of life to her.

There can be little doubt that she took to this way of life with avidity and skill. From what we now know of the never-changing basic activities of the Russian Intelligence machine – its methods and targets – its interest in gossip and scandal, and information about the rise and fall of people of influence, Darja was the right agent in the right place, even if, as seems likely she did not totally realise it. It was a perfect situation. Darja's brother was in the confidence of the Tsar, and was later to become the head of his Secret Police. In London there was the dull, decorous Ambassador, while his busy butterfly wife, flitting here and there, listening and provoking, passed on her thoughts on the facts she had garnered. As time went on she was to become more and more useful on a higher political level.

Apart from other considerations, royal personages were intrinsically interesting to her; she had been trained and reared to respect the head that wears the crown, even if it were cut down later.

But if she was generally agreeable to royalties, it has been said that it was from policy and not from temperament. Her innate temperament was sharply critical of those around her, and even royalty could fall under her disapproval – so long as they did not find out what she had said about them. She described the Duke of Clarence, later known to the English as the Sailor King, William IV, as the least educated of all the English princes. 'He had no knowledge, vulgar English habits, and manners, and his conversation was also vulgar. He was a good fellow with little intelligence, or rather, none at all. He had a numerous family by an actress.' The actress referred to was the unfortunate Mrs. Jordan, who bore him ten children, and supported him by her acting abilities. 'He had desired to marry two English heiresses in succession.'

Like scaly mermaids, the heiresses had slipped from the grasp of the future Sailor King. Darja noted that when she had first arrived in England, the Duke had had designs on a Russian Grand Duchess, and 'he courted me for that purpose. He did go to the Regent's Court often enough, but was treated by him almost as an imbecile.'

In the beginning, Darja had felt sorry for the Duke of Clarence, and he had dined very often at the Russian Embassy. But in the end he had bored the Countess – and she quietly dropped him. The Regent, fortunately, was not the least put out by this, his brother bored him as much as he bored Darja. That was one point on which they were totally in agreement.

There were occasions when the Duke of Clarence, and the Lievens were fellow guests at Brighton. In 1814, when the Pavilion was being rebuilt, the Lievens were lodged in a separate house, but they went every day to the Pavilion, to lunch, to walk, and to dine, and presumably for Darja to keep the Regent amused. She liked to retire early, and left before her husband. The carriage would be ordered for her, it would be announced in the drawing-room that it was at the door, and then the Regent would politely accompany her to the door and watch her drive away.

On one occasion the Duke of Clarence decided to take the Regent's place.

He was, as usual, after dinner, a little lively and unsteady on his legs. He walked slowly, and, having put me into the carriage – and then – just as they were going to raise the carriage-step, he pushed the footman roughly aside – and got into the carriage

beside me – without a hat, and ordered them to drive on. All this
was done so quickly that I had no time to stop it, but I felt very ill
at ease.

Hardly was he in the carriage when he said:

'Are you cold, Madame?'

'No, Monseigneur.'

(His conversation always began like that.)

'Permit me to take your hand.' (This was an extra.)

'It is unnecessary, Monseigneur.'

But this did not prevent him from taking my hand. Fear seized
me, for he was evidently drunk. With the other hand I hastened
to lower the carriage window as a precautionary measure.

Darja was racking her brains for some subject to distract him
from the obvious and drunken designs which he had on her person.
There she was alone in the carriage with him, and no one to protect
her. She did however know of one subject which was always
uppermost in his mind; it was the throne of Hanover. It was an
inheritance which might come to him, it had always been in his
family, and he was concerned about its future. She decided on a
ruse and announced that her husband had had a courier from
Vienna. He remained uninterested. What had the Congress of
Vienna to do with him, he asked? Darja replied: 'It is something
they have decided on the question of Hanover.'

He started. 'Hanover! You don't mean that!'

This touchy subject seems to have temporarily recalled the Duke
to his senses. For a few minutes the wine clouds parted, and he
released the Countess's hand. She decided on a further startling
announcement. 'Hanover is to be given to Prussia.' The Duke
jumped from his seat in the carriage. But he had no need to worry,
Westphalia and Saxony would be added to his lands – as
compensation.

Clarence broke into imprecations: 'God damn! Does my brother
know this?'

She looked wise, and said that the Regent did not know this yet.
'I beg you Monseigneur, do not tell him. It is a secret which I am
telling you.'

'We shall never allow that. Impossible! Castlereagh will be
attacked in the Commons.'

At this juncture the Duke relapsed into swearing and his sudden
attraction for his companion was totally forgotten in a stream of
abuse. By the time he had calmed down the carriage had drawn up
at the door of the Lievens' house, and she alighted in safety.

When her husband returned home later she confessed the whole adventure. 'Vraiment' Lieven was not at all inclined to find the incident funny, or to take it as lightly as his wife. 'What trouble you have just caused me! I shall have to explain to the Regent – and how *can* I explain to him?'

'Vraiment' was very angry with his wife, but she laughed. 'I found it a little comic that he was not willing to change the geography of Europe.'

But the following day the Countess decided to calm her husband down and wrote to the Regent to ask for an audience. 'He asked me to come at noon. I went to him – without telling my husband, and told him exactly what had happened the evening before, asking pardon for having disposed of Hanover in so cavalier a fashion.'

The Prince Regent dissolved into helpless laughter. 'I have never seen him so diverted.' Once the joke had begun the Regent decided to carry it on 'and prepared to mystify the Duke of Clarence by this exchange of territory, accepting Westphalia.' The Duke of Clarence was baffled by this complaisance on the part of his brother, the chief of the house of Hanover, and remained 'stupid, and stupified'.

But it had one good result. When Darja's carriage was announced, the Regent said: 'I promise you my brother will not conduct you to it any more.' He then gallantly took the lady's arm and led her to the door, and did this regularly until the last day of her visit to Brighton.

The attentions which the Regent lavished on the Countess Lieven underline the position she had reached. She was considered to be a leader of London Society. Madame de Boigne, the French Ambassadress, wrote that the Countess held first place in the Diplomatic Corps. She had been established for a long time in England, and had achieved a social importance and a diplomatic influence which was personal to her. This no one challenged.

There were, however, difficult moments, even when one had reached the top of the diplomatic tree. The arrival of the Princess Paul Esterhazy, noted Madame de Boigne, seemed to have disturbed the Countess. Austria was then the closest ally of the English cabinet, Castlereagh was of one mind with Metternich. Another disadvantage was that Paul Esterhazy was an intimate of the Regent, and his young wife was the grand niece of the old Queen. All these advantages held the seeds of social success, and Countess Lieven was worried. Apart from her advantages of birth and parentage, the Austrian Princess was younger, prettier, and had an advantage which Madame de Boigne described as *un embonpoint impertinent*, which could be translated in modern terms as charming breasts. This contrasted with the desperate, almost skeletal thinness of the Russian Ambassadress. But Darja had no need to feel jealousy for the Austrian Ambassadress never profited by her brilliant position, or her *embonpoint impertinent*.

Madame de Boigne draws a shrewd portrait of Darja. She was a woman of distinction. Her mind was 'exclusively applied to diplomacy rather than politics at this time.' The weakness of Darja, as Madame de Boigne saw her, was that everything was reduced to people and to personalities. 'A long stay in England had not served to enlarge her original Russian ideas.' Her reputation was that of a woman of intrigue, who could see events only as they profited her own country – Russia. 'In 1816, she was little loved, but greatly feared in London.'

Bonsi, as painted by Madame de Boigne, comes out as a curiously vague man. 'I do not know what he was. Certainly he was a man of breeding, and grand manners; speaking little, but to the point, cold but polite. Some few thought him profound, but most people thought him shallow. I saw him a great deal and I have no personal opinion about him. He was completely eclipsed by the incontestable superiority of his wife, who *affected* to be very attached and submissive towards him. One never saw her without him, whether walking, driving, in town, in the country, in society – everywhere they were together, and yet no one believed in the real love and affection of the ménage.'

Madame de Boigne's portrait of Darja could be said to be hostile. The French were no friends of Russia, but it does give a more sombre picture of the methods by which the Countess had succeeded, and that she was not only amusing, but feared.

How had she succeeded so well? She was not a beauty, although Lady Bessborough described her as pretty, and Harriet Granville remarked that she was 'en grande beauté' in 1839 when she was already fifty-four. The portrait of her by Lawrence, who always flattered his sitters, gives a good idea of her assets, and her defects: the long nose, the large ears, the slender neck and the large irregular mouth. Her enemies, like Chateaubriand, said that she had a sharp angular face, and others unkindly remarked on her reddish nose. This comment was related to her by an alleged friend. She replied with dignity: 'I know it only too well, but these are things which are *not* said.'

Her friends, and those who admired her remarked on her dark hair falling about her face in curls, and on the deep caressing look in her grey eyes. She was said by others to have a way of walking and moving which was graceful and sinuous. Harriet Granville remarked of someone else that the woman moved '*à la* Lieven, independent of her body.' Darja perhaps fell into the category of

3 Dorothea Christopherovna Lieven by Sir Thomas Lawrence. 'A charming face, a clever face'

those *jolies laides* whose features separately hold little attraction, and yet the whole ensemble has that indefinable fascination which evokes desire in men and friendship in women. To look at her picture is to see a woman who in many ways seems to have the attraction of an actress, like Gertrude Lawrence, who was not pretty, and yet who could light up the stage. To compare her to an actress is perhaps the best way to describe her attractions, for she played many parts during the course of her life.

A verse which was current at the time underlines the thought:

> Un air d'ennui et de mépris
> D'une reine de théâtre, la dignité factice;
> Des broderies, des bouderies,
> Des garnitures – comme quatre –
> Voilà l'ambassadrice à la façon de Barbarie.

Up to 1818 Darja's successes had been social and diplomatic. Her husband, that silent and possibly hollow man had always used her to purvey the gossip, the undercurrents of the town, and the political circles in England, but now he began to employ her to help him pen his despatches to Russia.

In 1818 the whole course of Darja's life was to be changed. From social and detailed local diplomacy her thoughts were turned totally towards international affairs, to politics on the grand scale, and politics at their summit. Suddenly she was to see the beauty of real power, and the scene was to be drawn for her by one man – Metternich.

CHAPTER SEVEN

Un bien joli petit congrès

Count Capo d'Istria, the Russian Foreign Minister at the Congress of Aix-la-Chapelle (Aachen),wrote to his wife that everything was going very well, and he had never before attended 'de plus joli petit congrès'.

For Madame Lieven the Congress was to have a profound and lasting significance. It was here that she met the Prince Metternich for the first time, and found the world of international diplomacy opening for her.

But back in St. Petersburg the natural talents of Darja, and her patriotic devotion to the Tsar – any Tsar – could be used in attempts to unravel not only the current cat's cradle but to try to forestall, and predict which way any cat might jump. In London, her gathering of social gossip had been in the nature of collecting small ammunition, but now her association with the great Metternich promoted her into the big league of Intelligence gathering. That she was genuinely fascinated by him was all to the good. Heart and head combined made things easier. But devotion to Russia and the Tsar was always paramount. So many questions to answer, so scant the information, till Darja arrived at Aix-la-Chapelle.

Could the Quadruple Alliance of Russia, Prussia, England and Austria gradually be allowed to include France in a Quintuple Alliance? If this did not take place would France be pushed into allying herself with Russia to the disadvantage of both Austria and England? Did Lord Castlereagh trust the fair words of the Prince Metternich? Did the English trust the Austrians, or the Austrians the Prussians? Did any of the Allies trust the French? The Conference became a five-sided dance with every participant looking over his shoulder.

And amidst the delicate manoeuvrings, and the worldly splendour of dinners and formal balls, Madame Lieven had met and fallen in love with the Prince Metternich.

As La Garde described him this was not surprising.

'His features were regular and handsome, his smile full of charm, his face expressed both nobility and benevolence, his walk full of *noblesse* and elegance. At first glance you were pleased to see in him one of those men whom nature had prodigally endowed with her most seductive features.'

A Russian diplomat Baron de Meyendorff expressed equal admiration:

I was struck by the distinguished bearing of the Prince, I found in him a kind of stiff grace which broke through his politeness, and the ironic expression of a face which had the imprint of calm and dignity. His hair fell into curls, his aquiline nose, his well-formed mouth, his high forehead and arched eyebrows formed a handsome whole of which the harmony was marred only by the fact that one of his blue eyes was quite immobile. When he laughed his face, usually so calm and difficult to read seemed suddenly too animated, as if thrown out of joint. A huge mouth opened like an arc, the eyebrows went up towards his forehead, and were unevenly separated. There was something of Mephistopheles in the grimace, and the voice of the Prince – ordinarily drawling, became harsh and high pitched when he joked.

Others also noted his nasal and drawling voice. But in spite of any defects there was universal praise for his bearing and his charm. Mrs. Trollope, Anthony's mother, who met him twenty years later, described him as being of medium height and very slim, his features handsome and regular, and his whole expression breathing sweetness and benevolence. But the lady perceptively noted that there were in his piercing blue eyes signs of quick and profound thought. Even a detractor like the Austro-American Selsfield (who wrote against the whole idea of Metternich's policies), was obliged to admit that although his exterior could be called slightly effeminate, it had to be agreed that he moved with grace and 'the blue eyes were full of charm, while the well-formed mouth was always breaking into a smile'.

As depicted by Lawrence in 1819 shortly after Metternich met Darja, who became for him 'ma bonne Dorothée', he was the perfect mirror image of the statesman of the *ancien régime*. The man who looks out from the portrait is amused, sceptical, elegant and detached from the common herd, whose common intelligence he had every reason to distrust. Had not the common people taken away his family inheritance, and driven him into the service of

81

4 Prince Metternich by Sir Thomas Lawrence; 'amused, sceptical, elegant and detached from the common herd'

Austria rather than Germany? Revolutions to his mind achieved little. Only stability and continuity and the preservation of the monarchies could achieve that *équilibre* after which he constantly strived.

He had grown up in the shadow of the French Revolution. He had seen the armies of Napoleon take part in the destruction of Europe. He had asked himself why he personally had been chosen to combat that great usurper Bonaparte.

His family was a great and powerful one, and traced its origins to the Middle Ages, it was said to the days of Henri I who on being told that one of his knights, Metter, would betray him, replied: 'Metter – nicht!' The suffix had been forever attached to the family name. The family gave illustrious servants to the Holy Roman Empire over many centuries: three of his ancestors became Prince Electors of Mainz, and from this eminence acquired rich lands – Winneburg, Bellstein, and Konigswart in Bohemia. These were all added to the demesne of the ancestral Castle of Metternich near Coblenz.

With this glittering and noble background, it was not surprising that to Metternich Napoleon was simply a *parvenu* of the worst kind who had destroyed his family fortunes and sequestrated his ancestral estates. Yet in combatting him the Prince was prepared to use every means. The daughter of the Austrian Emperor had been used as a pawn to flatter the vanity of Bonaparte and to attempt to satiate his appetite for further destructive conquests by a dynastic marriage. It had been a throw of diplomatic dice which had not succeeded. But Europe did not fail to note that Metternich had found it useful to dispose of a young woman to gain a breathing space for his system of *équilibre*. The maiden had been sacrificed, but the dragon had remained at large, and the battles had been recommenced only to terminate in 1815. Now the Arch Deceiver, as he had been called, was faced with the aftermath of Napoleon's wars.

It has been said that to understand Metternich it must be remembered that, although he was a great cosmopolitan aristocrat, his education was French, and yet he was German by blood. Some commentators see in his German blood the explanation of his qualities as well as his defects. He was accused by English and French alike of chicanery and double dealing. Lord Liverpool said that no one could have any confidence in him for he believed that politics consisted in finesse and tricks. In this way he created more difficulties for his government than if he had adopted a simpler way of proceeding. Talleyrand, contrasting the duc de Richelieu with Metternich, said that the former deceived, but never lied whereas

Metternich always lied, but never deceived. Napoleon's judgement of his adversary was that Metternich thought himself a great diplomat, but he was merely a great liar. Other commentators remarked that he liked complications because he lacked both the strength, and the depths of serious thought to carry through great affairs in a simple way.

Many comments on Metternich's character and behaviour cancel out the others. He was described as indolent and hard working, as trivial and well-read, as haughty and yet treating the great and the humble in the same affable manner. In spite of his reputation for *galanterie*, there seems to have been something feminine and agreeable in his nature, as if the need to be pleasant were part of his armoury, as it is part of a pretty woman's. Yet his self-confidence was overweening. He admitted openly and frankly that he had been born to be a great minister. His benevolent nature was an attribute in which he took great pleasure. 'I am like the orange tree – always in flower.'

Like the scent of the flowers he was always welcome, and in his own view always necessary, and always in command. 'All eyes are turned to the place where I find myself ... My soul never conceived anything narrow, I am above those things which occupy most men of affairs, I envisage a landscape which is infinitely greater than they can see, or wish to see.... I have never ceased to ask myself why fate chose me from so many millions of men continually to have to confront Napoleon?'

He was totally convinced of the love everyone bore towards him. 'My daughter would die of a broken heart if I died ... Nesselrode (the Russian Foreign Minister), has loved me personally for years... The Emperor Alexander said to me "Why are you not my Minister, we could conquer the world". The Emperor Franz sees in me, his most certain friend.'

Yet some of these men were penning missives to their subordinates or their governments which proved that the Arch Deceiver Metternich was himself deceived. Perhaps the differing views of a man's character stem from national prejudices. The English consider themselves to be truthful and straight thinking, the French consider the English not only stupid but perfidious. In France the Germans were considered to be full of duplicity and wanting in sincerity. But the Germans see themselves as proud, frank and brutal in their manner of thought. The German tongue itself leads naturally to expressing the truth. But Metternich, in spite of his German blood, was said by Talleyrand to use words not so much for expressing thought as for disguising it. In that sense his German blood must have betrayed him.

When Metternich met Madame Lieven at Aachen in 1818 he was over forty, and she was thirty-four. Both were in the flower of their intelligence, their influence and their attraction for the other sex. For her it was to be the turning point of her life. For him, a mere episode. They had much in common. They were both by blood and birth German in origin. They were both aristocrats bred and trained to take their place in the great world. They were both arch intriguers, having a fascination for the by-ways of court and diplomacy. Both had married young. Darja at fourteen, and Metternich at the age of twenty-three. He had made a dynastic marriage to Princess Elenora, the grand-daughter of Kaunitz, the greatest diplomat of the eighteenth century and Chancellor of Maria Thérèsa. Not only was Elenora of impeccable lineage, but she was also immensely rich. It was a unique opportunity for the scion of a family which had been ruined and dispossessed. The marriage offered a mending of family fortunes, and a chance to become a diplomat by inheritance. They were both chances which the future great Chancellor did not neglect to take.

The marriage took place on the 27 September 1795 at the then little known village of Austerlitz. The nuptials were shared with six peasant couples and followed by banquets, pheasant shooting, and country dancing. Metternich had taken the first step towards his future career in the forefront of diplomacy, while frequently remarking that great affairs fatigued him, and he would rather have given his life and talents to a scientific study, perhaps to medicine.

In the same way Clement Metternich could tell Madame Lieven, with total sincerity, that he had always respected the law, and had never consciously broken the happiness of any household. Yet the list of his mistresses was interesting, though he denied that it was extensive. Clement had found ladies to be more than compliant. But they were mostly gentlewomen of high birth and great beauty, though of varying nationalities. He had loved three Frenchwomen, Madame de Caumont, Caroline Murat, and Laure Junot, and three Russian Princesses – Bagration, de Sagan, and Madame Lieven. Yet although Metternich was to marry three times – each time he plumped for the solid virtues needed for marriage – choosing women from Austria. Like many philanderers he had great regard for the sentimental domestic virtues, and the sweetness and *gemutlichkeit* of hearth and home.

To Darja – his chère Dorothée, when in the first throes of his attraction to her – he was prepared to admit to a few noble and high-minded passions. He recalled the springtime memory of Marie Constance. 'I loved her as a young man loves, she loved me in all the innocence of her heart. I lived only for her, and for my studies. She had nothing to do, but to love me all day long; she passed her nights with her husband, but I believe she was more concerned with thoughts of myself than of him.'

It was an idyllic picture, somewhat marred by the fact that the seductive French emigrée, Marie Constance, shared her favours equally between her husband, and *two* young lovers – Metternich and the Marquis de Bouille, who in his riper years recalled Marie Constance with equal tenderness.

The atmosphere breathed all the cynicism and rotting delicacies of the old régime and *Les Liaisons Dangereuses*.

The Marquis de Bouille, recalling his rival Clement later in tranquillity, noted in him the measureless ambition, and inordinate vanity, under an exterior of elegance. But, from the high eminence he had achieved in the Councils of Europe the older Clement could look back with fond recollection on walks under the lime trees and could congratulate himself on the remembered favours of so exquisite a creature.

Nor were Darja's Russian rivals less formidable as tender memories of *le beau passé* in the mind of Metternich. At the time of his first diplomatic mission as Minister Plenipotentiary of the Austrian Emperor at the Court of Prussia in Dresden, he was only twenty-nine. It was here he felt a strong attraction to Russian women for the first time. Princess Catherine Bagration, daughter of Count Skavronski was (like the delicious Marie Constance) only twenty years old, and married to Count Bagration, afterwards to become the hero of Borodino.

Metternich's ladies of various races and charms all seem to evoke the same fervid recollections in their admirers. The sole exception to this catalogue of praise of Metternich's mistresses was Darja herself.

Nesselrode, the Russian Foreign Minister, noted of la Bagration 'that her whole body expressed an oriental languor and indolence.'

It was this irresistible combination of assets which caused Catherine de Bagration to bear a child nine months after her meeting with Metternich. In order to make the facts perfectly clear to the world, the daughter was baptised Clementine. At the time of the Congress of Vienna Catherine's conduct earned her the soubriquet of *bel ange nu*.

But in Wilhelmina de Biron de Courland, another Russian, Metternich had to admit failure. She had made him feel foolish by encouraging insignificant rivals. But finally after nearly twenty years he was forced to admit defeat: 'I abandoned her as a mathematician abandons the solution to squaring the circle – after many years of research. I had been mad – as the mathematician is mad . . .'

No doubt Madame Lieven was well aware that she had had many precursors whose attractions lingered in the memory of the man with whom she was to fall in love. Less beautiful than her lover's former mistresses, she had perhaps something infinitely more valuable – the talent to amuse, to interest, and that shared passion for intrigue which was as the breath of life to Metternich.

It was by a lucky chance that the Lievens were sent to Aix-la-Chapelle. Possibly the Tsar felt that, with their intimate knowledge of the English scene, and friendship with Lord Castlereagh, they could be of help in delicate negotiations, or possibly to point out the nuances of English conduct, as a barometer might indicate a storm or fair weather.

The Congress of Aix-la-Chapelle opened in the autumn of 1818. The Lievens had arrived late on the scene when some of the higher dignitaries were already drifting away. On 22 October the Countess Lieven was introduced to Prince Metternich in the drawing-room of Nesselrode, Chancellor to the Tsar of Russia. Nesselrode had met Metternich many years before in Dresden and remarked on his qualities. 'He is not without wit and intelligence . . . he is very amiable when he wishes to be, good-looking, almost always in love, but more often absent-minded, which is as dangerous in diplomacy as in love affairs.'

Possibly Nesselrode had no time to give Darja his true opinion of Metternich, or even if he had would it have altered the course of events, or of Darja's life? She was bored with her marriage which had lasted twenty years, she was only too conscious of her savoir faire, superior to that of her husband. The fruit was ripe for the plucking.

The backcloth of the brief love affair which was to follow was informal. The meetings were supposed to take place in the Town Hall, but in effect they were more often held at the house of one or other of the delegates, perhaps at the house of Lord Castlereagh, who was accompanied on his mission by his plump and pretentious wife, and sometimes at the house of Metternich, a house he had rented for 20,000 francs for the duration of his stay.

During the intervals between the meetings and the discussions, social life sparkled. The diplomats frequented the Kurhaus to take the waters, they gambled, or they strolled along the shady avenues of the town. Sometimes there were balloon ascents, once by two daring women astronauts. Concerts by Madame Catalini, the Brothers Ohrer and the cellist Lafon enlivened the day. And when the evening fell the candlelit fêtes included receptions and a formal dinner given by the Emperor of Austria. The following day the town dignitaries entertained the delegates to a ball at the Redoubt. Twice a week Lady Castlereagh gave soirées and all the Ministers were careful to attend. High politics – and gambling were the order of the evening. At first the most important of the plenipotentiaries frequented Lady Castlereagh's entertainments, but gradually they were lured away to the house of Prince Metternich who took it as quite natural that his hospitality was socially superior. 'I cannot leave out of account the inconceivable atmosphere of boredom which arose from attendance at this establishment...' he wrote to his wife. 'Everyone renounced the charms of milady, and fixed themselves on my drawing-room.'

On 10 October 1818, Count and Countess Lieven alighted from their carriage at Aix-la-Chapelle. A newspaper dated the 11 October announced the new arrivals: 'The Ambassador of Russia to the Court of St. James arrived in this town, having been called here by his Emperor.'

The town was beginning to empty. The principal object of the Congress, the evacuation of foreign troops from the French provinces, had been agreed. The Tsar of Russia and the King of Prussia were preparing to depart in order to review their troops near Denain and Sedan. An air of fatigue, or *après bal* appeared to pervade the town. Metternich complained to his wife about the musical entertainments offered – young prodigies, a boy of four and a half who played the double bass. He complained about the price of medicine, the high cost of souvenirs – he had bought nothing, and even the women – ugly and overripe. 'The same story for the women as for the shopkeepers – a total lack of patrons.'

But amongst the women of whom the Prince Metternich spoke so disdainfully was the Countess Lieven. It is possible that he had met her before, perhaps at the time of his journey to London in June of 1814. At that time the salon of the Russian Ambassadress already played an important role in the social and diplomatic life of the capital. It seems unlikely that the Chancellor could have failed to put in an appearance at the Russian Embassy. But of this first encounter, if it did take place in London, neither Prince Metternich nor the Countess Lieven had retained any durable recollection.

Up to the moment of meeting the Prince, Darja had considered him a man who was at one and the same time, cold, intimidating, and disagreeable, and for him she had many of the attributes given to her by her English detractors and caricaturists, being thin, indiscreet and gossipy. During the first few days of the Lievens' stay at Aix, these mutually unfavourable opinions did not change.

Nesselrode even went so far as to ask Prince Metternich, the cause of his coldness towards Dorothea Christopherovna, and attempted to improve relations between the couple, merely for the purpose of easing diplomatic contacts. Metternich had noticed the Countess Lieven for the first time at a soirée chez Nesselrode, who had managed obligingly to make the Prince see his compatriot in a better light. Possibly he had dropped a tactful word to the lady herself – it was injudicious to let personal feelings stand in the way of diplomacy ... who knows what a friendship could lead to? And suddenly the mutual charm began, like a hidden perfume, to exhale. Metternich found the lady had a certain style, and the lady found Metternich only too agreeable.

There was, of course for her, the contrast between her husband and the Prince. 'Vraiment' Lieven had not matured over the years, and his nickname continued to suit him, for he was permanently astonished at everything which occurred, an attitude of mind which may be common to some diplomats, but one which does not help to disentangle the motives of those who are not so easily bewildered. On this level Prince Metternich outshone poor Bonsi in the eyes of his bored wife.

Many writers, both male and female, while admitting that Darja had little beauty, tried to capture the attractions of her manners and her conversation. In an age which appreciated style and grace, she had both. The Duchesse de Sagan, while pointing out that she lacked heart, yet had to admit that her wit and her intelligence served as substitutes. Greville praised her finesse, and also agreed that she could be extremely charming – when she wished to be. Like Metternich, she combined both male and female qualities in her character, having a male intelligence which was serious and logical, but always tempered with that grace and suppleness which was seldom found except in a woman.

It was possible that for the first time Metternich had encountered a woman who could operate on his level of conversation, and yet was perceptive enough to appreciate the outstanding qualities of which he knew himself to be possessed.

Metternich, in writing to his chère Dorothée recalled that Napoleon had been the means of bringing them together. When they met chez Nesselrode their discussion about Bonaparte had drawn them into conversation. He had proved to be a good intermediary 'far more useful from the top of his rock than ever he was on his throne'. That meeting was the beginning of an amorous intrigue which was to dovetail into a correspondence which was to last for more than seven years.

Of Darja's ecstatic letters to her lover in the first years of their acquaintance only a few extracts remain. Her letters were returned to her by the Duke of Wellington, but she edited out the love passages, while leaving her political comments intact, and re-copied the extracts into a series of little notebooks which survived wars and revolutions. The result is that the Prince's letters, sentimental and pseudo-philosophical, remain as the sole witness of the beginnings of a love affair which, after the first few encounters, was more a political than a personal association.

But the beginning, like all beginnings, had a freshness and a charm which combined the fascination of a love intrigue with the great world of international diplomacy and politics. And the dangers which had to be overcome added to the dark enchantment of the circumstances. In Austria Metternich used his secretary Gentz as a go-between in *affaires de coeur*, now the Secretary of the Austrian Embassy in London was used in the same capacity. Neumann was the young diplomat so often mentioned as singing on social occasions to the accompaniment of Countess Lieven on the piano. This time he was turning the pages of a love duet sung by others.

Even the sending of the letters and the receipt of the replies entailed many careful precautions, not only against the prying eyes of husbands and wives, but against the busy police spies of other states only too ready to unseal letters in the hopes of finding useful political news for their masters.

Both lovers wrote to one another every day at the beginning of their *affaire*. Often the Prince would break off his long outpourings to the Countess, only to continue the next evening where he had left off. Each long missive then awaited the departure of the weekly diplomatic courier, for only then was it possible to send it by the safest of safe hands.

One of the letters from Darja survived intact because it had fallen into the hands of French agents. This makes quite clear the number of ruses which were necessary for the carrying on of this intimate correspondence. The letter was contained in four different covers. The first bore the name of the Baron de Binder, Counsellor of the Austrian Legation in Paris. The second, addressed to the same man, had a note scrawled on it in Neumann's handwriting: 'I have no need to recommend the enclosed to you, my dear friend.' The third was addressed to the faithful Chevalier de Floret, and the final precious letter bore no address, merely the seal of the Ambassadress, and it was this which was to be put into the hands of her lover, with the seal still unbroken.

Both lovers wrote in French, a language in which they had great facility, and it was a facility which perhaps led them sometimes into passages of high-flown banality. French is so beautiful a language that its very beauty can lead the writer, especially a foreigner, easily into the realms of exaggerated cliché. It was a fault of style which did not entirely elude the Prince Metternich. Yet in his letters to his chère Dorothée he paints a picture of himself as a man who found in woman a mirror to his own egotism.

It has been remarked that the style of his love letters differs little from the style of his diplomatic despatches. He studies and reflects on his own emotions, and the emotions which he has aroused in his mistress, as he would study the varying motives of some foreign diplomat. But those scraps of letters which remain from the self-censorship of Darja give the impression that the passion on her part was deeper and more genuine than that of her lover. She believed herself to have found a man she could admire, love, and respect, a man who was worthy of her. It is undeniable that a lover will read into the letters of a beloved more than appears on the paper. It was this self-deception, due to her own feelings to which Darja was to fall victim.

The history of her physical liaison with Metternich was of short duration, but in her mind it became one of the great love stories of the world, taking place against the backcloth of equally great events. In his letters to Darja, Metternich often complains that the world judges him incapable of loving. But the history of his amorous life proves that in the eyes of the despised bourgeoisie he knew the art only too well. He admits that, at first, he had misjudged her, but she had proved to him that she was attentive to those things which illuminate the essential woman. 'Even if the world had already given a different verdict about her.' It was perhaps a roundabout way of saying that he had heard the gossip about her, and had believed it – until he had really got to know her.

He went over those first hours of their coming together. 'My heart – that better side of myself – went out to meet you and had the happiness of not missing you, even for so short a time after our first encounter. I saw you, and I did not stare at you. You saw me – without looking at me.'

Then suddenly everything changed.

On the 25 October some of the eminent personages who still remained in Aix decided to enjoy a little diversion. Metternich sketched the journey in a letter to his wife. 'The day before yesterday, we made a little excursion to Spa with M. and Madame de Nesselrode, the Count and Countess Lieven, Zichy, Lebzeltern and the Prince of Hesse' and he concluded the list of those taking part with the ever-faithful de Floret, who was afterwards to prove so essential an intermediary.

It was obvious from the enthusiastic way he wrote that it had been a successful and amusing trip in the bright autumn weather. 'We stayed the night at Spa and in the morning we amused ourselves by driving about the neighbourhood. The weather was superb and Spa was empty. We were the only foreigners present, and the effect we made was complete. The journey from here to Spa is charming, nothing is more beautiful than the country of Limburg with its fields and numberless little dwellings.'

What the Prince did not add was that the attractions of the Countess made him leave his carriage and continue the journey at her side. They lunched together in a disagreeable little inn – but the most disagreeable inn can have its amusing attractions at the beginning of a love affair. The following day the charm had already taken effect, and the return to Aix marked a new step towards their liaison.

'I have such pleasure in seeing you again,' wrote Metternich to Darja, 'that it was I who proposed changing carriages so that I need not leave your side. I began to see that those who said you were a woman of great charm – were right. The road seemed so much shorter than the day before.'

From then on events moved swiftly to the charming conclusion. 'On 28 October, I paid my first, albeit formal visit to you. The hours which I passed seated at your feet proved to me that it was the right place for me. It seemed to me when I went back to my own house as if I had known you for many years ... On the 29th I did not see you. And on the 30th I found that the day before had been totally empty for me – cold and senseless. I leave aside the day you came to my abode:* you were on fire, my dear friend, you belonged to me ... Do not ask me what I have felt since then....'

Unfortunately for the lovers, Darja's great benefactress, the Dowager Tsarina of Russia, arrived at Aix, and with her was the Countess's mother-in-law, the formidable Baroness Lieven. Duty and affection alike compelled Bonsi and his wife to follow the Tsarina and his mother to Maastricht, and then on to Brussels. *Le Moniteur* announced the arrival of M. et Mme. de Lieven in Brussels on the 5 November.

Prince Metternich, still in Aix, felt that he had met a woman who was entirely to his taste and feeling, only to lose her, even if that loss were only temporary. 'I have experienced a whole period of my life in less than eight days. It would seem like a dream to me, if I did not understand myself. A person is all or nothing for me. My soul is not capable of feeling – or thinking – in half measures. I have

* The original gives the word *loge* which in the circumstances is taken to mean *logement*.

scarcely spoken to you, and yet today you form part of my whole existence. Those objects which lure the majority of men are without effect on me.'

These were words full of enchantment for Darja. She saw herself as singled out and set apart from the rest of womankind.

The Prince went on to amplify and expand his feelings.

The day when I felt that my thoughts blended with yours, that was the day when I felt no doubts at all that you would understand me, that your soul, and above all my heart walked on that line which I look upon as entirely my own. I felt that I could become your friend. I only needed to convince myself that I was not deceiving myself – in order to love you. Some force urged me to confide in you what you had already guessed. I am telling you nothing which you do not know already, but I felt the necessity to say it again – to you my love, to you my dear friend, a friend of only eight days, but for life. . . .

Perhaps we shall find one another again one day. I shall be then what I am today. So few friendships please me, but when they do, they do not end. Vow to keep a beautiful memory, and do not have any regrets. Leave me the consolation that if you had known me longer, you would have felt towards me no other sentiment than the one which you feel today. You see that I cling to every small crumb of comfort which can save me from my terrible grief; a man who is shipwrecked does not choose the spar which can save him, he seizes anything which is within his grasp – or he drowns.

These outpourings of the great Chancellor produce a curious effect on the reader, as if the writer were acting the part of the despairing lover before a mirror so that he could admire his own sincere expressions of grief.

'I spent a night which at one and the same time was terrible and comforting. Terrible because I did not close my eyes, and comforting because I thought so much about the object which is the sole centre of my thoughts. The object of my thoughts has become me, totally myself. Everything which is outside her is as nothing.'

He has to confess that there is another side of him which is still able to speak, to act, and to calculate, and it is on this 'reserve' as he calls it that he is able to carry on his official life – writing despatches, preparing for delicate negotiations, but his true treasure, that which makes for his inner happiness, is something quite apart which is separated from his everyday life. This is the part of his life which is occupied by love, and which belongs to his *chère amie*, as much as to himself. The other half of his life belongs to his country, to his position, and to his tasks as statesman. He would never offer to share *that* with her – he loves her far too deeply to expect her to accept so bad a bargain. 'I told you yesterday,' he confided to his chère Dorothée, 'that of all the certainties that which I have found the most difficult to grasp is the certainty of believing myself to be loved. Why do you inspire me with a security which I have known so little during the course of my life? Why have I no fear of indulging myself towards you with that feeling of security which I have never experienced before? Are you in truth – *myself*? In fact, I believe this, as one believes in something one does not understand.'

He then descends from this high plane to a discussion of practicalities. When will he see her? He will be at a tedious conference at Lady Castlereagh's; perhaps she will be able to send him a message?

At midnight he wrote to thank her for the wonderful day she had given him.

> You have given alms to a beggar. I saw you! I was able to tell you my feelings, I heard you say the one thing of which I had such need – I know it, and yet I wish to teach it to you every hour of my life. Am I really cold, my dear friend? Am I the man you imagined me to be in the moments which preceded our friendship ... Begin by believing me utterly, and end by loving me – love me with all your heart from this moment, tomorrow – and for ever, do not fear any regrets. I, who am *you*, will never betray you.
>
> Goodnight, I know with whom I am going to sleep, and with whom I am going to awake. I know so many things that I am totally astonished that I do not know your first name....

Her Christian name, and the day she was born are the two things which he feels he must know, they are necessary to him.

The spellbinding nature of these outpourings on Darja can be understood. The long monotony of her marriage had suddenly been illumined. She had become the *chère amie* of one of the greatest statesmen of his age. At last she felt herself to be loved by a man who was worthy of her.

The Lievens had arrived in Brussels on 5 November, but Metternich – after suffering from a lover's despair (for a full week or so) concluded his current diplomatic business, and had decided to follow his chère Dorothée. The *Journal des Debats* recorded

94

that the Prince Metternich was leaving for Brussels. The object of this journey, noted the journal, was unknown. The real objective of the journey was eagerly expecting her lover. His departure had been preceded by a series of letters, announcing first his arrival, then a delay. She must not be disappointed if he did not arrive till the 23rd. There could be the difference of a whole morning. He realised with despair in his heart that a morning is a great deal – it could be everything!

How could he tell his colleagues the reason he was drawn to Brussels? 'I follow the very worst of all professions.'

It was agreeable to sit down at midnight with the candles still burning, and pen a few despairing words after the business of the day. It was a relaxation and enabled Metternich to see himself in another dimension. The statesman who preferred to be the lover.

But at last, his business concluded, he arrived in Brussels, and sent her a note to say that she must send him some English newspapers to indicate when she was alone. He was taking a packet of them so that he could have a good pretext for sending de Floret to her. He would be in Brussels for the whole of Wednesday, Thursday and Friday – three days which would be his whole life!

On the night of the 26th, on the eve of her return to London, he had worked up to a despairing note again.

'My dear friend, you are going, and taking with you, my life, my happiness – everything!'

He was only able to write a short letter. Everything was so confused. Death could separate him from her, life could only bring her closer. Leaving death and despair aside, he gave her a complete itinerary of his journey home. Aix-la-Chapelle, Cologne, Coblenz, his estate at Johannisberg, Frankfurt, Munich, and so back to Vienna. During this journey home, his letters became progressively less despairing. From Coblenz he sent her a short history of his life (admitting to two great loves) and remarking that the world gave more women to his credit than he had ever encountered. He also sent her a short thought from the poet Richter.

> Die Erinnerung ist das einzige
> Paradies auf welchem wir nicht
> Vertrieben werden können!

Memory may be the only paradise from which lovers cannot be banished; it was a thought which perhaps lacked charm for a woman who felt she had found the one great love.

One night she had seen him in her dreams. He had taken her on his knee to speak softly to her, and she felt under her hand the heartbeats of her lover, heartbeats so loud that she woke with a start. 'It was my own heart which had replied ... my dearest, how sweet it is to love you. It is a thing of rapture.'

For the Chancellor a four-week rapture was over. Life had returned to normal and she was for him a happy memory. But a memory which perhaps could serve some useful political ends. Some time, some day....

Whatever precautions Metternich and Darja might take to keep their relationship secret, there can be little doubt that the harsh practical men in St. Petersburg knew about it, and approved, as they approved other means of gathering information. The official Ambassador, Count 'Vraiment' Lieven, would have included in his reports to the Tsar's Foreign Minister, despatching under safe diplomatic bag, answers to many of the questions which interested St. Petersburg – information which 'Vraiment's' wife had acquired in the course of her burgeoning friendship. There could be little other explanation for keeping Lieven, the dull nonentity, in his post as Ambassador. We shall never know whether Ambassador Lieven was urged by the Tsar, or his advisers, to be a *mari complaisant*, and told to turn a blind eye to Darja's infidelities. Or is it possible that he was so complacent that he did not notice them?

CHAPTER EIGHT

'L'esprit est toujours la dupe du coeur'

By the end of December Darja was back in London, and had taken to her bed in such danger from a chest and lung infection that she saw herself in her coffin. It is undeniable that her love for Metternich, which she had described to him as 'une chose ravissante', must have contributed to this illness. On the other hand, her cher Clément was in excellent spirits. How can he thank her enough for the wonderful letters which are his sole consolation? 'Yes, my dear dear friend, I know that you love me, that you love me as I wish to be loved, in a way which has only happened to me twice in my life.'

He had also sent her recommendations, one might almost say instructions, at the beginning of their fervent correspondence that she should be *good*, kind and affectionate to her husband. He stressed the importance of this. The inevitable result of this sage advice was that she found herself to be pregnant once again, and wrote in some distress to her lover on the subject. Metternich remained as good humoured about her pregnancy as he was about all other incidents in life.

'The Paris courier has interrupted my writing to you ... I will begin by the thing which interests me the most – after your love. It is your pregnancy. My dear friend, you have profited by my advice. I told you to be easy and pleasant in your married life. I do not know whether it is my advice which has made you pregnant, or whether you felt the need to become so. In any case – you are, and what can I say about it?' He was asking himself why she was so upset, was it because she felt the pregnancy might keep them apart. If she had harboured such a thought for a single moment she did not know him. 'I love you no less whether you are one or two. Pregnancies in *marriage* double the bonds, but they do not double the pleasure ... you wish for a daughter; that I can understand.' He hoped that she would have her desire. He understood her

97

difficulties. 'I have never broken up a marriage. I respect the law, I wish that everyone did the same.' As far as he was concerned Darja's pregnancy was only to be expected. She had resumed her married life.

'You think that I might be angry at your state, or rather the cause of that state. My dear friend, what do you want me to say? Was it not myself who counselled you to be loving in your marriage? I have not the slightest desire that your husband should not enjoy the fullness of his rights... You will have a beautiful child whom you will love well, and I will love because it will be yours...'

These were not quite the words which the love-stricken Darja wished to hear. She perhaps felt that a little jealousy would have been more fitting, and more in keeping with the writer of so many flowery, and sometimes despairing sentiments.

When writing to her family, on the other hand, Darja continued to be practical and full of the gossip and incidents of her Continental journeyings. Of the central happening which had affected her so profoundly she gave no indication.

On 1 January 1819 she wrote to her father from Brighton where she was staying with the Regent for the New Year. 'We are staying in the Prince's house, very well and comfortably lodged. He is always so pleasant and friendly to us ... The stay at Aix-la-Chapelle has been so interesting for him [Bonsi] on every level, and as for me I keep a really precious souvenir of it.' She allowed her father to think that it was Bonsi's diplomatic success which gave her this precious souvenir. Brussels had not been so interesting. In fact it had been extremely tiring because of all the fêtes and attendance on the Dowager Empress. It was almost impossible to find time to sleep. Or she might have added, to see her lover when he, at long last, arrived.

'My mother-in-law was so happy to find herself with us again. She was enchanted with my children. Paul is certainly the most handsome child, lively and clever. She parted from my husband with real sadness ... she seemed to be somewhat cast down and weak. From Brussels we went to Paris where we spent several weeks. The fall of the Duc de Richelieu has upset many people.'

The Duc de Richelieu, who had succeeded Talleyrand, found his position wholly untenable in view of the attitude of the *doctrinaires* and had been forced to resign. The Russians were partial to Richelieu as he had been in the Russian service at the time of the rise of Napoleon and the Empire, and had been Governor of Odessa. It is very difficult for modern people to understand an age when

Germans served the Russian Emperor, or a Corsican like Capo d'Istria could rise to be the Tsar's representative in so important a post as Paris.

To her brother Alexander Darja wrote in similar vein. How pleasant it was to see so many people from the Russian Court. She had seen so many old friends, and in so short a time 'that if I had not fallen ill on my return as a result of fatigue I would be tempted to think the whole journey to have been a dream. . . .' For her it had indeed been a dream, and the pleasure of that dream remained with her.

It has been remarked that the effusions of Metternich and Darja, those two worldly and cynical personages from the diplomatic world of the aristocracy, could not be other than superficial. Possibly on Metternich's part it was only an episode which could be used to his advantage, but on the part of his chère Dorothée, it had touched some well-spring in her heart which had sent her thoughts back to the beginning of her life, to the beginning of her emotional development. She must have voiced these thoughts to her lover. He tried to reassure her. She must not reproach him, for she will find him unchanging in his affection for her. 'My heart sought at eighteen what it has found at forty . . . If a cruel destiny meant that I did not see you for a long period of time, if our next encounter did not take place except at a very advanced age, our souls would still be as one.'

Why not reconcile herself to the fact that she cannot find her true heart in marriage?

You were a child when you were married. You were placed in a position which is not in tune with the nature of woman. The young girl has simply a need to love, nothing more; love presents itself to her as something spiritual; the body, the material part of it, does not touch her; she is totally ignorant of the force which is pushing her forwards, and which awakes in her an unknown feeling, which seems so full of enchantment. . . . The beginning becomes what should be the end . . . The soul becomes hungry under the weight of this regime. Marriage then seems a burden which is often too heavy to be borne, and an obstacle to true happiness. Life is then used up in desires, in searches, and in hopes which are deceptions, in errors of choice – and in regrets.

My dear friend, do you not see that I am right?

In what are *you* wrong? In trying to find in your husband the sole cause of all your regrets.

You love me – but if you had married *me* at fourteen, you would be no happier than you are now.

99

If it is love you are seeking – do not seek it in marriage.

Marriage was for the sole purpose of creating children, not to satisfy the heart's desire. 'The heart finishes by taking its rights, and I am absolutely convinced that good marriages would be more widespread if they took place between men of forty and women of thirty.'

By a curious chance these were the ages of Darja and her Clement. When writing to her he chose his words as carefully as he did those in his despatches. 'The world turns, my dear, according to the needs of society, the heart often has much affliction in submitting to the rules. But do not try to find the causes outside yourself.'

For once he wrote with great sincerity out of the depths of his experience. It was hard to live in a world where only consideration of family and advancement dictated the reasons for marrying. It was, of course, much easier for a man to adopt an attitude of love being a thing apart from marriage. But much as Metternich could manipulate political happenings perhaps he had not always been so adept at manipulating his own heart. The greatest of cynics, the coldest of hearts, and the most calculating of minds have moments of weakness. Moments, when, as Metternich wrote, the heart demands its rights.

If to read history is to live in the past, it should be possible to try to live in the bodies of the people of the past, and to see their surroundings as they did themselves, looking through their eyes and trying to understand with their hearts and their feelings. If to understand is to pardon, to write about the people of the past ought to be not only to pardon, but to understand them. Everyone, however great, or humble, is the prisoner of their country, their century, their class, and sometimes their religion.

Metternich and Countess Lieven were prisoners of their age, the age of Byron, the age of the great Romantics, when it was correct to be struck down by devastating passions, to feel profound sentiments, to shiver at the prospect of 'horrid chasms', or to be uplifted by the prospect of noble mountains. Who can deny that for a few brief moments both of them had felt a true sentiment and real feeling for one another? On Metternich's side it was speedily dismissed as totally impracticable, but on Darja's she held it to her heart as a wonderful might-have-been – or something which still could be. 'Comme il est doux de t'aimer – c'est une ravissante chose....'

This is perhaps borne out by the note which Metternich added to his sage and worldly counsels about how to conduct *affaires*

100

outside marriage in a sound and sensible way. 'Reading over your letter No. 9 I could not help laughing at your fury with Neumann because he yawned when you were speaking of me, and discussing us. My dear friend! Neumann is not in love with me, and God forbid that he should ever become so!' He went on to remark that the role of confidant was detestable, for there was nothing more tiresome than reading other people's love letters. Out of a thousand love letters there were very few, in his opinion, which did not seem to be the expression of folly, unreason, or merely sheer stupidity.

Darja had obviously expressed some jealousy. She had been told by two Englishwomen that he had been in love with both of them! 'Tell me the names of these two Englishwomen', and added he would never have considered such a crime as being in love with 'les insulaires'. They were obviously not to his taste. Certainly he had been six months in England when he was eighteen. He had, in fact, been twenty-one, but a man can be pardoned for taking three years from his age when he wishes to appear younger and more innocent than he was. 'Only tell me, my dear friend, which of your ladies is boasting of doing me so much honour.'

A month or so later he was alarmed by the news that she had been too ill to send him a letter by Neumann. 'My friend, do not frighten me in this way. I am afraid that you may have had an illness such as attacked you recently. The signs of a miscarriage are bad because they come back too easily.' He implored her to let him know that she was properly cared for – and she must send him a message by Neumann. He was not at all sure that she was wise to take the baths which had been recommended. Loving her as he did, he was afraid of everything. The only illness which he would permit her was a little cold in the head.

In the next letter his alarm still occupied his mind. He had dreamed that she was lying ill, with her husband, and Neumann beside her bed. Which one of these two was acting as her medical adviser he did not know, but if ever Neumann suggested a remedy to her, he implored her not to take his advice! 'I await with impatience the first letters from London – alas they are *so* long in arriving.'

In the month of March 1819 Metternich undertook an official journey to Italy, where amongst other visits, he was to see the Pope. En route he felt all the correct sentiments and expressed them in his letters to his chère Dorothée. The Alps had elevated, and yet crushed his soul. Then suddenly the sun had exhaled real heat and the spring flowers were opening. 'I send you the first one which I found with its petals unfolding, it is a little anemone.'

His German soul opened to the sunshine, to the flowers, to the peasants working amongst the olive trees. He did not actually quote 'Kennst du das land wo die citronen blühn', but in Rome itself in the course of his morning's walk he went into the garden of a convent. It was totally enclosed by high walls. Here he found the air heavy with the scent of orange trees, and adding to their heady perfume were the flowering bushes, and the delicate aroma of the lemon flowers. 'In this garden I picked a branch from the lemon tree on which were seventy ripe lemons. I had it packed, and sent it to my wife.' He makes no mention of asking the nuns' permission, but possibly the sight of an elegant nobleman hacking a branch off their lemon tree had made them speechless. He would, he added, have sent the lemons to his chère Dorothée, if he had only found a courier ready to leave for London, but there was none.

While Metternich described the pleasures of visiting the studio of the sculptor Canova, hearing a bad performance of Rossini's *Otello*, buying some large alabaster vases four feet high (at a reasonable price), and having a cheerful chat with the Pope, Darja was in England pregnant, ill, and far from happy. But when she was walking in the countryside, she fantasised. 'I have never seen two trees growing together without regretting that I am not a tree. Would you not have loved to be the other tree?'

It was the sentiment of the Darja who at fourteen had been so happy to wear the Tsarina's diamonds with her wedding dress. Just as speedily as the thought had come to her she dismissed it, as if she could see his ironical smile, amused and tolerant. 'Can you see us changed into two pieces of wood?'

She lives for his letters, they are so agreeable to read because he has such a fund of gaiety. 'You are the most good humoured man I have ever met and I love to laugh.' Perhaps at the core of her unhappiness in her marriage was Bonsi's lack of humour. In few accounts of social occasions does he sparkle. The impression which is given of his character and talents is that of a conscientious civil servant. One commentator has compared him to Karenin in Tolstoy's novel, and this comparison has some grain of truth. Many writers refer to Darja's air of ennui, and this seems always to have been part of her character; yet in society, and in her letters to Metternich, she was by turns amusing and sad, sparkling and cast down, but seldom suffering from that terrible *accidie* which assailed her in her marriage.

In May of 1819 she was still out of sorts and, writing to her brother, she admitted that she had been ailing ever since her return to England. 'I really believe that the little breath of continental air which I breathed has changed my feelings and that I have had enough of London fogs.' She would have been happy to hear of another appointment for Bonsi. 'But, as Nesselrode said to me, there is only Paris or Vienna, and Paris, Heaven preserve me from it...'

Vienna she did not comment upon. It was too near the centre of her thoughts. Her separation from her lover and her pregnancy increased her melancholy. It was useless for him to write: 'I love you at Carlsbad, as on the slopes of Vesuvius, and in the ruins of Paestum, and on the Champs Elysees,' if she were not there. She replied sighing: 'Good-bye till tomorrow. Tomorrow I will love you as on all the other days of my life...'

In September 1819 she came back to London from Middleton Park; in Oxfordshire where she had been staying for a few days with Lady Jersey.

My dear friend,
If only you had been there this summer what wonderful and happy chances there would have been for us to meet alone, and to be at our ease! I have been so much alone, sometimes for four or five days. How often I had said to myself in my solitude 'If only *he* were here!!!' Last night when evening was falling, as I came back into my apartments at Middleton, there was a wonderful moon. I stood for some time on the balcony of my bedroom. I heard someone walking in the room next to mine. I did not know who in the house party had been given to me as neighbour. But perhaps you would have been in that room if you had been staying with Lady Jersey. You would have walked on to my balcony, my dear friend. We would have spoken soft words to one another in low voices. The image of this thought must have pursued me all night because I dreamed and the dream was a delight.

She was with him. She heard his heartbeats, and now her heart was beating in the same way. Would her dream ever become reality? 'Mon Clément! Have you the time to dream?' Her dreaming was a source of more pain than pleasure to her, weighed down as she was with this new pregnancy. It was a pregnancy which had given rise to many amused and amusing comments. In spite of all the precautions of letters enfolded between triple covers by safe hands, the liaison had become well known.

In October of 1819, just before her confinement, Darja wrote to her brother Alexander: 'I expect you have heard what has happened to me, and that I am going to be confined again, in spite of the fact that I hardly knew I was pregnant.'

Six weeks after she had been dreaming of her cher Clément in the moonlight on the balcony at Middleton, she had a fourth son. After eighteen years of marriage, both Bonsi and Darja herself awaited the birth with the utmost apprehension, as did Metternich in spite of his easy attitude towards the event.

'My dear friend,' he wrote, 'It is impossible that by this time you have not been delivered of your burden. You told me that normally you were before the time. I am sure you will not delay this time. There must by now be another being in the world who has the right to my affections. My dear friend, give me news as soon as possible of what you do, and how you are.'

All the fears of husband and lover were resolved. Bonsi wrote to the family: 'In spite of the serious fears with which she had approached the birth, she had never had a happier confinement than this one. We would, of course, have preferred a girl, because three sons are enough, in spite of the hopes which they hold out for the future.'

The lying-in was happily concluded. But tongues continued to wag. Metternich was widely believed to be the father of the newly-born son. The Duchesse de Decazes, who arrived in London as Ambassadress of France in 1820, said that the child was christened 'l'enfant du congrès'.

But it had been eleven months since Metternich and Countess Lieven had parted. Even taking into account the primitive state of medical knowledge, an eleven-month pregnancy would have been more than a phenomenon. It can only be concluded that Darja's passion had been transferred into legal marital affections, and that though Metternich had not in fact been the father, he had been in essence a father by passion, and by proxy.

Darja wrote in some distress to her brother about the christening which seemed to have caused as much trouble as that of the Sleeping Princess in the fairy tale.

I must recount to you a series of idiocies on the part of my mother-in-law which have put us in an absurd situation. When I was confined, my husband immediately wrote to her, as well as to the Tsarina, and as the latter had always wished to be godmother to all my children, he told his mother that he left it to her to ask – or not – whether the Empress Mother wished to accede to this request, or whether she did not wish to be troubled.

As a result of this sentence my mother-in-law saw fit not only to say we wished the Empress Mother to be godmother, but that we also wished the Tsar to be godfather. Never had we thought of such a thing! If I had twenty-four children never would I have been so indiscreet to ask such a thing. The result is that she has totally mismanaged the affair, and has written that the Tsar and Tsarina have both accepted with pleasure to hold the child at the font, something which we would never have dreamed of . . .

This was not the end of the complications of the christening of the infant Lieven. Darja wrote angrily to her brother that she had told her mother-in-law that the Regent had already – early in the month of May last – asked if he himself could be godfather to the coming child, 'a request I could hardly refuse'. In addition the Prince Regent had graciously suggested that he should hold the child at the font, and wanted the boy to be called George.

It was very awkward. On the one hand she did not want to offend the Tsar and Tsarina, Rulers of all the Russias, and on the other hand she had not asked the Prince Regent for the high honour of having him as godfather to her son, and in addition having the honour of sharing his name. Would Alexander please make it clear that she had never asked the Regent to accord her this honour? In fact, she had hoped that the Regent had forgotten all about it, and in this belief had herself asked the Duke of Wellington, when he came to see her during her lying-in, whether *he* would like to hold the child at the font. Darja was extremely upset at the mounting number of godparents for her new son. 'Unfortunately the Regent did not let go of the idea and called my husband to him to speak about it again. Bonsi had nothing to do but to submit. The best of the affair is that in all this embarrassment and richness of godfathers my poor little boy is not yet a christian. First I was too ill, then the Regent was away, and now he has become King and there are three months of deep mourning, during which time there is absolutely no question of a baptism.'

But eventually the godfathers were sorted out. The Tsar and Tsarina declined the honour of being godparents, feeling that now the Regent was King the honour was the greater. The King of England held the infant at the baptismal font, and the child was called George. Wellington was given a promise that he should be godfather the next time, a promise which was fulfilled in 1825 when

Darja had her last child, Arthur.

During the years which followed Countess Lieven reached the apogee of her influence in England. If she was praised she was also condemned. The Regent, who had now been elevated to King in name as well as in fact, constantly called her to his side either to the 'Cottage' at Windsor, or the Pavilion at Brighton. But his incessant attentions perhaps did her more harm than good in English society. The women in the social round and about the Court feared and distrusted her. Ministers complained that she intrigued far too often with the Opposition. Foreigners, quite rightly, were hardly expected to meddle in affairs which were solely for the English to arrange in their own way.

Prince Esterhazy told the duc de Decazes – in the strictest confidence – that he was seriously concerned, and indeed upset 'at the secret correspondence which Madame de Lieven kept up with Prince Metternich.' Louis XVIII also warned his Ambassador in London to take the greatest care in his dealings with the Russian Ambassadress, and to be warned against the 'perfidies of Madame de Lieven and her "chèr z'amant"' – as he called Metternich.

The *chose ravissante* had diplomatic repercussions far beyond the thoughts of Darja as she stood on the balcony on the moonlight dreaming of her lover. But even her detractors had to admit that she had a sprightly wit, that she brought life and sparkle to social occasions. Her sheer ability, amusing conversation, and intelligence drew eminent men into her circle and kept them as friends over the years. Once again this happy fusion of personal inclinations and opportunities provided Bonsi with titbits of information for onward transmission to St. Petersburg and the Tsar.

During the hunting season, when all of aristocratic London left the city behind in order to pursue foxes over the fields, and shoot birds in the autumn woods around their country estates, the three ambassadresses of Russia, Austria and France were much thrown into one another's company. The young French woman, scarcely twenty years old, was taken under the wing of Darja. The duchesse de Decazes wrote very kindly of her. 'When I was ill, which happened to me very often, the Countess wrote me little notes. I have kept a good number of them – they are concise and affectionate. She always had a great fear of catching illnesses. A few days after my departure for France, my son had scarlet fever, and she walked every morning under my windows to know from my own lips how I was.'

The duchesse added that Madame Lieven led a very busy life. According to fellow diplomats and politicians perhaps it was a little too busy in the winter of 1820/21. It was generally believed that she directed the affairs of the Russian Embassy and sometimes, through her correspondence with Metternich, even interfered in the affairs of Austria.

Several times a week she would write to the Tsarina. 'Sometimes', wrote the Duchesse de Decazes, 'I would arrive at the house of Madame de Lieven at the moment when she was finishing her letter to her sovereign. She would tell me what she had written, and ask if I had any gossip to add. The Tsarina loved news, details about fashions, what everyone was wearing, and relished any little scandals about society.'

Apart from her diplomatic intrigues, Countess Lieven was an excellent hostess. Her receptions, dinners and the way she organised her Embassy were much praised, though possibly there were criticisms of the way she organised Bonsi, and his correspondence.

1820 brought no reunion of the lovers, but it brought great sadness to Metternich himself. On the 6 May he lost his daughter Clementine. By a terrible irony the portrait which Thomas Lawrence had painted of the girl arrived, complete in all its flush of early beauty, just after she had died. She was to be the first of the Prince's children to die in adolescence. Like Darja herself, Metternich was devoted to his children, and his letters reveal a deep melancholy at his loss. 'She seemed destined for a happy future, because of her gentle and amiable qualities of character. She was a flower which shrivelled at the moment of budding, and in common with other delicate flowers she was not able to withstand the chilling wind. All the doctors are agreed that without this last terrible winter which we have had – she would have survived.'

No letter of condolence for this great blow seems to have survived to show what words of comfort Darja sent her lover on the loss of his beloved child. Or perhaps she had excised the outpourings of her heart when she copied her letters into her notebooks. What remained in the remaining edited letters was gossip – gossip about the Cato Street conspiracy – everyone had wanted the honour of cutting Castlereagh's throat. Two of the conspirators were to cut off the heads of various unfavoured politicians, the third had the happiness of holding the bag into which they were to be put. The conspirators were hanged – that was a natural result – but Darja was appalled at the ferocity of the mob. It was like a holiday; they had thronged the streets wearing masks and banging drums, playing musical instruments and dancing. It was like a carnival. And the conspirators themselves? What had made them act in the way they did, and why did Brandt die crying 'Long Live Liberty!'? It made her sad to think of the aberrations of mind and imagination which were represented by Thistlewood and his fellow conspirators. What dominated their minds at the moment of death?

In these little asides and sudden thoughts a different side of the social Darja is glimpsed, a side which had never been, and perhaps would never be developed.

She was concerned that her cher Clément was so *affairé* and worried. This was not the path of happiness, he knew that yet his ambition drove him on, although his heart rejected that path. 'Men wear out their existence in promising themselves happiness and tranquillity. They reckon with everything except the flight of time, and end their days without achieving that happiness. How discordant are our intellects and our wills! In each of us, what virtues and what littlenesses.' Was this an appeal, or an attempt to show what happiness they could have achieved together should the world and ambitions be able to be set aside?

Just as suddenly her dark thoughts were dispelled and the letter ended with a description of the King's new favourite, Lady Conyngham. She had been very coldly received by society. The whole incident had revealed the English in a different light. The 'accession' of the King's new mistress had embarrassed them, and there was a definite reluctance even to greet her, just a few muffled how-do-you-do's were heard. But that will come, in time people get accustomed to everything. At Ascot the King had not been well received, and she went on to describe how, she, the King and Lady Conyngham got into the same carriage and on the return to the 'Cottage' had been overtaken by a storm. But the King seemed oblivious to everything except his new inamorata. Once he was back in his own home, he begged for music. The Countess must play for him, as she did in the old days. She agreed and sat down at the piano. He was so overcome by the music that for five minutes he could not speak, and then a flood of tears poured down his cheeks. 'I have never seen a man more in love.'

Like the good performer she had taught herself to be, Darja could switch from the cynically comic to the pathetic with hardly a change of tone or tempo. In the same letter she describes Lord Liverpool sitting at her feet on a little footstool. It had been remarked that he seemed to take a very great interest in her, as she told Metternich and added, 'I quite like Prime Ministers.'

She also liked Kings, Tsars, Princesses, Foreign Ministers, and anyone or everyone who looked likely to be in the social, political

108

or diplomatic ascendant – or who might have information for Bonsi, and St. Petersburg.

It was often remarked that she had a swift eye for anyone who was climbing the ladder to power. Her social position was reinforced by her official position as one of the 'dragons' at Almack's.

A leader of fashion – Darja had only to appear at Court with her diamonds linked across her gown in trails for this to become the mode – her self-confidence in the twenties of the century grew apace and she had constituted herself to be the one person who could explain the Russians and the English to one another. After eight years in London, the Tsar's Ambassador in Paris remarked that she enjoyed a complete success.

Like many *grandes mondaines* who spend their days and evenings on the fatiguing social round, Darja liked to feel that she was happier away from the bustle of town. 'This is the epoch of obligatory pleasures in London,' she wrote to her brother Alexander, 'personally they bore me. I look forward to the time when, instead of going to a rout, I can go off to sleep, to the hootings of owls.'

She looked forward to going to her place in the country; there was the beautiful English turf and the green leaves, and the fresh air untainted by the fogs of the city. The pleasures of England which so bored her at the beginning of her stay were now creeping into her inner consciousness and becoming part of her new feelings about the country.

Her marriage was not all it seemed to be on the surface, and there were many current stories and gossip which seemed to prove that Darja's complaints about her husband had some foundation, although the myth of a happy marriage was preserved. Even George IV seems to have relegated Count Lieven to a minor role. On one occasion he sent for him, and spent a long time discussing indifferent topics. Bonsi went away without discovering why he had been summoned for a conversation of banal small talk. As he left the King asked him to return on the following day, and the same thing happened, nothing of any consequence was said. It later turned out that George much admired Bonsi's coiffure and the way his *jolis cheveux* were arranged and had decided to take a good look before having a new wig made.

But if Bonsi had proved a disappointment to her, Darja was much concerned with the education and the future of her children, and often wrote to her brother about their prowess and their progress in their lessons. It was admitted that she was a good and conscientious mother, and devoted to her sons.

But Darja's joy in them was coming to an end. Bonsi had decided to spend a couple of months in St. Petersburg in 1821. 'He has need of a holiday to look after his private affairs, to get in touch with Russia, to mix with his fellow countrymen again. Eight years of absence almost makes a foreigner of one, and that is a condition to be avoided. He is going to ask for a few months leave of absence during the fine weather. He will go to Russia with the two elder boys, the other is too small to face so long a journey.'

Not only had Bonsi decided to have a holiday on his native soil, but he had also decided that the two elder sons should return to Russia to complete their education. Alexander and Constantine were sent to stay with their grandmother Lieven for some weeks, and then their father had arranged for their studying at the University of Dorpat in the province of Riga. They had been sent back to their native Baltic background after so many years of English education. It must have been as much of a wrench for them as it was for their mother. Paul, the third son was to be sent to Paris. Bonsi was perhaps, in his careful way, attempting to assure their future. Two were to be Russian educated, and the third was to be kept at the centre of diplomatic activity.

At the end of 1820 she wrote to her brother about Paul:

I have to thank you for a letter to myself, which we have just received with the many details that you give us about our boy. I am delighted to know that he is at school, and equally pleased to find that you are prepared to show some sternness in dealing with him. I have been really anxious about the Court favours he has received. He has his faults, and what he needs to overcome them is rigid supervision rather than indulgence. He has always been extremely idle and it was partly because he thereby hindered his brothers' progress that we thought it advisable to separate them, and it must be allowed that since their departure they have been going on famously.

Now only her last born, the royally sponsored George, was to be left with her. It was a disappointment to her not to see her brother and her dear father but Alexander must understand that 'it would be impossible for me to leave my small boy here. He is a sweet gentle creature – I wish you could see him.' And then a sigh for the *beau passé* escaped her. 'Whenever shall we see one another again?'

If Darja had to submit to the separation from her sons, Metternich had suffered a second blow. His eldest daughter, who had married the Count Joseph Esterhazy, and about whom he had often written to Countess Lieven, also died of the same mysterious

5 Christopher Lieven by Sir Thomas Lawrence. 'George IV admired Bonsi's coiffeur and took a good look before having a new wig made'

illness which had carried off her sister. 'I break myself upon the wheel of duty', he wrote to her, 'as a man plunged into despair throws himself on the enemy batteries. I no longer live to feel but to act. How I love that child! On her part she loved me as more than a father. For so many long years, she was my best and closest friend.'

This time Darja allowed herself, with some propriety, to express her grief at her lover's loss. 'I have learned of the death of your daughter, believe me, mon Prince, that I enter sincerely into your affliction.' This edited extract adds nothing else but goes on to chat about the Neapolitan revolution and ends with a typically contemporary high-flown sentiment 'Adieu mon Prince, I suffer in your grief, as I shall rejoice in your glory!'

It is impossible not to feel that her letters, so carefully edited, were also painstakingly re-written. She was always aware of posterity's eyes upon her and perhaps also conscious that her correspondence with 'mon Prince' would make a contribution to the history of her time.

In the year when he had lost two of his daughters, Metternich became nervous about the health of his delicate wife and his three remaining children. All of them suffered from that scourge of the nineteenth century, delicate lungs. The climate of Vienna, which had already carried off his favourite daughter, he now felt too harsh for the rest of his family. The sun of Italy would have been his choice for their health's sake, but the uncertainty of political crises and possible revolutions precluded that country as a healthy refuge for his family. He decided to send them to Paris, and once again returned to his work as to a drug.

Although the lovers had the sorrow of separation from their children, the year 1821 was to bring them together again. The unlikely and adipose Cupid was said to be George IV. He had always had a passion for intrigue, and it seems unlikely that he could have been unaware of the gossip surrounding Metternich and the Countess. He could possibly have been an unconscious accomplice in arranging a rapturous reunion of the lovers. The Count Lieven was busy and happy in Russia, cementing his contacts with the Court. It seemed to his wife that, as in a carefully contrived comedy, the absence of her husband was an advantage to be enjoyed.

But when she wrote to her father the facts were more carefully arranged. She had been in Hanover for eight days, the King of England insisted that she should come, and Lord Londonderry had sent a special courier to Frankfurt 'to hasten my arrival'. What a great pity that Bonsi was not here. She had hurried into Hanover,

112

hoping to find him, imagine her disappointment! The Prince Metternich had arrived also hoping to see Bonsi, and *both* of them had been disappointed. She added that couriers had been sent to tell her husband that King George could not stay much longer as he was indisposed. Darja expressed renewed astonishment, and indeed dismay at the absence of Bonsi.

'In spite of the fact that I am here at the King's express invitation, I am totally put out in being without my husband, and I cannot express how much this upsets me.'

She had mentioned Metternich's name only once, as if by not commenting on his presence, which so concerned her, she could keep her feelings hidden. By a curious coincidence Metternich had already left by the time Bonsi arrived from Russia. He was complacent and satisfied with his visit to his native country, leaving, as he remarked, without having asked for, or obtained any special favours for himself or his family. His letter describing his successful visit seems like a Russian version of Mr. Collins speaking of Lady Catherine de Burgh.

The gracious esteem and confidence of our adorable Monarch, the flattering welcome held out to me by persons of consequence, the reunion with so many relations whom I had not seen for so many long years, or whose acquaintance I had not yet made, the chance to get closer to a fatherland which is being developed and transformed with such surprising rapidity, are only a few of the objects which have given me such unimaginable pleasure – and have even been of real use to me.

And so, while Bonsi was making himself useful and helpful to royal and eminent personages, Clement and his chère Dorothée were able to enjoy a whole week of passionate philosophising.

It must be hoped that cher Clément was able to bring himself to echo the sentiment 'comme il est doux de t'aimer'.

CHAPTER NINE

'What a loss for us all...'

The head of Lord Castlereagh was one of the heads which the Cato Street conspirators had planned to parade on pikes through the City of London. They had marginally anticipated fact – for on 12 August 1822 he cut his jugular vein with a penknife.

It was on the eve of the Congress of Verona when, yet again, the future of Europe was to be discussed. Castlereagh (or Lord Londonderry as he had become in 1816) had been at the head of foreign affairs in Europe, in England, and in Ireland for more than twenty years. The high point of his career, as of Metternich's, had been the settlement achieved by the European allies, after the defeat of Napoleon. To contain the power of Russia was one of the planks of Castlereagh's policy, and as a consequence of this, he naturally became one of the targets of the Countess Lieven's attentions.

The beginnings of their acquaintanceship had been unhappy, and dated back to 1814, when the Tsar, after the penultimate defeat of Napoleon, had been posturing and adopting what Castlereagh called a 'chevaleresque attitude. He has a personal feeling about Paris, and seems to seek for the occasion of entering, with his magnificent guards, into the enemy's capital.' Castlereagh was neither disposed to let the Russians take all the credit for the victory, or to let them dictate the future course of French history by imposing a new government on France. (It might be noted, several wars later, that Russia's aims hardly seem to change in method or direction.)

The Tsar Alexander informed Castlereagh that the Prince Regent had no desire for a peace with Napoleon, that the Regent had informed Count Lieven that he was in favour of a Bourbon restoration. This information had come to Count Lieven by way of his wife who was in the confidence of the Regent and had used her friendship, with what seemed to her a good effect.

Her adored Tsar had thus been made privy to the Regent's

114

thinking. This manner of passing on information did not recommend itself to Castlereagh. It seemed to him to be more the action of a spy, than that of an ambassador's wife who had no call to act as a direct contact between the two rulers, thus avoiding Britain's ministers.

Castlereagh replied coldly to the Tsar that any information which the Tsar had received from the Prince Regent by way of Count Lieven had not been brought to *his* knowledge, and he would consider it his duty, as a servant of the Crown, to give totally different advice. Thus Countess Lieven's relations with Castlereagh had begun in bitterness. But, possibly through Castlereagh's awareness of her love affair with Metternich, and the fact that, as Foreign Minister, he had always regarded Austria as the natural ally of Britain, his relations with the Countess began subtly to change.

In 1820, at the time of the Queen's trial, Castlereagh had gone down to his country house at Cray for a few day's relaxation and the Countess was among his visitors. She hated to fail with anyone, and by this time had set herself to captivate Castlereagh. It is hard, looking at her arrogant face set on a long neck, the watchful eyes, the mouth with its sarcastic half-smile to recapture the charm of the woman. But it was there as Lady Granville makes plain. 'Madame de Lieven, delightful as she is, comes too seldom, and goes too early to make me reckon upon her, and my pleasure in my at-homes ceases if I have not someone's brains besides my own pour amuser mon monde.'

The Countess had taken care to meet Castlereagh as often as possible, and, by the time of her visit to Cray, she was achieving her object in becoming one of his close friends. She regaled Prince Metternich with the details. She had been shown round the Minister's country house. It had been much enlarged and he was obviously very proud of it, and with no reason to be, according to Darja. 'What taste in furnishing! The story of Don Quixote carpets his study, and Sancho is being tossed in a blanket just in front of his desk. He says that it gives him a pleasant sensation, and he thinks its position is excellent. Join me in laughing!'

A month later she was down at Cray again for a fête. 'We tried to be very gay. He himself insisted on waltzing with me – heavens what hard work it was to keep the Minister revolving! I am a very suitable person to make that kind of sacrifice, not as regards physical resources, but as regards goodwill.' She went on to recount that while she was keeping the Minister revolving, those members of the party 'who had some sentimental preoccupations went for a stroll. It was a dark night; the little paths were well-

115

screened with thick laurel bushes, and the great majority of the guests gave us the slip . . . There were some comic scenes.'

The Countess added a comment on the curious moral attitudes of English married women which always seemed to her to be both hypocritical – and surprising. In the end with the marked absence of the couples engaged in amorous pursuits, the ballroom was left only to little girls, a few old women, and herself endlessly waltzing with the master of the house, sacrificing herself at the call of duty . . . Even when writing of the deserted ballroom to her lover, the Countess manages to get in a derogatory remark about Bonsi. She describes the little girls as having the dancing ability of her husband.

Castlereagh may have shown himself to be a poor dancer, but the Countess was proving to be a good diplomat, and she began to understand the qualities of the man and to appreciate his integrity, and his intelligence. He in his turn, in spite of his original doubts, began to confide in her. It is possible that in the back of his mind he wished her to convey his thoughts and feelings to Metternich. Castlereagh could hardly have been unaware of the fact that she carried on a constant and intimate correspondence with the Prince, and she could have been a useful channel to disseminate not only policies, but ideas of policies which were forming in his mind. If so, Darja was becoming like a railway junction, handling a good deal of two-way traffic. Goods changed trains at Bonsi, but were always loyally carried on to St. Petersburg and the Tsar.

It was by now some years since the 'final' settlement after the Napoleonic wars, and the whole situation was changing. The men who had made the peace had relied on the principle of 'legality'. They had restored the Bourbons to France, and in the aftermath of the wars, the populace had been only too pleased that the killing should stop, and that the men should come home, and the farms and fields be restored. But by 1820 the wars had been forgotten, men's minds turned to their present ills, and against their present rulers. Piedmont and Naples rose against the Austrians who crushed them. Castlereagh was content to see this done, the Austrians were the allies of the British in the Mediterranean, and Metternich was a bulwark against Russian expansionism.

But then a more difficult and more potentially dangerous revolt began. The Greeks rose against the Turks, and massacred every Turk they could find. The Turks, incensed against these unbelievers, decided to strike at the heart of the Greek religion. On Easter Sunday they killed the Greek Patriarch and exposed his body on the doors of his cathedral. Many other Greek bishops were torn from their altars and killed, like so many human sacrifices, on the steps of their churches. The Tsar, the Countess's beloved Emperor, like the emblem of his Imperial eagle, had a double look. On one hand he could gain prestige by protecting the Christians against the hordes of Islam, and on the other he could gain a much coveted warm-water port in the Mediterranean.

Any differences which might have divided Castlereagh and Metternich over the years were speedily remedied. The danger of Russia drew Austria and Britain closer together. Previously there had been sharp differences. Metternich was an interventionist, and both he and the Tsar were demanding that Britain should help to put down uprisings in Spain. Metternich himself had tried to repress liberal ideas with his Carlsbad Decrees against the Universities and the press. The stamping out of revolution was the paramount aim of Prince Metternich, but Castlereagh stood firm for non-intervention. Not that Britain was herself immune from the general revolutionary ferment. Countess Lieven described how at a dinner party at the house of Lord Castlereagh, she had asked him if it were true that he went about in the streets armed. He did not answer, but for a reply produced two pistols which he laid on the table in front of him. The Countess was much impressed by the cool courage of Castlereagh. He had told her that he was undisturbed by the mob in the streets; the only thing which would inconvenience him would be if they began to pull down his house.

The Countess remarked in a letter to Metternich, 'Few men have Lord Castlereagh's intrepid coolness but more than once nothing but his unruffled appearance has overawed the mob.'

Apart from his international troubles Castlereagh was beset with the petty quarrels of the women who surrounded him, quarrels which ended in social snubs and absurd behaviour. Lady Castlereagh had an intense dislike of the King's mistress, Lady Conyngham. This not only caused social difficulties but also poisoned the relations between the King and Castlereagh himself, causing the latter much embarrassment. It was in this context that he began to confide in the Countess, who was trying to patch up the quarrels. With her Continental attitude towards mistresses, lovers, and love affairs, and her intense admiration of any form of royalty however stupid or decadent, the Countess obviously took the view that anything which the King had decided upon was good and acceptable, even his ageing mistress.

She draws a quick vignette of life at the King's seaside residence. 'Since we left Brighton, the King has seen nobody. Love which allowed nothing to interfere with it is all very fine; but how extraordinary when its object is Lady Conyngham! Not an idea in her head; not a word to say for herself; nothing but a hand to accept pearls and diamonds with, and an enormous balcony to wear them on.'

Darja found the atmosphere at Brighton irresistibly funny, especially when the King presented her with a new 'Order', a portrait of himself on a blue ribbon. The reason she had been given this privilege first was merely so that Lady Conyngham could then wear it herself – with propriety.

But to Castlereagh the bitterness of the quarrels between his wife Emily, and Lady Conyngham were hardly a matter for cynical amusement. In Countess Lieven's relaxing company Castlereagh began to unburden himself, and to find relief in her amusing gossipy conversation. At the time of the King's visit to Hanover, he had fallen in with the King's plans that the Countess should be invited as an intermediary for him with the King. 'Vraiment' had luckily been detained in Russia. Emily was not invited and so the way was open to effect a reconciliation between the King and Castlereagh, which Metternich and his *chère amie* now proceeded to engineer. Prince Metternich was to be persuaded to co-operate in preventing the Tsar going to war with Turkey, and the Countess and her lover were intent on healing the quarrel between the King and Castlereagh. Under the subtle influence of the Austrian Chancellor and the Russian Ambassadress, the King's ever volatile mood changed, and he smiled on Castlereagh again. Deep within himself Castlereagh felt this cordiality as a humiliation. He had needed two foreigners to heal the breach with his own sovereign. But for the moment, in the euphoria of the meeting with Metternich, and his increasingly warm relations with the Countess, this was forgotten.

By the end of November the Countess was back in London. She wrote to Metternich of the intense pleasure Lord Castlereagh had on his reunion with her. He had come into the room with open arms 'and I simply had to open mine half-way so that we gave each other a kind of semi-tender embrace'. They had naturally talked a great deal about Metternich, and Castlereagh, in what she thought to be a rather simple and naive way, asked if Metternich liked him. His bitterness about the necessity of the influence and good offices of the two foreigners was temporarily forgotten. He went on to remark how easy he felt in the Prince's company, and looking at the Countess he added: 'It is the same with you – my ideas are all fluid.'

The King who, according to Darja, liked to encourage *affaires de coeur* amongst his friends and acquaintances, invited his Ministers down to Brighton, and took the greatest care to tell Castlereagh that Countess Lieven would be there. But on that occasion Castlereagh had little chance for his friendship to ripen – for the

King monopolised the Countess himself, and Castlereagh, who was flanked at dinner by members of the Opposition party, was reduced to eating two large helpings of roast mutton. But back in London Castlereagh found out that the Countess took a daily walk in Kensington Gardens, the only place where, according to her, there was any air. Castlereagh managed to ride in the Park at the same hour, and he would get off his horse and walk slowly up and down with her talking of all the subjects which obsessed him, and amused her – Metternich, the King, the political complications, the quarrels of his wife and the reigning favourite.

Darja felt that he really was very fond of her, but it was a tender friendship. She reassured Metternich: 'If you hear any remark about my intimacy with him please do not think there is any harm in it.' This reassurance was perhaps not as necessary to Metternich as it was to herself. But she went on to explain the reasons for their intimacy. Castlereagh knew very few people in society, for most of the men and women in the social swim were of the other party, and women did not find him amusing. There was another thing which intrigued and amused her – Castlereagh's French, which was most original. He used the most curious comparisons. When speaking about Austria he had told her: 'We regard her as the pivot of Europe, and our shoulder is always ready to support her; we are like a lover whom she will always find waiting for her; and we like her to help her other lover Russia who is perhaps not always so faithful, but must be treated all the better for that very reason.'

Darja began to admire him more and more. His aristocratic air of distinction attracted her, and she was drawn to him by her understanding of the deep melancholy which she felt clung about him, and which, with her Russian background, she entirely understood. Amongst his other confidences he admitted how deeply the quarrel between his wife Emily, and Lady Conyngham had affected him. He confessed that it disturbed him night and day. The Countess, always ready to take a hand in negotiations, decided that something must be done and she managed to persuade Lady Conyngham to call on Emily, but at the last minute the favourite decided not to give way, and refused to go. This petty quarrel between petty women was carried on at all levels, and the quarrel reached new heights when the King had to give a large dinner for an official visit to England of the Princess of Denmark. The list was naturally headed by Castlereagh and his wife. As soon as Lady Conyngham saw those names on the list – she refused to attend the dinner. The King was reduced to using the good offices of his friend Countess Lieven, asking her to plead with his mistress to change her mind. A week went by in which the dinner was ordered – and

119

6 Lord Castlereagh by Sir Thomas Lawrence. 'His aristocratic air of distinction attracted Dorothea'

cancelled – no less than three times. Eventually Countess Lieven managed to persuade Lady Conyngham to allow Castlereagh's wife to be included in the official guest list. Castlereagh was relieved, but his wife then proceeded to vitiate the atmosphere by sitting next to the King at the ball, which followed the official dinner, thus displacing the royal favourite, who was more than ever incensed.

Some days later Castlereagh told the Countess how delighted he was that Emily had eventually been invited, and asked how this had been engineered. The Countess, only too pleased to display her prowess at domestic diplomacy, told Castlereagh the truth. She expected him to express his pleasure at her good offices, but instead he went white with anger and said: 'You have shown me our position clearly. Things cannot go on like this. We cannot put up with a Lady Conyngham who is powerful enough to offer us such affronts.'

The Countess tried to soothe Castlereagh's ruffled feelings. It was neither important, nor serious. Lady Conyngham was merely a superficial inconvenience who must be appeased rather than opposed. But Castlereagh, already at the end of his tether, could not see it in that light. 'From now on I shall be nothing more than His Majesty's very humble servant and we shall see how long these relations will last – if they do not – I shall resign. I have done enough for my country, and my master, to be independent in that respect and nothing shall stop me.'

The Countess could not see how such trivial matters as dinner invitations and who sat next to whom at routs or balls should lead to the resignation of a Minister. She intimated as much to Castlereagh, but he said: 'I cannot sacrifice my honour and my pride; both are more wounded than I can say. I repeat, things cannot remain as they are. I have served my master with all my heart, but I am in a position to serve him no longer. Let him give orders to Lord Liverpool, the Duke of Wellington, or to whomever he pleases. Whatever it may mean to me, I can no longer receive them, if he thinks that through the patronage of a *foreigner*, I can accept without difficulty an act to which my position alone entitles me.'

The word 'foreigner', thrown at her like an insult struck Darja like a blow. All their good relations, all the good offices which she had performed for Castlereagh vis-à-vis the King seemed to disappear.

Later on Castlereagh had calmed down sufficiently to be able to discuss foreign affairs more rationally. He spoke in a calmer and more reasoned manner about the proposed journey which he was to make with the King. Yet another Congress was to discuss the endless problems which now hung over the former Allies – the uprisings in Spain, the revolution in Greece, and the possible recognition of the Spanish colonies. Castlereagh was happy that all the arrangements had been made for the foreign journeyings. This piece of intelligence was at variance with the facts as the Countess herself knew them. Lady Conyngham had raised her diamond studded head yet again. She wished only to appear at the King's side in the glittering capitals. The King wanted her by his side throughout the whole journey and he was petty about the whole project. If Lady Conyngham was not by his side – he would not go at all.

At this point Darja may have given some indication that she could take a hand in calming down the domestic storm. Once again Castlereagh took her intervention in the wrong way. 'The King's journey will or will not take place; that is no more my concern. I wash my hands of it. The King has Liverpool – let him arrange with him. I shall accept his orders and if I continue to serve him I shall decide, according to whether my wife is, or is not included in the expedition, what course I have to take.'

The Countess still held to her view that the whole matter was too trivial to be taken at such a tragic level. But, unknown to her, tragedy was in the air, its dark wings were already spreading themselves over the mind of Castlereagh. He began to mutter about treachery. The Duke of Wellington – he seemed to be a friend, but was a traitor. Finally he turned on the Countess: 'And you! You are also a traitor!'

Darja, who at the beginning of her life had seen in St. Petersburg real treacheries and real betrayals, was for once at a loss. The man she had considered to be a friend, and whom she had tried to help, had cut her to the heart. In tears she left the house, and on the way home in her carriage she turned to her husband and recounted the conversation.

The Count Lieven, often prone to find fault with his wife, was convinced that she had said something to upset Castlereagh. She insisted that this was not the case, and with great precision went over the exact course of the conversation.

For once the Count did not use his favourite phrase: 'Vraiment' – he looked at his wife, and said blankly, 'Well, either I am mad – or he is!'

After his outburst against Darja, Castlereagh went round to his brother's house. He was greatly agitated, and repeated all the allegations which he had made against the Countess. It was she who was trying to force him to resign. She had managed to insinuate the Duke of Wellington into the favour of the King. She wanted the Duke to succeed him. The reason was that she wanted to see someone more amenable to Russia in his shoes, someone whom she could manipulate. She was well aware that Wellington was not a friend of his and wished to supplant him.

It was true that Countess Lieven was an *intrigante*. She certainly had some influence with the King, if only because she had always taken a more sensible and worldly view of Lady Conyngham, but she had never acted against Castlereagh.

After his agitated outburst to his brother, Lord Stewart, Castlereagh burst into tears – and so did his brother. Charles Stewart had never before seen this controlled man in such a state of agitation and emotion. The next morning Charles went round to see the Countess. In a state of distress himself, he explained what had happened, and the allegations which his brother had made against her.

Puzzled and distressed the Countess said: 'Whatever influence I have had, I have used actively and loyally in his service.' She went on to point out that Castlereagh had many proofs of this. 'As for the Duke, Castlereagh has not a more sincere friend than he.'

There was something in all of this which was difficult to understand. Was it possible that her husband, normally not the most perceptive of men, had managed to penetrate to the truth? Was Castlereagh mad? Darja mentioned the curious state of mind in which she had left Castlereagh. His brother brushed this aside. Castlereagh was disgusted with everything. 'One more reason for disgust – this women's quarrel. The cup has overflowed ... and the distrust he feels of all his colleagues.'

The Countess became more and more amazed. Was it not more sensible to be pleased that Castlereagh had friends like Wellington and herself *near* the King, and his favourite, rather than enemies? 'I am as sure of the Duke as I am of myself. He is incapable of dishonesty. And what good would it do him to harm your brother?'

At this point Lord Stewart broke down and sobbed. The background to Castlereagh's agitation was his wife's ceaseless petty nagging. She would quarrel far into the night, endlessly repeating her grievances against Lady Conyngham, the slights she had suffered. Sleepless and disturbed by his parliamentary worries, Charles Stewart confided to Darja that his brother was broken hearted, and he himself feared that his mind would collapse.

Darja said that she hoped time would destroy the suspicions in Castlereagh's mind. She had decided to act, and set off for the 'Cottage' at Windsor where she was closeted with the King all day long. Once again she seemed to be achieving her objective in patching up all the difficulties with Lady Conyngham about the King's journey. She wrote to Metternich describing how she had achieved this admirable result. She had said everything she could to flatter the King's pride, his love of pleasure and his small vanities. The plan which had evolved was that Florence was to be visited after Vienna, and of course, Paris. 'It was really extremely funny. They thought Florence was twice as far from here as Vienna. They did not know which way one went – so I began by teaching them geography.'

The favourite was dying to be seen at the King's side on an official European journey. The King on the other hand, whose health was hardly brilliant, was for staying comfortably where he was. The Countess countered his objections by making a long speech about the dangers of Jacobinism, and painting a rosy picture of the enormous moral boost which the presence of the King of England at the Congress would produce in Europe. She mentioned her Tsar, and the fact that it would be an admirable chance to efface the memories of his visit to England in 1814. 'In short I tried to remember all the King's vulnerable points, and really we have never been so near achieving our ends.'

The brief description which Darja gives of her visit to what was known as the 'Cottage Coterie' paints an admirable picture of her methods – flattery combined with a knowledgeable attitude, and the ability to keep the end in view while using the vulnerable weaknesses of others. She constantly remarked in her letters what a good courtier she was, in the context of many of her activities, and she was well aware of her ability to use this quality to good purpose. She had been trained from a young age in a court where a mistake could lead to disgrace, and even to death. Consequently, the manipulation of a weak and vain King was child's play to this experienced woman. Although the companions of the King seemed to her to be ridiculous, and the picture she painted of the ageing mistress hung with jewels, and the doting King, has in many respects the qualities of a caricature, she never forgot that he had that magic aura of kingship. In the back of her mind and imagination kings and emperors had the sublime virtue of being set apart from other men whatever their demerits and vices.

Satisfied that she had persuaded the King of the glory to be gathered by his Continental journey, she went back to London. When she drove up to her house in her carriage, she found Lord Stewart inside the house waiting for her. He had come round to find out what had been decided.

This time the Countess kept her own counsel. She was no longer eager to boast of her diplomatic prowess; the insulting use of the word 'foreigner' remained in her mind. As she wrote to Metternich: 'I begin to suspect that, though certain people may need my help in that quarter, they are a little offended at the influence I exercise.' This was small minded, she had always shown Castlereagh every kind of confidence. He should forget that she was the Russian Ambassador's wife, and remember that she was his friend.

Yet she could not help remembering a curious encounter in Kensington Gardens when she had been taking her usual walk, and had seen Castlereagh wrapped in a cloak walking towards her. He saluted her and began to walk along beside her, but his whole manner was strange and curiously remote. She did not mention the projected journey. For some moments she had the feeling that he wanted to confide in her, as if the barrier of silence between them could be broken. He made some remarks indicating his distrust of her, and when she became angry, he looked at her with a strangely sad smile which gave her an icy feeling round her heart.

Suddenly he looked at her and said: 'Good God, can I trust you?'

She asked him to look into her face, and say what he saw there. He told her it was a charming, and a clever face. Blushing she said: 'No, my lord, nothing of that. But an honest face.'

In her soul she knew that they had been real friends, and that this detached man with his cold aristocratic manner had confided in her more than in anyone else, and yet now a great chasm yawned between them. It was as if he were on the ledge of a rock and no amount of help on her part could rescue him.

All this passed through her mind as she talked to Charles Stewart who, as she wrote to Metternich, 'disclosed to me his brother's suspicions'. It had become firmly fixed in Castlereagh's mind that Wellington wished to supplant him, and go on the journey. Stewart went on: 'If Wellington moves up a step, my brother will resign, for he will never suffer this rival – or indeed any rival. These fancies seem to him all the more real in view of the enmity that exists between the two women, and the general unwillingness to let Lady Londonderry [Castlereagh's wife] go on the journey.'

The Countess went on to list all the reasons for disbelieving these delusions. 'I gave twenty different proofs that it was quite the contrary.' Wellington would not be at all popular, he was invited only because he was part of the set in which she herself moved. 'To tell the truth, I am astonished at all this intrigue and at the illusory terrors that have been conjured up, and I foresee that nothing good will come of it.'

On 10 June she wrote again to Metternich – Castlereagh looked ghastly, and he seemed to have aged five years in a week, and was a broken man. She feared that Lord Stewart was not helping, and that his own suspicions may have taken root in his brother's mind. She recalled that Castlereagh did not like her husband to talk business with Wellington, and had been very prickly on that subject. The reason was quite simple, the Duke was much easier to deal with, more open, more frank, and above all – because he had no responsibility – he was always ready to be persuaded. In Castlereagh's mind the reasons for the Countess introducing the Duke into the King's circles were obvious – he was to replace him.

As far as she was concerned that would have been merely to exchange one difficulty for another. She had more confidence in Castlereagh than in the Duke. 'Why on earth has Castlereagh these suspicions?' Surely he could see what was in her heart? She again decided to act, and went off to see Lady Conyngham, and had roused her enthusiasm for the glory which would accrue to the King if only she could persuade him definitely to undertake the journey. Darja went on to outline the absolute necessity of the English Foreign Minister (Castlereagh) being at the Congress. There would be a difficulty in getting him there – the King's journey made the perfect excuse. The favourite swallowed the honeyed words, and two hours later the King sent for Castlereagh.

Later the Countess went to dine with Castlereagh. Her mind was full of alternating hopes and fears, but when he met her he seemed radiant. They fell into a teasing conversation much in their former manner when they had been close friends. The Countess gave him a message from Metternich, and he replied that he himself had had a long and friendly letter from the Prince. She asked Castlereagh what reply she might give to Metternich, when she wrote and finally he said, 'Tell him I am hoping to see him soon.'

After dinner Lord Stewart came up to her and said: 'I congratulate you. You must be proud of yourself. You have made the King obey you on every point. My brother found him as prepared as if he were under orders. Everything you wish is done, and we must all run at your bidding.'

The Countess wrote that Lord Stewart looked angry. Again in the back of her mind the insulting word 'foreigner' lingered. To be considered an interfering foreigner when she was trying to pour oil on the troubled waters of domestic friction! Perhaps in her mind Darja pondered whether all these petty displays of malice were not only the work of Emily, Castlereagh's wife, but that Charles Stewart had not calmed his brother's worst fears. They all resented her good offices on their behalf with the King.

Four days later Darja wrote of finding Lady Conyngham red-eyed and in tears. The favourite had had a letter from the King. Everything was changed. He had decided to go – not to the Continent – but to Scotland! The Countess implored the favourite not to let the King take any irrevocable decision, but at that moment the Marchioness's son came in. The King was with his Ministers. 'That finished it!'

Count Lieven was told officially that the continental journey was now given up. The King was going to Scotland, and couriers had already been despatched announcing his imminent arrival in Edinburgh.

But the complications of the abandoned journey continued to send their ripples round and round the social pond. The effect had been, as the Countess noticed, to bring the King's coterie closer to the Opposition, and as a result there was a good deal of animosity towards the Government. Darja was not anxious to be regaled with the satisfaction which was going to be expressed about the failure of her efforts to promote the King's journey. Her plan was to prevent the favourite sitting next to Lord Grey when they dined at the house of Lady Cowper, who was a stalwart of the Opposition. She made Lord Grey sit next to her at table and, by the time they had reached the dessert, she had managed to make him believe that she was encouraging him. Later in the drawing-room Grey sat beside her again, and in this way Darja was able to prevent any secret talks with the favourite. But suddenly all these carefully laid plans fell apart. Lady Conyngham remarked in a loud voice: 'When is Londonderry [Castlereagh] going to the Congress?'

Lord Grey pricked up his ears. 'What? Londonderry? What Congress? Is there to *be* a Congress?'

Lady Conyngham replied that of course there was to be a Congress. If that were so, said Lord Grey, they should send him, he would know what to do there.

'What would you do?'

'Break it up immediately, and send the Holy Alliance to the devil!'

Darja ended her letter to Metternich by remarking that it was all a nice mess. A gross understatement for things were moving slowly and inexorably to a climax.

Castlereagh's mind was increasingly filled not only with the stupidities of his wife and the King's mistress, but with even darker delusions.

In July of 1822 the Bishop of Clogher, son of the Earl of Roden, had been arrested on a charge of 'having committed an act of criminal association with a private soldier in a common ale-house in Westminster'.

As his melancholia and delusions crowded in on his disordered mind, Castlereagh began to believe that he was being blackmailed as a result of committing the same crime as the Bishop. The truth seems to have been that he had visited a brothel and that, as a means of blackmail, a man in woman's clothes had been substituted for the expected prostitute. Castlereagh began to mutter that he would rather face death than disgrace. But in spite of the black miasmic thoughts which fogged his brain he went doggedly on with his work, and proceeded with his projects for the Congress.

He had arranged with Metternich his detailed plans. Britain and Austria were to combine in an alliance to prevent, not only another war in Europe, but also to keep the Russians out of the Mediterranean. At the last minute the delicate balance of diplomacy was put at risk, for the Turks massacred the Greek population at Scio. Castlereagh sent an official protest to Turkey. The British Ambassador delivered the protest, and managed to persuade the Porte to give way on the four points which Russia had demanded.

No one seems to have noticed the increasing strain under which Castlereagh was working. His wife should have been aware of his excessive nervousness, and the fears which attacked him. But she seems to have been more concerned with her plans for her brilliant appearance at the Congress. Now that the King and his favourite were off on a jaunt to Scotland, there was nothing to prevent her shining as the first lady of the Congress.

But the shadows were drawing ever closer in Castlereagh's mind. He said to his secretary, Lord George Seymour: 'My mind is, as it were – gone.' And he put his hand to his forehead.

He went down to his country house at Cray, where Seymour accompanied him. In the afternoon Castlereagh was walking towards the river which ran at the end of the garden, and he looked so cast down that Seymour followed him, and tried to start a conversation. But Castlereagh did not seem to be present at all. Seymour tried to bring him back to himself by talking about the projected journey. He personally was much looking forward to seeing old friends and diplomatic acquaintances.

Castlereagh looked at him: 'At any other time I should have liked it very much, but I am quite worn out here', and again he tapped his forehead, 'quite worn out, and this fresh load of responsibility now put upon me is more than I can bear.'

Alarmed at this confession, Seymour went to Emily and voiced his fears about the state of her husband. But Emily brushed him aside – her husband was merely tired. Eager to be off on her journey she ignored the warning signs.

Burden upon burden had been laid upon him, and now the

overloaded beast was sinking in its shafts. He was fifty-three and had been in politics since he was twenty-one. At the Foreign Office he still wrote most of his despatches with his own hand. He was Leader of the House of Commons, and, after the retirement of Lord Sidmouth in 1821, took on the further work of the Home Secretary.

He had never been popular. Almost every party at home and abroad hated or feared him, and all for different reasons. The Irish patriots because of the Union, the Irish Protestants because of the emancipation of the Catholics, the Whigs because he had continued the war against Napoleon, the French legitimists because he had tried to make a negotiated peace with Napoleon in 1814. Even the English Tories regarded him as an Irishman, although he belonged to the Protestant Ascendancy. The Romantics attacked him. Shelley had written:

> I met Murder on the way,
> He had a mask like Castlereagh,
> Very smooth he looked, yet grim
> Seven bloodhounds followed him.

Byron was especially bitter against him. In lines tinctured with venom he described him as an intellectual eunuch, a cold-blooded, smooth-faced placid miscreant, and the most vulgar tool that Tyranny could want.

> States to be curb'd and thoughts to be confined,
> Conspiracy or Congress to be made –
> Cobbling at manacles for all mankind –
> A tinkering slave-maker, who mends old chains
> With God and man's abhorrence for its gains.

The Romantics, always immoderate, always speaking in superlatives abhorred the middle way, and brushed aside the evidence of their own immoderation, or in some cases, as with Shelley, did not live long enough to see the results of revolutions, nor have time to reflect that new chains can be forged by new men.

Castlereagh, in spite of his faults, had held Europe together. He had chosen Wellington to combat the French in Spain, a happy choice which had led to their final defeat. And now this man, so long execrated and for so many different reasons was tired – tired to death. So many years, so many conferences, so much opposition, so many enemies on every side.

The day after his brief conversation with Seymour he drove up to

London to take his formal leave of the King before setting out for the Conference. Emily went as far as the Palace with him. Possibly she was still hoping against hope that his strange condition would not be noticed. At his audience with the King he showed him the instructions and notes which he had drawn up for the Congress. The King began to read the paper out loud, and suddenly he noticed that Castlereagh was not listening. His eyes were on the ceiling, and rolling from one side to the other in a very odd manner. The King, disturbed, asked what was the matter. Castlereagh replied that it was his insufferable footman John who was at the door, and would not go away although he had constantly been told to do so.

King George looked at his Minister and realising that something was very wrong with him said: 'You are ill, my Lord. Go home and have yourself bled.'

But Castlereagh looked round, his whole attitude was one of terror. 'Have you heard the news – the terrible news? I am a fugitive from justice. I am accused of the same crime as the Bishop of Clogher.'

The King attempted to soothe him, but Castlereagh continued to speak, the words pouring out from him, while his eyes were full of fear. 'A warrant has been issued for my arrest. They are looking for me. I have ordered my horses, and I am going to fly to Portsmouth and there embark for France... I shall leave by the little gate in your garden.'

'My Lord,' said the King, 'you forget yourself. This pleasantry is misplaced – entirely misplaced.'

In reply Castlereagh merely laughed sarcastically. 'I know well that you *also* are my enemy. Everyone hates and shuns me. When I walk down the streets people take the opposite side to avoid meeting me.'

The King, now seriously upset, tried to reassure Castlereagh, but nothing soothed him. The King was his good friend. He was ill. 'You have a fever, have yourself bled, and chase away your fit of blue devils.'

But Castlereagh continued to accuse himself of every crime, even producing alleged blackmailing letters to prove the truth of what he was saying.

Then, just as suddenly, he broke down. 'I am mad. I know I am mad. I have known it for some time.' With tears in his eyes, he implored the King to keep his secret, and not to divulge it to his colleagues.

The King was now thoroughly alarmed. As soon as Castlereagh left him, he spoke to Wellington, and asked him to send urgently for Castlereagh's doctor. He also wrote an affectionate letter to Castlereagh himself, strongly urging him to seek swift medical advice. And finally George wrote to Lord Liverpool making it plain that he was very nervous about Castlereagh's mental state, and requested Liverpool to come at once.

As soon as Wellington had left the King's presence he managed to overtake Castlereagh who was still muttering about being pursued, and the necessity of escape. Wellington, in his usual blunt way, rode straight at the fence. 'From what you have said I am bound to warn you that you cannot be in your right mind.'

'Since you say so, I fear it must be so. I have an oppression in my head which distresses me perpetually, and makes me fear that my ideas are indeed in disorder.'

Wellington sent for the doctor to go to Castlereagh: he bled the wretched man, making him even weaker than before.

On Wednesday 13 August Countess Lieven wrote to tell Metternich that she had been sent for by Lady Conyngham two days before, but the favourite was then taken ill, and Darja had not been able to see her. 'She had wanted to tell me, in confidence, that Lord Londonderry [Castlereagh] was mad, so that I might warn my husband secretly that he could not go to the Continent.'

But when eventually she went round to see the King's mistress, Darja had not yet heard the news. No one except the King, Wellington, and Lord Liverpool suspected Castlereagh's condition. So when Countess Lieven went into Lady Conyngham's room she congratulated her – it happened to be the King's birthday. But almost directly her elder son came in 'as pale as death, and said: "Londonderry is dead!" Lady Conyngham clutched her head in her hands and cried: "Good God, he has killed himself."'

Lady Conyngham's son said he thought not, Lord Londonderry had had an apoplectic fit, but she repeated firmly that he was mad and must have killed himself.

The Countess Lieven was unable to speak, she was so overcome with emotion at hearing the terrible news. As she later wrote to Metternich: 'Besides mourning Lord Londonderry as a friend, you have to mourn him as a Minister – perhaps the only man in England who understood European politics ... what a loss for us all ... I cannot get over it. I see him in front of me all the time; that noble face, so serene and so handsome! The circumstances of his death seem to me incredible. Imagine leaving a madman alone for a second!... He had nobody there except his wife, and what a wife!'

When Castlereagh had talked with his doctor, Bankhead, the

night before, again his mind was full of delusions and accusations of crimes. He could not go to the Continent until his name was cleared. Eventually the doctor managed to calm him down and he went to bed with his wife as usual. As a precaution, his pistols and his razors had been taken away from him. At seven in the morning the doctor knocked at the door, and the maid told him: 'My lady is getting up.' Five minutes later when the doctor came back he was told: 'My Lord has just entered his dressing-room.' Dr. Bankhead immediately went to him.

The Countess narrated the end. 'He cried "Let me fall in your arms, it is all over." The doctor ran to him; at that moment streams of blood gushed from an artery in the neck, directly connected to the heart. In his right hand, he was holding a little penknife with which he used to cut his nails. He fell stone dead.'

A few days before his death Castlereagh had said to Count Lieven: 'Je sens mon cerveau ebranlé' and he had repeated the phrase to M. de Werther, the Prussian Minister. The Countess wrote: 'It did not strike them, they took it to mean that he had a headache, as his French was rather peculiar.'

But *ebranlé* means shaken and he had chosen a word which meant exactly what he wished to express. His mind was shaken and his whole being in dissolution. The handsome, cold man who had achieved so much, and felt he had achieved so little, was self-destroyed.

Even the manner of his death brought no charity from the pen of Byron.

> So he has cut his throat at last! He! Who?
> The man who cut his country's long ago.

He was buried in the Abbey next to Pitt and Fox. But controversy pursued him to the grave, as the Countess recounted: 'For some days, abominable notices have been placarded everywhere urging the people not to allow the body of a suicide to defile the sanctuary of Westminster. On this subject Cobbett has been publishing disgraceful articles, which are read with avidity by the lower classes. As a result, the mob has collected round Londonderry's town house, and has been shouting the most insulting accusations.'

And Byron, writing in Italy a preface to some cantos of *Don Juan* was on the side of the mob. 'It may at least serve as some consolation to the nations, that their oppressors are not happy, and in some instances judge so justly of their own actions, as to anticipate the sentence of mankind.'

132

Some hirelings made an attempt to raise a cheer as the coffin was carried into the Abbey, but, as Lord Clancarty wrote: 'This attempt was received with such indignation on the part of the crowd, that the exciting parties were not induced to renew their efforts.' Byron might have felt himself to have lost caste to find himself on the side of the hirelings.

Others wrote of the deep feeling of grief amongst all descriptions of persons, 'for his Memory is already beginning to be cherished by those who opposed his measures'. There is nothing which causes a statesman to achieve greater popularity amongst fellow politicians than being safely buried in the Abbey. Praise can then be lavished without fear of political complications.

But by Darja, Castlereagh was sincerely mourned, both as a friend, and a man of noble bearing and integrity.

CHAPTER TEN

'*I will regret Verona*'

Once the funeral was over, the death of a Foreign Secretary, like the death of a king, posed the question of the succession. Much as she mourned her friend Castlereagh, the Countess was naturally anxious to know who was to take his place at the coming Congress of Verona. Her informant was Wellington, who on his way back from the funeral called on her and chatted for two hours. She asked him point blank: 'Are you going to be Minister for Foreign Affairs?'

'No, I don't want to be; that would mean deviating from my position and my career. I should be compelled to adopt the opinions of my party and my individual opinions would no longer be free.' He preferred to keep his ideas quite independent, and he wanted to 'stick to them'. Obviously if the King demanded that he should become Foreign Secretary he would do so, but frankly he had no ambitions in that direction.

He went on to outline his ideas about foreign policy, which perhaps ring curiously on modern English ears as they smack much less of faction than our modern attitudes. No one man was responsible for the policy of his country, 'that policy is already marked out, and the Cabinet cannot turn aside from it. Let England abandon that policy and you plunge Europe and consequently yourselves into chaos ... I have such confidence in the system that I believe that if Lord Grey (of the Opposition) were to become Minister today he would do just as we do.'

Wellington posed the continuity of fore gn policy as an axiom to be pursued, which was difficult for the Countess to understand, as she was always partisan.

At the end of August Darja was down at Brighton, but had heard nothing except rumours. She complained to Prince Metternich of her gloomy life. Is this, she asked herself the way she should be using her intelligence? She was puzzled that people so much stupider than herself seemed to have a hundred times more sense:

134

she realised that true intelligence consisted in being happy – and she was not happy. Perhaps this was an appeal to Metternich himself, but in her edited correspondence sentimental passages have been eliminated. She must find a way of amusing herself, and she saw no means of distraction in 'this lovely island'. She was obviously hoping to see Metternich if and when she managed to get to the Congress of Verona and the uncertainty of whether she would see her lover again was obviously in the forefront of her mind. At the beginning of September she wrote that she had no further news. 'Really, we have grown very unceremonious – we have quite forgotten to be polite to one another.'

But eventually the cabals and the corridor-diplomacy were resolved, and, in spite of the King's antipathy to him, Canning was named as Foreign Secretary, and the Duke of Wellington, recovered from a sudden illness, was able to accompany him.

In October of 1822 she wrote to her brother Alexander from Verona saying that the Congress was one of the most interesting she had attended. No doubt the presence of Prince Metternich accounted for her enthusiasm. All Europe, she wrote, seemed to find themselves there – the Tsar, the King of Sardinia, many Italian princelings, and – representing France – Chateaubriand, whom the Countess does not mention. The reasons for this are quite clear. They had taken a great dislike to one another. Darja was not struck by the prestige of the great writer, an opinion she shared with her English friends and acquaintances. She also paid scant attention to the beautiful Juliette de Récamier, Chateaubriand's mistress. The only reference she makes to the women at the Congress was to remark that the feminine element was 'weak'.

But writers always have the last word. Writing of his stay in England, Chateaubriand mentions the Countess Lieven who had had

> various absurd troubles with Madame d'Osmond [wife of the previous French Ambassador in London] and with George IV. As she was bold and seemed to be well received at court the Countess Lieven had become extremely fashionable. People considered her witty, but they supposed her husband was not; M. Lieven was much superior to Madame. She was sharp featured with a forbidding face – a commonplace woman, tiring, arid, who had only one form of conversation – everyday politics; for the rest she knew nothing and she hid the paucity of her ideas by the abundance of her words. When she found herself with people of merit or distinction, her sterility made her dumb; she clothed her nullity behind an air of bored superiority as if she had

the right to be bored.

Chateaubriand described her as the 'dowager' of the Congress of Verona. In his *Mémoirs d'Outre Tombe* the secret of her liaison with Metternich was first given openly to the world. He wrote that much of her subsequent fame and influence came from the fact that she had had the honour of seeing Prince Metternich at those hours when, being tired from the weight of great matters, he amused himself in *effiloquer la soie*, as one might say 'by silken dalliance'. There was indeed little friendliness between the Countess and the Count de Chateaubriand. It would seem that underneath the French Ambassador with his grand house in Portland Place, Darja could perceive the parvenu writer from the provinces. There were other reasons for her considering the French Ambassador lacking in finesse. He entertained the actor Laffont because Laffont's wife was his mistress. 'He is keeping her and she does the honours of his house. He spends his evenings in her company, and discourses to her for hours of fame, of enthusiasms – and even of virtue!'

An *affaire* should be conducted on a much higher level than that, and with people of distinction. Darja described Chateaubriand as like a hunchback – without a hump. His old-fashioned romantic attitude was tiresome to her and she remarked that he wore on his sleeve a worn-out heart which could be bought – only there were no bidders. When the French Ambassador told the Countess that he was finding London tedious, she proposed introducing him to some intelligent women. He immediately replied that he would very much prefer the company of stupid women. It was an ill-concealed insult to Darja herself, and she did not forgive it.

Another possible cause for his distrust and dislike of the Countess was that Chateaubriand was not a success at the Congress of Verona. The grandees present were unaware of his fame. The Queen of Sardinia had the stupidity to ask him whether he was any relation of the Chateaubriand who wrote those *tracts*. Metternich had made the Frenchman unpopular with the Tsar. Pozzo di Borgo, the Russian Ambassador to Paris, labelled him 'an old child of fifty'. All the foreign representatives at the Congress were experienced in that kind of gathering. They knew when to advance, when to retreat, when to stand firm, and they knew the different nuances of social behaviour. Chateaubriand annoyed and irritated everyone by his mixture of pride and shyness. When Metternich proposed to let him into the secret of the correct way of making macaroni, the writer/ambassador dubbed the Chancellor 'a mediocrity'.

But it was in this social and political sphere that Darja was in her element, as she outlined to her brother Alexander. 'Here we have been for two months sitting in Congress. Europe is quite interesting, and the circle in which I live puts me in a position altogether conformable to my curiosity and my taste. Every evening the Congress assembles chez moi. Both Count Nesselrode and Prince Metternich urged me to allow this as a resource for them, and I find every advantage in such an arrangement, because it brings me into daily contact with those who are most noteworthy, either by the part they play in Europe, or by their personal attractions.' In far away St. Petersburg the information gatherers would also 'find every advantage in such an arrangement'.

Then, for the first time in her correspondence with her family, she mentions the Prince as a friend. 'I already knew Prince Metternich fairly well by meeting him on several occasions, but here I have associated with him on the most friendly terms.'

Their liaison had been resumed. But there were difficulties in the relationship. And with some of her other relationships. The Duke of Wellington, one of the best and firmest of her English friends, came to see her constantly. These two stars, Metternich and Wellington, were 'looked upon unfavourably in the Tsar's ante-chamber, and have completely deprived me of the society of my fellow countrymen, so that at Verona I see all Europe – except Russia.'

The reason seems clear – the more she was seen mixing with fellow Russians the less she would be trusted by diplomats of other nationalities. There were exceptions, and she was happy that Nesselrode, the Russian Foreign Minister, did call on her, as did Pozzo di Borga and Tatischeff, the Russian Ambassador to Austria.

She went on to remark with some acerbity: 'I am sorry to find that those who should be on the best of terms with me are precisely those who keep me as much at a distance as they would an enemy. Because I have spent ten years in England they look upon me as an Englishwoman, and because I see Prince Metternich daily, they think me an Austrian.'

There were grave difficulties in carrying on an *affaire* with a statesman of another country, however distinguished he might be, and while the Russian Ambassadors were prepared to profit by the Countess's knowledge and the gossip which she could so assiduously collect, the lesser fry were not prepared to become too closely associated with her, lest any political difficulties should ensue with the all-powerful Tsar. Death or exile were troubles to be avoided. A fall from grace could happen only too quickly with even the most benevolent of autocrats. Some might even wonder if the

137

Countess had not already become tainted with ideas of freedom which could prove unhealthy in St. Petersburg.

> I have some suspicions that the Tsar realises the ill-will which is held against me, and that he disapproved of these attitudes. I know that attempts have been made to draw him into this cabal against me, but the plot has failed completely. He treats me with the greatest kindness and I flatter myself that he understands me completely. As for my own attitude, I have made every possible advance to the Russians, and they have responded in the way I have recounted; I remained polite with them whenever I saw them, but not at all worried by their petty gossip, nor in any way put out by it.

If she were not worried by the attitude of the Russians, she was certainly worried about the Tsar and very careful to nurture her relationship with him. She was abroad. Her enemies were at Court and not unaware of her vulnerability.

The Congress was dispersing. The Duke of Wellington had already left, and soon she and her husband would be gone. 'I will regret Verona, I have passed such an agreeable time here.'

When writing to Alexander she added that her husband had been very busy and fully employed at every moment of the day. No doubt that added to the pleasant ambience of Verona: a busy husband would enable a wife to slip out to agreeable encounters with a distinguished gentleman, who, although his company may have led to difficulties with fellow countrymen, was sufficiently the lode-star of her life to make such encounters worthwhile. But now it was already December and she had to think of returning to London. She and Bonsi were to go back there; she wondered for how long. 'It is already ten years since we arrived in England, it is a long time.'

Every now and again she returned to her refrain: surely it was about time that Bonsi was moved elsewhere? She had often told Count Nesselrode that it would be pleasant if he could think of 'finding us another place, when the convenience of the service might allow such a chance. The choice is not great, it is true, because it falls simply between Paris and Vienna.'

The surmise must be that her reports forwarded from London, a victorious and powerful capital where she was well dug in with the King and his Ministers, were likely to be, and remain, more useful than if she were in defeated France, or in Vienna where her sole access to top level information would be through her suspect association with Metternich – and how long would he, or it, endure? So she was a permanency in London. A move for Bonsi seemed a forlorn hope. Vienna had been given to Tatischeff who, she had to admit, had great ability, and 'of course, Pozzo is getting on splendidly in Paris'.

She added that possibly her brother might not be seeing the Tsar before the end of January, but perhaps Alexander could speak about her to Nesselrode? 'He will be able to give you all my news ... I love him with all my heart and I trust him completely as the most loyal and sure friend I have in the world. I love his wife, and I much regret that she has not been here in Verona – she is a woman of intelligence and spirit.'

Compliments could hardly be overdone when writing home. It was not easy for the Lievens to carry out their duties in London, and at the same time to be aware of the undercurrents and complications in far away St. Petersburg. Again and again she returned to the fact that London was so bad for her health. But once back in London she seemed to settle down. Old friends, garnered over so many years, drew her back into the social bustle.

At Verona, as at so many Congresses, nothing of any great import had been settled. At the opening of the Parliamentary Session of 1823 the King's speech stated that 'he had declined to be a party to any of the proceedings at Verona which could be deemed an interference in the internal concerns of Spain on the part of Foreign Powers'. As he had not personally been at Verona at all, this statement was strictly true. In the debate which followed, Mr. Brougham, unfurling the banner of freedom, wished to have no truck with allies whose aim was to stifle the liberties of Spain. Unlike the Countess, he did not see Russia as the champion of civilisation. 'Resistance to this band of congregated despots was a matter of duty.' Mr. Peel mildly protested against the invectives levelled against our glorious allies – had not Russia recently failed to go to war with Turkey? The Tsar, that beloved of the Countess, was not universally beloved, nor were his posturings taken at their face-value in countries other than his own.

In February of 1823 the wife of Darja's brother Constantine died, and he was returning to Russia. 'My first intention', wrote Darja, 'was to accompany him, but my husband would not allow me to do so in my present state of health.'

Since she had returned to London from Verona she had scarcely left her bedroom, and felt it to be very doubtful whether she would improve before the fine weather came. 'I cannot bear the cold.' Darja never made the least of her ailments, and very often they served as useful excuses for refusing to do things which she had no intention of doing in any case. She was approaching forty years of age, she no longer loved her husband and there seemed to be no prospect of being transferred to Vienna and Metternich. Letters were no substitute for the presence of a lover. Or perhaps her meeting with Metternich at Verona had made it clear that opportunities for meeting him would entail endless difficulties.

She was a success in England, but the longer she stayed the more empty her success seemed to her. She was now totally accepted by the aristocratic English circles in which she moved. Her oddnesses and quirks of character were equally accepted. Lady Granville was not the only one in society who found that Darja 'comes too seldom and goes too early'.

If her fellow countrymen distrusted or feared her, *tant pis*, the Tsar at least was well aware of her uses, the greatest of which was her intimacy with George IV and her intricate knowledge of the undercurrents of English politics. Although her relationship with Metternich may have cooled, she still continued to write to him, most vividly about the King. He had aged a good deal, but he still amused her with his attitudes. The latest was that he was disposed to adore her little boy George. She had been surprised to find the absolute ecstacy with which everyone about the Court spoke of her son. She was aware that he was a nice child, but surely hardly so outstanding. But now the King had discovered in him an amazing likeness to himself. She could well see what would happen. 'Up to the present, he says it as a joke; in a few days he will be saying it meaningfully; later he will let it be understood that he has good reasons for saying it.'

George IV had been able to convince himself that he was present, and had given gallant service, in the foreign wars, and he was now disposed to claim Darja's child. On the strength of being little George's godfather, he was advancing a claim to being his father.

Reverting to the late Congress, the Countess told Metternich that she had had a long conversation with the King about it, and he was of exactly the same mind as herself (and Metternich), about the service and disservice which Wellington had done at Verona. The King considered that all his Ministers were fools, that Canning was inexperienced in European affairs having only just taken on his role as Foreign Minister. As he saw it, Wellington was the only one who knew anything about European affairs, and who knew the sovereigns personally and the heads of their cabinets. It was for this reason that he, the King, had insisted that Wellington should go to Verona, although he was well aware of the Duke's faults. 'He sets about a question like a battery of cannon.' This was bound to do harm to Verona where conciliation should have been the order of the day.

Darja, in her role of careful courtier, had then remarked how much the King himself had been missed at the Congress. Canning was undoubtedly distrusted, and it was her opinion, she told the King, that it would be useful if he could take a more active hand in affairs. Since the sad death of Castlereagh, there was no friend to the Allies in the Cabinet – only the King himself.

It was obvious to the King, as it was not clear to the Countess, that George was no Tsar, and that his powers of interfering were strictly limited, but he was not going to make this plain to a Russian lady, however much of an amusing friend she might seem to be.

7 The 'Cottage' at Windsor entailed a deadly routine

The King accepted the compliments graciously. He admitted that it was true *he* was the only friend of the Allies, but added cautiously. 'We have to be careful of our situation.' Metternich he regarded as the first statesman in Europe. The difficulty with Metternich was that he relied too much on his own capabilities. The disadvantage of that was the fact that he could jeopardise the position of others. George admitted that he felt himself to be in a strong position. There were few men of second rate abilities in the Cabinet. Another point was that Canning was so unpopular that, as the King saw it, he needed his sovereign, to remain in office as Foreign Secretary.

Darja's letters, written to Metternich in the form of a journal give a vivid impression of life at the 'Cottage' at Windsor, or by the sea

141

at the Pavilion at Brighton. The hot stifling rooms, the rich food, the lack of air and exercise, the boredom of guests who were not so well disposed to act as courtiers as herself. She wrote about the increasingly precarious health of the King. Now he was lame, now he was better, now he had gout and had been in bed for two days. The boredom was all enveloping. At Brighton she could sometimes escape, but a holiday at the 'Cottage' entailed a deadly routine in which she felt a prisoner. She rose at nine and went straight into the garden. Once dressed, she took luncheon with the King at eleven o'clock, and then they usually talked till one. This was the nub and certainty of her day, the *raison d'être* of her being there. In these two hours of intimate conversation who knows what essential pieces of gossip of political usefulness she might glean? Like a diligent bird, alert and ready for any crumbs which might fall from the King's table, she was always there. Always ready, in spite of the boredom, to file away pieces of knowledge to pass on to her beloved Tsar. But it was knowledge which was hard earned. Like a maid or a butler, the only free time she had was from one till two in the afternoon. From two till four it was time for more talk, either while driving around the countryside, or boating on the river. Courtiers had to earn their keep.

Returned from carriage or boating exercise, there was a mere half-an-hour for changing one's *toilette*, and then it was 'on parade' again for dinner. After dinner the long evening stretched ahead until midnight. A long blank period enlivened only by herself playing the piano, or joining in a card game. She found herself becoming more and more stupid. If she looked into her mind she was quite certain that she would find nothing in it. It was a well which had dried up, even a beating would have brought no sensible idea out of her. There must be better ways of spending an evening. She looked about her – there was the King gazing at Lady Conyngham with an expression in which sleep battled with sentimentality. Lady Conyngham's gaze was fixed on the wonderful emerald on her arm. Her daughter toyed with an equally beautiful ruby which hung round her neck. These were the spoils of the favourite's boredom. Darja's spoils were only the snippets of information which she was able to send overseas.

Lady Conyngham's obvious cupidity amused her. When the King was ill the favourite had remarked, looking round her pretty room, filled with the spoils of her liaison, 'It would be a pity to lose all this.'

In the spring of 1823 Wellington had said to Darja that he gave the King only eight months to live. Lady Conyngham seemed to have the same idea. The Countess wrote: 'I notice many arrangements being made in the Marchioness's household that look as if she were taking precautions.'

It was obvious to the Countess Lieven that the King enjoyed hardly an hour's good health, and sometimes he was ill for three or four weeks at a time. It was only to be expected – the regime was suffocating – with the lack of air and exercise from which his guest, as well as himself, suffered. She herself was far from well. She asked herself whether she was going into a decline, and told Metternich that she felt she could become absolutely useless to him at this rate.

Lady Granville's letters underline the accuracy of Darja's picture of life at Brighton. She describes the King as 'claiming to be ill' but being able to 'scud into dinner' with Lieven on one arm and the Marchioness on the other. Harriet Granville also complains about the heat, the lack of air, and the over-eating. 'The King will force me to eat and drink – syllabubs, meringues, ices etc, so that I am as bilious as possible.' Not surprisingly she describes the Marchioness as grown much fatter and with twice the number of bracelets and rings as before. The great lack was someone to laugh *with* – there was plenty to laugh *at*.

As for Darja, there was little doubt that a courtier had to earn his, or her keep, and she was a triple courtier. Paying court to the King so that she could pay court to Metternich by post, and to the Tsar by proxy, through Nesselrode.

Harriet Granville did not take to the boredom of Brighton so easily, and she made her feelings more than plain. It was quite obvious to Darja that Harriet hated to be either embarrassed or bored, and was longing to get away from the Pavilion in order to make fun of the royal household for the amusement of her friends. 'Harriet gets impatient when she sees me putting up with it all, as if I enjoyed it.'

In some ways Darja did enjoy it for it gave her pen material for scenes of high comedy. But occasionally friendship with the King, assiduously cultivated for many years, palled, she had to admit to herself that she was increasingly and totally bored. Nothing seemed any longer to excite or amuse her. She was even finding it difficult to enquire what was going on. But that attitude, as she realised, had its disadvantages. What would Metternich say in reply to her total lack of news, gossip or political titbits? 'It will no longer be worth your while to await my letters so impatiently, as once you used to honour them by doing.'

And in the midst of her boredom, looking round at the fat bejewelled Marchioness and the sickly King, she remembered Verona. There were better ways of spending the evenings.

In 1823 her father died, and this was to her a bitter blow. She

8 George IV by James Gillray. 'He will force me to eat and drink – syllabubs, meringues, ices etc.'

retreated into intense grief. The loss of loved ones was always to affect her very deeply. It was a curious contradiction in her character that though she lived her life on a worldly cynical level, there was in her soul a deep attachment to some ideal past when she was young, and the world was opening up its riches to her. She was overwhelmed by the loss of her father, and although she realised that, in the natural order of things, a father would die before his child, and even that he was old and failing, yet the fact that she had been separated from him for more than twelve years, in some strange way made it more difficult for her to accept the deep sadness of his death. She had, after all, been his favourite child, and at the end he had asked for her. He had wanted to bless her once again, and she had not been there to receive his blessing. 'That is the real misery. This will be a grief to me for many a day...'

Nor did the appalling English weather improve her spirits. The rains, the mists which were half ice-cold, and half damp affected her chest. The thick yellow vapours of the London fog which seeped into the rooms, and blotted out the whole town – while outside the very hooves of the horses passing the street seemed to be muffled, giving her the feeling of being in an absolute void. It was impossible to describe the melancholy and monotony into which the blotting out of the sun plunged her spirits. She had been laughing at the English people for more than ten years when they blamed their lack of cheerfulness on the weather, but she had now succumbed to the same influences herself. But she realised her faults and her virtues, and they were contradictory. She was both active and lazy. Cheerful and melancholy. Brave and cowardly. As changeable as the English weather.

But, in spite of her lack of spirits, she braced herself to go out into society, taking advantage of brief social encounters to 'discover whatever it is in my interest to find out'.

There was little doubt about her cleverness; she had known that she was cleverer than her husband from early on in her marriage, and since they had come to London it had become increasingly apparent to her that she was the lynchpin of the Russian Embassy. The disseminator, and the collector of news.

But there was one thing which she did lack, and that was deep thought and any philosophical basis to her thoughts. They skimmed across the surface of the waters of politics, like dragon-flies, and were as quickly gone. She seldom read, and this characteristic was often remarked upon by others. The only books which she recommends are poetry by Byron and books by Walter Scott, which would be the equivalent of recommending the best sellers of today. And it was, of course, much *à la mode* to be totally *éblouie* by the passion of Byron. Even Lady Granville, normally so amusingly cynical, found Byron affecting. She had found *Cain* 'really wicked and yet so filled with feeling and passion' that, after reading it, she could 'neither see nor hear'.

The Countess does choose to commend Shakespeare, extolling his grasp of life and the amazing understanding he has of people, somewhat invalidated in her view by the fact that he had given Bohemia a sea-coast. Darja was touchy on points of geography.

In most respects she remained the same girl who had left the *pension de jeunes filles* at the age of fourteen – very conscious of social status, quick to suffer from ennui. Although she operated in the field of international politics, she had retained all the trivialities of society women of any age. That quick ability to seize on the lions who were about to spring to the forefront of power, and the equally well developed ability to perceive the flagging powers of the lion about to be set upon by the pride. There was little room in her world for the wounded lion. The pride of power moves on with the strong lions which were ready to dominate the plain. And she would move with them.

The King might be sick and ailing, but while he was still King, she remained his close friend. That was natural and right.

She wrote to her brother that the King was insisting that she should go down to Windsor on the grounds that a stay at the 'Cottage' would do her good. 'But Windsor life will assuredly do me harm; late dinners and long evenings do not suit me.'

Then there were the exigencies of the task.

'How can I, in my situation here do otherwise than bend to its requirements? The more so, too, as by not complying I should be preventing my husband from being brought in closer contact with the King. You don't believe me when I say that I have had enough of this life of an ambassadress in England ... but what is the good of getting people to like you, when etiquette forbids your forming intimacies?'

She was being disingenuous. Her intimacies and her knowledge of the intimacies of others formed the basis of her power, and of her use to her husband.

'Do not imagine, I entreat you,' she wrote to Alexander, 'that this complaint arises from pride, and please don't speak to others about it.' She remained aware of the gossip about the Court and was not disposed to jeopardise her position. 'Those who do not understand my feelings will think me vain, and God knows that I am not that – only sick and sad hearted. My husband is very busy – fresh points are continually arising – I can only hope that they won't get tangled.'

146

Without stating the facts directly, she was saying that she hoped that Bonsi was handling the information which she gleaned for him in the correct and most suitable way. 'There is need, not only of the greatest care, but of much will on the part of all concerned to avoid the rocks which beset the course of affairs.'

The forces of reaction working for the restoration of authority which had prevailed right up to the Congress of Verona were gradually disintegrating all over Europe. At the time of the great Congresses, men of similar mind had met on the same level of thought, but now Wellington and Metternich represented the past.

As a slight amelioration of her lot, and possibly as a reward for her services, Nesselrode gave permission for the Lievens to move from their house in Harley Street to a much grander house in Dover Street.

She now began to interfere even more actively in her husband's job. She read his despatches, and with her impatient mind, saw that Bonsi's effusions could be more succinctly précised so as not to cause boredom to the recipient – the powerful Count Nesselrode. She attached her shortened versions to the official despatch. Nesselrode, who no doubt had been as bored by Count Lieven's long-windedness as his wife, was pleased, and wrote to ask her to continue her efforts in this direction. From that time she began to take upon herself the task of giving more and more political angles to her letters. The gossipy basis of her life began to decline. She had smelled the heady scent of real power, perhaps thinking to herself how much better she could do her husband's job than he did himself.

She also began to use her influence with the King in a more definite way. Down at Windsor she became more and more involved with the 'Cottage Coterie'. George IV had surrounded himself with foreigners who flattered and amused him. Apart from Countess Lieven, there was Count Münster, his Hanoverian Minister. (It may be recalled that at this time the King was still authoritarian ruler of Hanover.) In his heart of hearts he would have liked to rule England as he ruled Hanover, without the necessity of parties, factions, or changes of government. Life was so much simpler if a King could govern his own country without such trivial complications.

Other foreigners who were entertained at the 'Cottage' were Prince Paul Esterhazy, the Austrian Ambassador, and Neumann (the go-between and post office of Metternich and Darja), and Prince Polignac. The only English people present were the diamond-hung favourite, Lady Conyngham, and Sir William Knighton, contemptuously referred to by the Countess as the 'man

147

midwife', a slighting reference to his former profession of *accoucheur*.

No doubt the fact that only French was spoken aided the Windsor cabal. At the 'Cottage', in the rich atmosphere of syllabubs, heat, and meringues all the foreigners were plotting. A plan was afoot 'pour faire sauter M. Canning'. They all disliked M. Canning, for his ideas were far too liberal, he was trying to foster liberalism all over Europe, and even in South America. The 'Cottage Coterie' having put their heads together, had decided that Canning was antipathetic to their ideas. The King was on their side. He had accepted Canning as his Foreign Minister with the greatest distaste. In fact his letter to Canning had been almost insulting, and Canning himself had remarked that it was the equivalent of giving him a ticket to Almack's and writing on the back, 'Admit the rogue.'

Although the King was of the same mind as the foreigners of the 'Cottage Coterie', he knew more about English politics, and their reality, than they did. To dismiss Canning was not going to be as easy as they might imagine. He agreed with them about Canning: 'He doesn't know the first thing about his job; he has no tact, no judgement and idea of decorum.'

In the spring of 1823 the plot was set *en train*. Some of Canning's disgruntled colleagues were inclined to join in. Politicians can always see pickings for themselves in the downfall of a colleague.

Countess Lieven with her ultra-aristocratic attitude towards politics, considered Canning at that time as a radical, which was tantamount to being a tool of revolution. She wrote immediately to inform Metternich of the progress of the plot: 'You can rely on it, decidedly they are working to get rid of Canning. And indeed, when I think of the numbers of honest folk who are scheming against him, and *who* they are – the King, the heir to the throne, all the ministers, and their supporters, who in fact, comprise the majority of the two Houses, when I think that Canning's party consists of half a dozen fools, that his supposed popularity with the Opposition is a farce, and that he is so vain that he runs into traps like a blind man, I cannot help conjecturing, that the efforts of the right side will be crowned with success.'

But they were not.

Canning found out what was going on, and confronted his adversaries head on. He published a relevant State paper, and followed it up with two speeches in the House of Commons which defended his policy. France had no call to intervene in Spain to restore Ferdinand VI. England would not intervene, but he, Canning, hoped that the party which represented the true constitution of Spain would win.

The reactionaries were appalled. Metternich, Countess Lieven, and all the ultras including, of course, the Tsar, who had by this time shed a good many of his liberal principles, were loud in their condemnation of the fiendish Canning. In the current opinion of Darja, Canning hardly fell into the category of gentleman. But gentleman or not, Canning had a large majority in the House of Commons. His policies were triumphant and in the heat and the syllabubs the 'Cottage Coterie' diminished in power and prestige. The plot had failed because the King's power – unlike the Tsar's – was limited, and he knew it.

CHAPTER ELEVEN

When in Rome . . .

In the autumn of 1823, worn out with political intrigues, boredom and retreating into ill-health as was her custom, Darja decided on a recuperative trip to Italy. There is little doubt that she did this in the hopes of reviving her liaison with Metternich who had apparently held out hopes that he would meet her there.

At first her letters to him were lively and cheerful. She was in Paris, she was busy – she had met Pozzo who 'treats me as you used to treat me when we first knew one another'.

Although Darja edited her letter-journals so that only her political acumen, and that of her lover would be apparent, the impression remains that there were little sentences with which she was loth to part, and the general tenor of a woman writing to a man whom she loves also remains. She looked back to the past when Metternich was amusing her, and she was listening. Pozzo finds her a good listener, and a man who feels himself to be understood becomes warmly attached to the good listener. The underlying thought is that perhaps those times could come again. Perhaps in Italy. . . .

But the journey was likely to be long, and she had received so much conflicting advice about it. One recommended this road, and one that, and she almost felt that one set of travellers could be talking of China and the other of Canada. She had received some extremely gloomy letters from Bonsi in London – and written him a sad one in return. There was little doubt, she felt, that she needed a journey to the warm South, as her health was undermined. She was beset by troubles and distress. The distress had affected her legs, causing Harriet Granville to remark sarcastically, 'I have never heard of sentimental knees before.'

This remark seems to pinpoint the fact that her distress and her ill-health were largely a reaction to the onset of middle age, and a reaching-out to her erstwhile lover.

150

Suddenly, while she was in Paris, the whole outlook for the 'ultras' – the right-wing reactionaries – changed. The French had invaded Spain, and re-established Ferdinand VII. The Russians in Paris took this as a personal triumph for their Tsar. Darja was delighted, and so was Pozzo; in fact he was enraptured. The only thing which the Countess regretted was that she was not in England to enjoy Canning's discomfiture. As for Pozzo, he had spent his whole time in her rooms, but 'I assure you,' she wrote to Metternich, 'he is not in love with me.' It was, perhaps, not necessary to reassure Metternich on this score, but she was not yet aware of the fact that their separation was permanent.

The whole journey had upset her. Even the start of it had been full of gloom. The King was angry with her for leaving, the Duke of Wellington had come down from Scotland especially to say an equally gloomy good-bye to her. The Duke of York even deserted his pursuit of the fox, that essential centre of autumn affairs in England, to see her once again. Her husband insisted on going as far as Dover with her. Altogether it was as if she were about to cross the Styx instead of the English channel.

And now here she was – stuck in Geneva. The weather was quite as disgusting as it had been in England. It had never stopped raining for two days and the fog was so thick that it was impossible to tell which were the mountains and which was the lake. On the way she had been nearly poisoned at Châlons, so much so that she had been convinced of imminent death.

But her gloom was short lived for on the following day the sun came out, and she was enraptured by the smiling countryside, the mountains, Mont Blanc glittering in the sunshine, and the golden leaved trees reflected in the waters of the lake. It was astonishing; the charming view had held her attention for quite half-an-hour. She had good reason for her fears about her journey, for the carriage nearly overturned and she reported to Metternich that she had never been nearer to death, and could not understand why she had not found herself at the foot of a precipice. She vowed she would never cross the Simplon again in October, and perhaps not even in summer. Then she remembered her cher Clément's lyrical letters when he himself had made the descent into Italy, and there was no doubt that he had not exaggerated in his descriptions. What a stupendous sight it was to descend to Domodossola, and what a heart-lifting view!

She had written of the dangers of her journey to Lady Granville, but ended on a happy note. Arrived in Milan, half-dead with fright, her spirits had soared. The weather was like July, and there she had found Lady Granville's brother, the Duke of Devonshire, uncommonly well, in boisterous spirits – all kindness and civility. He carried on as if he were in London; dinner parties every day, and two private boxes at La Scala.

But to Metternich she wrote in less happy mood. 'So I find you are not coming to Italy after all. Then why did you ask *me* to come?'

Now she was left high and dry. She had left her family, her comfortable home, all her friends, and her social life, and even her intellectual pursuits – for what?

Admittedly she was in ecstasies over the landscape and the countryside – Lake Maggiore and Isola Bella – how beautiful! She had taken a long walk all the way from Bavena to Arona. The sun was warm, the road winding along the lake, and above the blue mountains clothed with vineyards. How beautiful everything was – if only there were some newspapers, even the *Moniteur* did not penetrate to this countryside. Nor did her unaccompanied state please or amuse her. She even toyed with the idea of going back to Geneva. Meanwhile she was becoming irritated, not only with Metternich's disgraceful failure to arrive in the smiling countryside of vines and mountains, but also with his politics. Capo felt that sooner or later the Tsar would feel the humiliation of being ruled by an Austrian Minister. 'Here if you will not mind my saying so, I secretly applauded Capo d'Istria.' The Countess's political feelings were as volatile as her reactions to the weather, and always geared to some personal viewpoint.

She retained very unpleasant recollections of Milan. The more so, possibly, because it was there she had received the definite news that Metternich was not coming to meet her. Everything irritated her. A dozen times she was upset at having to arrange everything for herself. She preferred that someone else should take the responsibility for her travelling arrangements. Here she was, wandering about Italy all alone, and she found her position, quite frankly, unnatural.

Bonsi did not seem to be happier than his wandering wife, for each of his letters to her was more pathetic than the last. She felt that it would only take a small hint on her part for him to implore her to come back. As for herself the slightest encouragement would impel her to go back to her normal way of life. What was she staying in Italy *for*? Perhaps she was afraid to retreat, for she had used her frail health as an excuse to leave her husband. To go back to England in the middle of winter made her former excuses implausible. But in spite of her misgivings she decided to journey on to Florence. She compared herself to Madame de Sévigné who had said that what she saw tired her, and what she had not seen

152

worried her.

By November she was in Florence awaiting news from Metternich – she had heard that he was back in Vienna. What could she tell him about Florence? He must know without her needing to tell him that she disliked it. Her health had, in spite of everything, improved and she had totally forgotten that her legs had pained her. In fact she was even growing fat, and when she told her new acquaintances that she had come to Italy for her health, they had all laughed heartily.

It is difficult to avoid the feeling that the Countess reported her small social successes in an attempt to show her lover that she was not as heartbroken at the disappointment of his not coming as he might have felt her to be. Although she had little news to impart to him, could he perhaps go back to his old habit of writing every day, and sending his letters once a week as he had done five years ago? Their correspondence had been so interesting to her, and he had recounted so many things which were far outside her own knowledge. Now she felt impoverished, and hurt. 'Encourage me, it is the only way to set me writing.' She felt herself to be stagnating.

While the world saw her as an arch-intriguer she saw herself as merely a sounding board for other people's opinions. But her view of herself was not only as a talker but as a listener, an amanuensis sitting at the feet of great men absorbing their wisdom. Yet when she did comment on the great men of the period, Metternich excepted, it was often with derision, or with amusement. Perhaps, in her own mind, she remained the *jeune fille riante* she had once been. To the great world her face was quite different. Even her dead friend Castlereagh had said it was 'a charming face, a clever face'. When she herself had said it was an honest face, Castlereagh had dropped his eyes, and had not replied.

Metternich never took her at her own valuation. He saw her as a child, crying one day, and laughing the next, attempting not to be aggravated by life, and yet always, *au fond*, good-humoured. Her letters to him from Italy certainly show her to be laughing and crying, but perhaps not always so good humoured as she had seemed when he had (as she recalled) sat at her feet reading. 'As far as I can remember', he wrote, 'I *read* very little, and I remember equally well how I tidied you into *decency*.' Every word she had said remained in his memory, he wrote politely.

And now she was in Rome, the Rome which he had described so vividly and charmingly to her. She remembered his description of his apartments – twenty-five magnificent salons filled with beautiful objects. She remembered how he had written of wishing that she were at his side to look – even for a single instant – from the window of his great salon. 'A decorative painter who decided to put on his canvas all which is laid out before me would be accused of exaggeration and even of madness. I have in front of me the famous horses which give to the Quirinal the name of Monte Cavallo.' In the background he could see St. Peter's, and the Vatican, and he looked down on the old City – the Colosseum, the columns of Trajan and Antonine, the Forum, and a hundred palaces each more beautiful than the last. The City was quite different from what he had imagined, it was like a person whose character one had guessed at, and who turns out to be quite different from one's imaginings. He had felt that Rome would be old and sombre, but although it was antique, it was superb, dazzling – and new. And there was the Vatican, wrote Metternich, and so many beautiful things, that the soul was uplifted and yet oppressed by so much beauty. And the Gallerias of the Vatican – salons painted by Raphael, frescoes as clear as the day they were painted, each figure as divine as the mind which had conceived it. 'Dearest friend, I am here at the zenith of my feelings, and I believe Rome to be the Zenith of the world.' She remembered his letters, but could not attempt to vie with his descriptions, but she had at least hoped that he would have been there to savour the beauties of the city and the passing moments with her. But although her lover was not there she was determined to show the correct artistic feelings. How beautiful Rome was – she had arrived two days ago in the most brilliant sunshine – sunshine in December! She was mad with joy, the sight of St. Peter's had reduced her to tears. It was impossible to arrive in Rome without some trembling of the soul. It was an overwhelming experience and she had wanted to see everything straight away – St. Peter's, the Pantheon, the Capitol, the Forum, the Colosseum. . . .

But little by little her overwhelming feelings died down, and she was reverting to her normal gossipy social life. She had had two visits – Prince Philippe of Homburg and Count Walmoden. They had come straight from Vienna bringing her news that had really upset her. Prince Metternich was not in the best of health. What was he doing putting himself in the hands of a doctor who knew nothing, a man who had forbidden him to go out? If Metternich stayed cooped up in his apartments from where is he to get his strength? What he needed was air, exercise, peace of mind – and above all – some distraction. He should not be worried, or tired by events – or even by people. Let Canning and his machinations take care of themselves. Metternich will never be able to mould Canning's views to his own way of thinking. He must first consider getting well, later there will be time to worry about politics . . .

154

'Come to Italy!'

But time passed and he did not come, so at least she would try to make her life sound amusing. The Duc de Laval, the French Ambassador, was full of attentions to her, Madame Apponyi polite, the widow of the late Duke of Devonshire (Elizabeth Foster) assiduous in her *politesses*, Lord Kinnaird (very witty) had kept her amused. She had dined with him, a fact which would make her husband very worried, but it was no good being prudish in politics, at least not when in Rome. M. de Laval was also of the company and she hastened to reassure Metternich that de Laval was not a Jacobin. Lord Dudley and Lord Kinnaird were rivals in wit and kept the dinner party as lively as could be. Darja admitted that she had a great penchant for witty people – she needed them – but although that could be a failing, it was something which she could not help.

There were hazards in Rome. There was the hazard of cold. When she was asked out to dinner, she always enquired whether there were any mosaics, and if her hosts waxed lyrical about their antique mosaic floors, of such great charm and beauty, she made certain she would be cold, and stayed at home. Winter was winter in Italy as elsewhere, and, as far as she was concerned, many of these fine palazzos were like ice palaces.

She had had some causes for amusement. When walking along the banks of the Tiber, her amusing friend M. de Laval appeared on horseback, but he was not horsed for long. Suddenly he was flung off, and she feared he was going to roll straight down into the swollen Tiber. This did not surprise her, as de Laval, apart from not being able to see very well, was a very bad rider. She ran up to him in great alarm, but found him unharmed, and far from being his usual witty urbane self – he was very angry and demanded: 'What in the – ' she was doing there, adding, what if he *had* fallen off, what was that to do with *her*? She had great difficulty in not laughing, but some people find a point of honour in the fidelity of wives, and some in sticking on to a horse.

On the other hand she had stopped laughing at the Duchess of Devonshire sighing after her Cardinal – she *could* be very unhappy. But the ostentation of the Duchess's pangs of love was something which she herself could not accept. 'At no age should a woman dispense with reserve about her relations with a man.' Perhaps there lingered a thought in the back of Darja's mind that she trembled on the verge of this danger.

Rome still enchanted her. She had visited the tomb of Cecilia Metella, and, as she stood there, she could see her cher Clément admiring the aqueducts stretching away across the Campagna. She felt that 'we two' could live so happily in Rome. She knew that he was quite enchanted by it, and she was ready to be totally enchanted. 'Together we should make a happy and harmonious household.'

Running through all her letters, even with their excisions, is the regret that Rome, cher Clément, and chère Dorothée could not make a harmonious whole. Rome was amusing, there was plenty to see, plenty of people to amuse her, plenty of gossip to be had. But she had seen it as a background to love, and it had proved to be merely a holiday from London.

There were other irritations – the courier had arrived – and there was no letter from him. She was angry – when she found no letters from him it was always a calamity, but in Rome, so far from the centre of things, it was a double calamity. As a punishment for his lack of thought for her, she was going out to dine with Lord Dudley – and if he had harsh words to say about Metternich, well and good, she would agree with the noble peer, and become the enemy of Austria. In fact, she was about to change from being a close ally to being an enemy. It was not good policy on the part of cher Clément to be so remiss as not to write to her.

She covered her hurt with chat of treaties and allies, but the feelings of the woman shine through. She was beginning to realise that her love was an illusion. Had she been used as she had used others? But she was not going to show herself to be unduly upset – at least not on the surface. He would not believe how beautiful she had become while in Italy. The journey back to London would blunt the edge of this miracle which had happened to her looks. Quel dommage!

The last part of her stay in Rome was beset with a drama concerning her son Paul. It was a ridiculous sequence of events brought about by the duc de Laval. Paul had decided that he had been insulted at a masked ball in the house of Demidoff but when he found out that the 'mask' was a mere painter of pictures, he had naturally become angry at the idea of dealing with someone of so low a station in life, and had stated categorically that he could hardly demand satisfaction of a mere artist. The duc de Laval had then rather stupidly interfered, and used his authority to try to get the painter to apologise to Paul. That was as far as it should have gone. But then gossip began, people alleged that Paul – in order to avoid the duel – had asked de Laval to intervene. The rumours came back to Paul, who very naturally decided that he must fight to protect his honour, and would confront the very first man who spoke to him about the affair. The unlucky first man was the marquis de Bonneval. Having consulted various friends as to the right course to follow, he chose his seconds and challenged the unfortunate marquis. Dignity and honour were preserved.

The chosen weapons were pistols. The first shot went wide, and the Frenchman, (very wisely as it was not really his affair) wanted the duel stopped. But Paul insisted on it continuing and then the marquis apologised. Paul's seconds decided that honour had been satisfied. The result was that the whole of society in Rome was full of her son's praises. Even the old Marquess of Hastings had come up to her, his eyes brimming with tears, and had offered his congratulations on her son's conduct. Paul was a true gentleman. She was so happy that he had behaved so correctly, but thankful that she had known nothing about the duel – until it was over. Darja's emotions where her children were concerned were always extreme. When they were ill she was sunk in despair, when she had to part from them, gloom overtook her. But this time, through her son's delicacy and thoughtfulness, all was well.

Paul, who seemed to be suffering from bad luck, tore his leg above the ankle, and this delayed the Countess's departure from Rome. As the surgeon considered the wound to be very critical, she would be delayed for nearly a fortnight. Meanwhile she had received Metternich's no. 154, which as far as she could see contained nothing but bad news. The trouble with writing letters with such long gaps between them was that by the time the answer came it was easy to have forgotten what one had written. She was grateful for all the kind things he said about her letters. Perhaps she ought to copy her letters, because from the moment she put her seal on the packet she totally forgot what she had written, or what had made him laugh or cry.

In spite of everything, up to the last weeks of her stay, she still felt it possible that Metternich might change his mind and come to Italy. On the eve of her departure she wrote that perhaps his letters would arrive before she left, but she had the feeling that nothing which they contained would make her extend her stay ... she tried not to express her regrets but a faint glimmer of a hope that he might come still remained. She was beginning to accept that perhaps theirs was merely a love affair which was gradually disappearing like the mist over the fields on a summer morning. Meanwhile she was extremely bad tempered at being delayed in Rome. Metternich was obviously not coming, and there was nothing to keep her, except the slow healing of her son's leg which did worry her.

But she solved this problem in her typically arrogant way – she merely hired the surgeon to go on the journey with her, travelling by way of the Adriatic and expressing all the right sentiments about the coastline from Fano to Rimini. Her journey was made all the more pleasant because it was Holy Week, and only a heretic like herself would travel at such a time. The roads were clear, she was able to bowl along with no other travellers to compete for the post horses. The towns were full of people in their holiday clothes, and the countryside was awakened after the winter. The freshness, the tender sky, the empty road, and the budding trees – everything seemed new. Change, travel, and now the prospect of London with its gossip and politics at the end of the journey, lifted her spirits.

Bonsi met her at Dover, and they took two days to travel to London, where the whirl of social life began again. Wellington, Canning, the Government, the Opposition – Darja was once more on what she had now come to regard as her native heath, and she needed time to sort out her ideas, and allow everything she had heard to settle down.

But no sooner had she begun her old life in London again, than there was talk of her visiting Russia. King George had offered her his yacht, which would make the journey so much shorter and more pleasant. She was always more comfortable travelling by sea than by land. When she travelled over land she could do nothing but eat and sleep, and only alighted from her carriage to go to bed at the inn. Her fatigue was too great even to write letters. But a journey in the king's yacht seemed a more agreeable idea. On the other hand if she went by land she could pass by Metternich's estate at Johannisberg, and she wondered whether he would be there on 8 June? When writing to Metternich, Darja liked to convey the impression that the meeting was to be concerned with deep political matters which she would more easily be able to relate personally.

In the event, she got only as far as Dover. To her cher Clément she wrote that the reason for her sudden change of plan was simple – she feared she was once again pregnant. The tender meeting at Dover with Bonsi, and the slow peaceful journey back to London, had produced the inevitable result of marital reunion. Originally this inconvenient fact did not deter her from proceeding with plans for her visit to Russia. Her doctors could see no reason why she should not go, and she had a shrewd idea that it was time for her to get in touch with goings-on at the Russian Court. It was one thing to know exactly what was happening in London, and to write all the political news to her beloved Emperor, but quite another to renew her respects in person. But Darja was now in her fortieth year, and this was her sixth child. By the time she had reached Dover, on the first stage of her journey to Russia, she was already feeling weak and suffering from sickness. The idea of sea-sickness had always been something which she shrank from, and her pregnancy had increased her fears. She was compelled to take to her bed. Bonsi, for once, put his foot down. Whatever the opinion of the doctors, his wife was not to travel. Darja tried to remonstrate with him, but he was adamant, and now the whole project had fallen to the ground.

The next months of her journals to Metternich were filled with all the political gossip of the day. The King sent affectionate messages and was eager to talk about Pozzo di Borgo, the Russian Ambassador in Paris. What a low opinion George had of him! Naturally Darja wanted to hear what the King had to say about Canning, who now seemed to be in the ascendant. But there seemed to be no way of pulling King George round to the subject, except in a roundabout way. Obviously the King was becoming more cagey. Perhaps he had learned his lesson from the débâcle over the 'Cottage Coterie'.

There was so much going on that it was difficult to know where to begin. Lord Grey had told her she would be very surprised at all the changes which had taken place in her six months' absence. The health of Lord Liverpool, the Prime Minister, was not good – it could be possible that he would retire – would Canning succeed him? In that event a good many ministers would be compelled to go.

She had discussed the whole imbroglio with the Duke of Wellington – he had been sounded out as to the possibility of becoming Prime Minister. On the other hand if the King appointed Canning – no one would serve under him. 'He would be thrown out twenty times before one of us budged.'

The Countess had teasingly suggested that perhaps the Duke's lack of debating power might be a disadvantage. But he took that fence at a gallop: 'To begin with – I can learn. If I want it, it will come back to me. And even if I can't, the Duke of Portland had no more idea of speaking than I have; and yet he was at the head of the administration.'

Mere oratory was fudge as far as the Duke was concerned. The main idea was to get on with the job in hand.

And so she was gradually drawn back into the life she knew. Dining here, gossiping there, staying with the King at Windsor. The King himself was highly delighted with the news of her pregnancy, and glad to have her as a guest on call to amuse him. He was even more attentive to her now that she was getting fat, for he liked fat women. The favourite, Lady Conyngham, had on more than one occasion taken to sulking in the garden as a result of the King's attentions to Darja. But the months seemed to her to go by very slowly, and there would be many more before she and

Metternich could meet. The thought saddened her, but 'there is something soothing in the impossible' and when she came to reflect about it: 'hope kills more than it keeps alive'.

Her hopes were dwindling. And she was bored. In August, down at Brighton there was nothing to do but yawn and listen to the Duke of York's long stories. Schönburg had followed her down to Brighton. He was a bore too, but she had a feeling of friendliness towards him for he often saw Metternich, and when he was talking of 'mon Prince' she listened with the greatest attention. Poor Schönburg thought his own charms were making an impression! For most of the time she was quiet and indolent – in the mornings she sat and watched the sea, in the afternoons a carriage drive and after dinner a party of cards.

Darja's political allegiances were as capricious as her social engagements were various. She was shrewd, but perhaps not perceptive enough, and, in concentrating on the day-to-day events in politics and society, perhaps she ignored many deep currents of feeling on the part of her English hosts. Her sharp tongue and her fluctuating friendships must have made her more enemies than she realised; but now she was in the high noon of her influence and the friendship of the King protected her. Her capacity to make fun of others was noted, and perhaps not forgotten, as she fondly thought, when making the rounds of the English country houses, showing her countrymen the beauty and luxury of living, and yet criticising her hosts at the same time. In October in the shooting season she had taken the Ozarovskys to visit Lord Salisbury's house at Hatfield. A mixed party of 'diplomats, Ministers, pretty women, jealous husbands, perfumed dandies, long dark corridors, chapels, towers, bats-in-the-bed-curtains – everything you need for a romance – or at any rate an *affaire*.' An *affaire* was not a possibility for her.

There were some advantages in ailing. When she was staying with the King at Windsor, she had fallen ill and the King was in his element fussing over her, and insisting that she should be bled in his presence. She had to admit that she had enjoyed being spoiled and fussed over, and because when the King had responded to her illness in this fashion the whole of his Court had followed his example.

In spite of her pregnancy, the rivers of political talk went on. Would it not be a good idea if Metternich patched up his difficulties with Wellington? The King had told her that he hated Canning. But Canning had gone to see the Duke's brother, the Marquess Wellesley. The Duke did not agree with his brother. Liverpool, Canning, Lady Conyngham, the Duke of York, the kaleidoscope of long forgotten cabals whirled round.

Down at the 'Cottage' in September the heat had been intense and most of the hot nights had been spent boating on the lake, dining in the open air, and then departing by boat again. There were disadvantages in the royal favour. Inspired by the still lake, the moonlight on the water and the dark trees, the King began a long dissertation on Eternity, God and Religion. Darja confided to her cher Clément that a speech by the King about Religion, or even God, was quite enough to make anyone lose *all* respect for any form of worship. She had felt like a schoolgirl again, with an intense desire to giggle which was suppressed only by stuffing a handkerchief into her mouth. Then he began to sing, and Darja was made to sing with him. At last the comedy was over, and they reached the shore. But the hot weather continued and the boating parties went on. Her popularity with the King and his brother was all very well on dry land, but in a small boat she was wedged between two sets of fat royal thighs – the sweating royal pair, the heat and the motion of the boat brought on an attack of acute nausea. Fortunately she was able to tell her husband in Russian what ailed her, and Bonsi rescued her. There was no doubt that two pairs of royal thighs in twenty-five degrees (Centigrade) of heat was too much for anyone, especially someone in as delicate a state as herself.

In February of 1825 Darja was delivered of her inconvenient child. She wrote to Metternich: 'I have a fifth son – it is very stupid.'

She made a slow recovery and after seventeen days was still moving only from her bed to a couch and not allowed visitors. But there were consolations. Delivered of her burden, she could again think of her visit to Russia, and Metternich's coming visit to Paris. They had become used to being 400 leagues apart; how were they to get used to being at a mere two days distance from one another?

Metternich's journey to Paris was neither to do with politics nor with renewing the fires of old loves. His wife was ill. She had lived in Paris for many years, for after the death of his two daughters, Metternich had sent his wife and children away from the 'fatal climate of Vienna' as he called it. He did not hurry away on hearing of his wife's illness, for he was used, as he put it, to making sacrifices to his duty and to 'reason'. He admitted that the state of his wife moved him more than anything in the world, and he would hurry to her side – as soon as he could see his way clear. Politics dominated even the approach of the wings of death. 'If I am obliged to go to Paris, my journey might well be misconstrued by Canning. He would see the sole and sad cause of my going there as a pretext for other business. His error would leave me absolutely cold, and yet – it could have evil consequences.'

But in the end he was forced to go, the journey had become inevitable, politics or no politics, and he left Vienna for the bedside of his dying wife. While watching beside his wife, he noted that the Paris papers were much occupied in commenting on his arrival, and drawing their own conclusions, and in London 'they attach even more importance to my sudden appearance in the rival capital'.

His wife gently slipped away without uttering a single complaint. Metternich wrote that 'this best of mothers, this beautiful soul went to Heaven, and returned to the bosom of God with a sweet and peaceful confidence in his paternal grace'. And he added that his marriage to her had never been troubled by a single cloud. 'Her heart and her conscience were as pure at the moment when she had drawn her last sigh as during every hour of her whole life which had always been totally devoted to her duties as wife and mother.' They had been married for thirty years. It was thirty years since he wed her to re-gild his family escutcheon, thirty years since the village fête in her Austrian village home. Having dried his tears, and rendered his homage to the memory of a good woman, he went on to comment that his presence in Paris at the present time would not fail to have good results.

Darja was upset that he should be so near – and yet so far. Would it not be possible for him to cross to England? If only she could be with him, but she realised that he must have no distractions from his duties as a husband. That above all was sacred, and yet – she could have soothed his sadness and helped him overcome his sorrow.

To a woman who lived life to the full as she did, and relished every detail of the passing pageant, death, the death of anyone at all close to her, affected her in a particularly poignant way, as if it were some insult to her whole tenor of existence. She was especially stricken because she had heard a rumour that Madame de Metternich had improved. What about the poor children? Victor especially must be in a terrible state. One consolation was that he was at an age when a mother's tenderness was a pleasure rather than a necessity. 'But those poor little girls! What a loss! If I had any right to ask you for them, how tenderly I should care for them! The children of Madame de Metternich would always be dear to me.'

Apart from indulging in grief, there were the usual political moves afoot. The King had asked Metternich to come to Windsor on a visit. This plan seemed perfect to Darja. She had seen Wellington, and he had suggested that Metternich should embark at Dieppe, and go from Dieppe to Brighton. At Brighton he would find herself, and Wellington; and from Brighton it would be simple to travel to Windsor, and then to leave England – without seeing Canning at all. Wellington saw this as an admirable plan which would please friends and infuriate the enemy – Canning. It is difficult not to feel that some of the details of this secret journey were more an attempt on the part of Darja to see her former lover than a political ploy on the part of Wellington. Wellington, according to Darja, was delighted with the whole idea and was certain that Metternich 'would jump at it'. Then the cool light of reason told her that Metternich was too wise to jump at anything.

In April of 1825 she was down at Brighton again, looking out at the sea which separated her from France. In a mere ten hours she could get to Paris, but she had to remain this side of the sea. 'What a poor creature a woman is!' Nothing consoled her, his letters were even less frequent than when he was in the Ballhausplatz in Vienna. But when he left Paris at the end of the month, he travelled to the Midi and to Italy. Italy! She remembered Verona and its amphitheatre. There was nothing like a journey; to travel was to leave politics behind. One could stop thinking and leave one's heart open to all the sensations of beauty and sentiment. Perhaps he could find a place in his thoughts for her?

It is odd to remark these two very political creatures, so full of the correct sentiments about love and death, and noting their own feelings about these primary emotions. Yet it is hard to make out how much was posturing and how much sincerity. On his part she had merely been one woman like another, more amusing perhaps, and yet merely a traveller whom a man might meet in a wayside inn, choose as a companion for the night – and then travel on cherishing the thought of an amusing incident which had whiled away the idle hours. Yet in her case she had been an incident with useful political consequences and no ties. As a spymaster might engage an agent to collect information for him so Metternich used Darja. The death of his wife perhaps posed other reasons for carefulness in his relations with her. No longer tied, he was less free.

She continued to write her letters full of gossip and political undercurrents for his delectation, but his letters became fewer and fewer, and further and further apart.

In the spring of 1826 Darja heard some gossip which did not please her. Lady Georgina Wellesley had been on a visit to Vienna and was full of praise for and interest in the doings of Prince Metternich. All the doings of the Prince were recounted to the Countess. Some things she was pleased to hear, and others were hardly to her taste. Amongst the latter she included the news of his daily visits to a certain Mademoiselle Leykam. Was she to be his future wife – or merely his mistress? She also heard of the lowly nature of the lady's background, and, with a misguided touch of asperity, mentioned that her father and mother could hardly be the reason for the assiduity of his attentions; indeed gossip said the girl was not only very young but very pretty. 'So much for the constancy of men!' She could not imagine his taking notice of a little girl, what if it were the other way round and she had found herself a young boy? It would look ridiculous for her to bother with a boy. She would rather kill herself.

But all these recriminations, and sarcastic references to the background of the girl were in vain. On 5 November 1827, in strict secrecy, on the day the news of the battle of Navarino reached Vienna, the marriage between Marie-Antoinette von Leykam and the Prince Metternich took place at a little village in the suburb of Hetzendorf. The doors of the church were closed to the curious. There were present Metternich's mother, his sister, wife of the Duke of Württemberg, and the witnesses, his brother, Joseph, and his brother-in-law, von Kaunitz.

He had married for love, the love he had never really felt for Darja. 'My eyes are not blinded,' he wrote during his engagement, 'my heart has not succumbed to the sad influence of passion, it is warm and peaceful, serene and disciplined.'

But whatever he might think, and however he might overlay his feelings with reason, an ageing man had fallen under the spell of a young girl thirty-three years his junior. She was described as an enchanting creature, with the gaiety of a Viennese and a touch of Italian blood. The sight of her made the pens of her admirers run into descriptions rivalling the brush of a Fragonard or a Lawrence. A charming figure, her oval face set off by a tiny smiling mouth, tumbling blonde curls, an expression which was at one and the same time, soft and melancholy, intelligent and lively, with artistic tastes, and when she moved it was with a poetic grace.

It was a formidable picture to confront a political lady of forty who had borne six children. Metternich wrote to the Countess Zichy that, in spite of the evil gossip which surrounded his motives, he was happy in the path he was to follow. Nothing anyone could say would alter the affections of his heart, nor the first solace of his private life – the necessity for a real home.

Darja, back in London, preferred to listen to the slanders. The girl's background was hardly aristocratic – she was descended from a coachman from Wetzlar. Her father was married in Naples, there was some talk of an opera singer, and on *that* subject several tales which were hardly agreeable were circulating around Vienna. Darja was very happy to repeat the *bon mot* of Madame de Coigny: 'The

Knight of the Holy Alliance has now ended by making a *mésalliance*.'

Metternich ignored all the gossip: he had found happiness, and sunshine and gaiety had come into the gloomy Chancellery. The young Princess brought all manner of people together – artists, musicians, and diplomats. And the Prince himself had found something he had sought for so long 'a being who would belong to him forever, cherish him, and shield him from every care'.

This intense happiness was short lived. Marie Antoinette died fourteen months later in childbed leaving a son 'fat, ugly, healthy and well-formed'. The son of Metternich and his beloved lived on to become Austrian Ambassador at the Court of Napoleon III.

But the romance which Darja had for so long cherished in her heart, and, in spite of the cynical overtones of her letters, had believed in, was now over for her. In a letter to him written a year before his marriage she said that their hearts and minds were well matched. It would be very hard for either of them to find people of their own calibre. 'You will find no one better than me. If you meet your like – show him to me. Adieu.'

That was a point which Darja, for all her sharp eyes, sarcastic tongue, and witty pen had overlooked. He did not want anyone like himself. It was hard to live with oneself, one needed a softly lit mirror which gave back the image of a pleasant less sharply defined world.

On the death of his wife he wrote a letter which threw light on his deepest feelings. It is said by some to have been written to *une belle inconnue*, and by others to Countess Lieven. In view of the tone of her last letter to him, and her remarks about his marriage it is hard to believe that she had written him *une lettre de condoléance* on the loss of his wife, but it is always a possibility.

I thank you from the bottom of my heart for your two last letters, and feel myself totally at ease with you in my grief – which is extreme.

Yes, my dear friend, I have suffered the greatest unhappiness which could have befallen me. I have lost half of my existence. My home, my domestic happiness, that part of my life which belonged to myself alone, and helped me to support the other part of my life which does not belong to me. Everything has perished around me, and in me.

Referring to his search for a bride he explained:

I was quite detached in my calculations, and I sought for a long time before choosing. What I wished for was a being who would always belong to me, and would relieve me of every care, and all the necessity for worry, a young person who would never have the slightest need to be a mother to my daughters, but simply their elder sister.

This being – I found. Alone and without a family the day she entered into my life, beautiful as an angel, and an angel by all her qualities. This being whom I had found, death has snatched away from me after fourteen months of happiness! My life has ebbed away with hers.

I would have written to you after my tragedy, but I lacked the force. I threw myself into public affairs as a murderer seeks to hide in the forest.

The sacrifice has been made; it is without return or remedy. Public sympathy has given me some solace, and I take this expression of sympathy as homage to she who has gone.

The more I am pitied, the more I have lost.

Adieu, my dear Friend.

In the close alliance of love and death in the heart of cher Clément, there was no further place for chère Dorothée.

A cynic has written that love is only the beginning of hatred. That was to be the postscript to the story of the political lovers, Darja and 'mon prince'.

CHAPTER TWELVE

To visit our beloved Emperor...

While Metternich had been burying one wife and marrying another, Darja recovered from her confinement, and was able to write to her brother Alexander of her steady return to strength, and incidentally to busy herself about the complicated threads of political activity. So much to be found out – and passed on.

It is difficult to avoid the thought that with the decline of her *affaire* with Metternich, she had bolstered up her self-confidence with an even more frenetic zeal, not only in the domestic politics of England (in which she would have done much better to take a less passionate interest) but also in the field of international politics as it concerned her own country. She had seen the webs of power being spun by Metternich, and this had fascinated her. In her own right, as a woman, she had no power, but she could usurp the power of Bonsi, and little by little this is what she did. It was said that, in many instances, she acted totally without informing him of her actions. 'Vraiment', and his family, had managed to get to the positions they held by caution, by loyalty to the Imperial Crown, and by advancing slowly as a snail peering out of its shell from time to time to make certain of its terrain. Darja was more impetuous, and she felt that her way was pleasing to the Tsar.

With her return to health, she also returned to the idea of picking up the threads of Russian thought. Two of her sons had returned to Russia, where both of them were destined either for the Army, or the Diplomatic Service, the natural inheritance of any member of the Lieven family. But at the moment they were serving in the army.

The Countess was not entirely pleased with their situation. 'If you have any influence in the matter, dear Alexander, try and get my poor boys made officers. I confess it will be a shock to me to find them in the garb of corporals, and it seems to me that their apprenticeship has been long enough. In what branch of the service are they serving – cavalry or infantry? The cavalry of the Guard is too expensive. They *must* be in the Army, but where and under whom?'

It was all important to set their feet on the right rungs of the ladder. Her reasons for sending her sons back to Russia were expressed quite simply when she wrote about her son Paul:

'Our reason for wishing him to make his debut in Russia was to awaken in him a love for his own country; we have endeavoured to make him understand his duties towards it. In what concerns his tastes and affections he will need freedom of choice – that is the outcome of his stay in this country – but the fruits of his learning will not be limited to this. If your ideas on this subject do not agree with mine, wait until we meet; do not let us fall to disputing, especially on paper. My departure is fixed for 1st June.'

The political background to her visit was the idea that the Holy Alliance, the principles of legitimacy and absolute rule which had been upheld for so long by Metternich, were things of the past. Metternich was to be consigned to the dustbin of history, and Canning was to be promoted as the friend of Russia. Canning, however, was not being used, he was making use of the Countess as his emissary to the Tsar.

She told her own story with some disingenuousness.

I knew the invariable hostility of Prince Metternich to the Greek cause. I had more than once given him sincere warnings on the need of ending the Eastern business in good faith, on the clear-sighted view of Russia in this business, and on the danger of finally bringing the Tsar to recognise that he had been the dupe of difficulties improvised by Austria. My advice remained without result. I felt deeply the humiliating situation in which Russia was, and I left in June 1825 for Petersburg, but without any fixed plan, but with the firm resolution of telling the Tsar the truth if he did me the honour to speak to me of his affairs. It was not at all probable. The Tsar chatted with me no more than with anyone else.

It took her some time to attain her objective. In the meanwhile, she was enjoying being back on her native soil, finding again the background of her youth, 'the maternal goodness of the Tsarina, with joy – even the unwonted etiquette of the Court, the old routine of the courtiers, frivolous things which have their serious side in a monarchical country.'

From her long stay in England she had forgotten the ambience of her own country. The sharp contrasts between the immense luxury of the huge apartments filled with Italian, French and Flemish masterpieces of painting, the vast salons filled with marble and porphyry – and the total squalor of bug-filled beds and filthy servants sleeping on the stairs, and in the corridors.

But the luxury in Russia was such that it came as a dream of a totally different planet. Writing some few years later, Lady Londonderry described a fête at Court.

We drove to the door and staircase of the Empress Mother, from which we were shown to the Salle Blanche where we found an immense number of people collected, the gallery around it filled with spectators. There are above two hundred maids of honour all wearing the cipher-and-crown in diamonds on their shoulders, and distinguished by their red and gold trains. The *dames d'honneur,* and the *dames à portrait* are dressed in green and gold, the maids of honour of the Grand Duchesses in light blue. These colours are prohibited for others. After passing through a *salle* full of magnificent troops the procession arrived, a great cortège of *fourriers de la cour,* gentleman of the Chamber, Chamberlains etc. and at last the Tsar in the uniform of Hetman of the Cossacks leading in the Tsarina in full Russian costume with a red velvet and gold train and her cap and gown a blaze of jewels, followed by the Grand Duchesses. These were all dressed in pale blue velvet and swansdown. They proceeded through the *Salle des Maréchaux,* a long gallery filled with Dawe's paintings, to the chapel which is white and magnificently gilt, very lofty and with the transparent Greek screen. The Tsar and Tsarina stood in front; behind them the Grand Duchesses, and then were ranged the whole Court, the ladies on one side, the men opposite. The heat was excessive. The Grand Duchess Olga fainted, and a maid of honour suffered in a far less refined manner, Madame Nesselrode remarking in her usual imperturbable manner: 'Pauvre petite chatte, *elle degosille.'*

Even Darja was impressed with the vastness of everything after the informality of English country-house living. 'Tsarkoe Selo is the Versailles of our Paris, a very imperial, very magnificent residence ... much gilded within and without. The gardens are vast and much adorned with strange-looking statues.'

The Tsar had an apartment prepared for Countess Lieven and the

---

* An intense search in various French dictionaries and consultation with a French friend has not revealed the exact meaning of this word, but in the context it should mean 'been sick', vomited or puked. *Degober* is apparently the modern French slang for this. Perhaps it would be more polite to leave it in French!

Tsarina conducted her to it. 'I crossed the long *enfilades* of halls and galleries and was installed in a rich apartment, where I waited for the arrival of the Tsar. It all seemed to me *icy*. Space, magnificence, solitude are all so sad.'

Eventually she was ushered into the presence. 'The Tsar received me with the familiar good humour that I had always had from him. He was so isolated from all contact with man that his habits had become monastic, and his mind so suspicious that the sight even of a person like me seemed to embarrass him. I do not know why, but this embarrassment gave me courage. I answered his banal questions in such a way as to interest him a little.'

All this was written in her journal, in the light of hindsight, but it is to be presumed that in the cold magnificence of the palace, in the strange detached presence of the Tsar, Emperor of all the Russias, her lord and master, Darja felt some of the awe which she had felt as a girl. Little by little the Tsar became more friendly: 'He referred to things and persons. He spoke to me only of business and my answers were reserved and firm.' She proceeded with caution. It was dangerous to show oneself as being either ultra or liberal. 'I would not show myself to be either for or against Mr. Canning, for whom the Tsar had a deep hatred.'

The Tsar spoke to her of the weakness and carelessness of other Cabinets. 'I said to him: "Put your foot down, Sire, and you will make the whole world tremble"... I made him speak much himself ... finally after an hour and a half's tête à tête I must have made an impression on his mind, since he did me the honour to speak of me to my brother after this interview saying: "I left your sister a young woman; I have found her a stateswoman."'

This was the impression which Darja had of herself. She had moved on. She was now not only the intimate of Prime Ministers and the King of England, but of the beloved Tsar himself. She decided, prudently, not to mention anything which the Tsar had said to her, except of course to Nesselrode, his Foreign Minister. And then she could not resist contrasting her own boldly simple attitude with that of Nesselrode.

I found him of the same political sentiments as myself, but in such an attitude of fear towards his master that he had never dared to discuss the probity of Metternich. He was a little frightened at the boldness of my talk with the Tsar which I had repeated to him, but seeing my good courage and the reserve of my behaviour, he communicated to me from his side what might help me in the vague idea which I had formed. It was reduced to this: to detach ourselves from Austria and re-approach England

... my conversation with the Tsar had been so cautious that I regarded it, for my own part, only as a good foundation.

Darja then went on to award herself all the credit for the Tsar's changed views about Austria. Nesselrode had told her that the Tsar had detached himself totally from Metternich's suggestion of imposing on the Grand Duke of Baden an edict forbidding debates in the Baden Parliament, the aim of which was to stem the unhealthy flow of revolutionary or liberal ideas which he saw flooding over Europe. Her truthfulness about her audience with the Tsar, and subsequent interview with Nesselrode is somewhat invalidated by the account she gave of her relations with Metternich. She had made the acquaintance of Prince Metternich at the Congress of Aix-la-Chapelle and 'a warm correspondence continued ... in our respective positions, politics necessarily had the greatest share.'

If Darja, no longer the *petite pensionnaire* from the Smolny Institute, thought that her relations with Metternich were unknown to her beloved Tsar, she was wrong. Like many intriguers, she was herself intrigued against. 'The Emperor thought,' she wrote, 'that I had some knowledge of Metternich's intimate views and was therefore curious to make me speak about him. The little I had dared to say had been enough to justify the irritation he had begun to feel secretly against him. It increased from day to day.' She went on to write that she had informed Count Lebzeltern, the Austrian Ambassador at the Russian Court, that if matters were not arranged with Turkey 'he could be sure that we should take up the matter ourselves, and declare war on that power'.

This was not entirely the truth. In May of 1825, after the break-up of the Conference at St. Petersburg, the Tsar already planned a war against Turkey. Metternich, always anxious to keep his Holy Alliance together, tried to prevent this. Lebzeltern had come to consult Countess Lieven about all these difficulties, and – as she tactfully put it – 'he did it with entire confidence for he knew of my relations with his Chief.'

She remained for four weeks in Russia and was satisfied with her mission. The Tsar had visited her twice at Pavlovsk, had listened to her news from England, and had discussed Metternich with her. He was not pleased with Metternich's attitudes because he did not follow a straight line, but on the other hand he felt Canning to be a Jacobin, which in modern terms could be simply termed a non-authoritarian.

The Tsar himself had begun his career full of the liberal ideas

171

instilled in him by his Swiss tutor, La Harpe, but gradually the insinuating practicalities of power had changed him. Metternich said of Alexander: 'I found the Emperor a Jacobin – I have made him an Ultra; it only remains to make a tyrant of him.'

Darja, her intense devotion to her lord and master paramount in her mind, wrote: 'The Tsar would never have become that. God had marked his soul with the seal of goodness, but he was full of terrors. He remained humiliated, irresolute, *combattu.*'

The Tsar decided to use his Ambassador's wife for a little under-cover diplomacy. The Russians saw the Turkish power crumbling, and the Tsar felt himself abandoned by his allies. His people were demanding war. Everybody had interfered in the affairs of Greece, only he, the Tsar, had remained pure. He had not even a single agent in Greece. (This was also not true, but the aggrandisement of Russia and her advance towards the Mediterranean had to be given the cloak of a noble crusade.) What the Tsar proposed was that Countess Lieven should take a message to London – that Russia and England allied could control events, and establish in the East an order of things conformable to the interest of Europe, and the laws of religion and humanity.

Of course, Russia could make no open advances to England but the Tsar would welcome the ideas of the English Cabinet – when Lord Strangways arrived in Russia, he should be furnished with new instructions. All this was conveyed to the Countess by Nesselrode. She listened with delight and astonishment, and admitted that it was going to be very difficult for her to carry out this mission.

'Here was Nesselrode, the most cautious and discreet of Ministers compelled to entrust the most confidential, most intimate and most bold political projects to a woman. It was new, and something to laugh at.'

It also proved to her that she had totally superseded dear Bonsi. He might have the honour of being called Ambassador, but she was asked to carry out the important projects. She was not unaware of the difficulties. Canning was isolated in the Cabinet. All the Ministers were pro-Turkish, and against the Greek revolution. How was she to begin?

'A woman knows how to make people speak', said Count Nesselrode, 'and that is precisely why the Tsar considers you a unique opportunity, and your presence here has been for him like a revelation.'

'But what an incredible idea!' Darja exclaimed. 'The Tsar then wishes to break the Alliance. He desires a separate engagement with England, and in agreement with her, to drive the Turks from

Europe. To erect in their place, a Christian power; in a word to overthrow everything.'

At this point, according to Darja's account, Count Nesselrode put his hands to his head, and looked around fearfully. 'My God! If the Tsar heard you! Ah, well, it is possible that is what he dreams of.' Then, with a despairing gesture, the Count pushed his glasses up to his forehead and leaned back in his chair. It was not, after all, easy to deal with the vagaries of an absolute ruler.

The Countess was equally aware of the dangers and insisted on putting her instructions in writing. The Count read over what she had written, and said, 'That is the true wish of the Tsar.' They also agreed between them that it should not be made obvious that Darja was taking on Bonsi's functions. *La paix du menage* was to be preserved. She was to tell her husband everything which had happened, and although she would put the matters to the parties in question, he should 'take the question in hand'.

Count Nesselrode did not sign the instructions, but with the greatest prudence wrote a simple note to Count Lieven: 'Believe all the bearer tells you.'

It was quite obvious that both the Tsar and Nesselrode were using the Countess as an agent. Her instructions were written by herself. Nothing had been signed by anyone, and the words 'Believe all the bearer tells you' could apply to any circumstances, or be denied in any circumstances.

Darja, elated by her newly acknowledged importance, saw herself speeding across Europe like a courier, or a feldjäger. Actually she did not arrive in London until 28 September, which was twice the length of time taken by a courier.

In October of 1826 Countess Lieven took up her pen again to write to Metternich, anxious to impress upon him her importance. 'The Tsar took me for a man; he treated me as one, as regards confidence, and as a woman as regards attentions and consideration.'

Everyone in Russia had spoiled her. The Empress Mother dissolved in tears when she left. There had been nothing but compliments and praise for her on all sides. Then she could not forbear a sarcastic aside, perhaps to show her erstwhile lover that she had not lost her sharp observation of the stupidities of others: 'It was not worth the trouble to disparage me, since I was there only for a few weeks, and people who are leaving soon are always popular.'

Darja's journal was filled with the chronicle of her return to the inner politics of London. She had seen Wellington and Canning, and of course, the King. She liked to think that it was her influence which had brought the King and Canning together but there is little evidence that this was true. The King had become reconciled to the increasing power of Canning for some time.

Bonsi was moving forward in his usual snail-like way. On 5 October he wrote to Nesselrode: 'the return of my wife has put me in possession of the little letter which you entrusted to her, and by which you authorise me to hear by word of mouth all the details of the last interview you had together.' He had as yet done nothing, as he felt it better to move gradually. It was all very well for his wife flying about Europe accepting instructions, but it was he who had to carry them out. 'I regard our affairs as going on well in this country, my conduct will prove to you that I have understood the sense of the "living despatch" [his wife].'

Darja, as usual, was more disposed to give herself the credit. 'There grew up between the King and Mr. Canning, and myself, a tacit custom of doing one another good turns, which perfectly smoothed the path for me to ask in my turn for more serious assistance from the Minister. I raised the question of Greece by slow degrees.'

She did give a small pat on the back to Bonsi. 'I owe my husband the justice to say, that on his side, he set out very cleverly to draw Mr. Canning into the path we desired.' She then went on to outline the process of the negotiations – with some discrepancies. Wellington was pro-Turkish, and a rival to Canning, both with the King, and in the Cabinet. In 1825 she had considered Canning as not being 'sincere', yet by 1827 she was writing to Earl Grey that 'Canning was a true hearted man, and his heart was in the right place.' The Countess's opinions about people and circumstances varied with her instructions and her political alliances.

It is difficult not to remark that Darja's own heart seldom remained in the right place for long. Like some seismograph or sensitive barometer her allegiances to people whether they were rulers of great countries, or mistresses of Kings and Ministers, descended with the descent of their power and influences, or rose with their ascent. If she had a great talent it was for making certain that she had judged correctly.

Up to the present – time and circumstance had been on her side. Both Tsar and King were her confidants, and she had become the intimate of Canning, her former enemy.

Mr. Canning had taken a fancy to Brighton, so Bonsi decided he could not do better than spend a good deal of time there. It was as well to be near the target. 'We spend about four days out of ten in London.' Although it was already October the weather was superb, the days just like July, and not a yellow leaf to be seen.

But then the blow fell. The Tsar Alexander died at Taganrog on 1 December 1825.

When the news reached Darja, she was overcome. 'Oh my brother, what a misfortune has stricken us. A courier from Count Nesselrode brought us the frightful news today; today the day of his birth, we learn of his death! This tragic news has been circulating for a week, but I could not reconcile myself to believe it, my heart recoiled from the idea that the Tsar no longer existed. One must have a firm belief in religion to resign oneself to such a blow of Providence.' She reacted in true Russian fashion to the sorrowful news. She wanted to be in Russia itself; she wished to see everyone around her in tears. 'Ah! Our tears are in truth sincere.'

There were ambiguities in the succession. At first the Countess had acknowledged Constantine as her Emperor, but it speedily became clear that this was a mistake. The Tsar had died without issue, and by the laws of succession his younger brother should have inherited the throne. But Constantine was generally thought to be dissipated and an unsuitable candidate to wield such enormous power. There were other complications: he had married a Polish countess morganatically, and renounced his rights to the throne. Whether he intended to comply with the terms of this renunciation once the distant prospect of power had become a reality is not known. But once the news of Alexander's death reached St. Petersburg, Prince Peter Lapouchkin broke the seal of a packet left by the late Tsar to be opened on his death.

It contained a letter from the Grand Duke Constantine dated 14 January 1822 formally renouncing all rights to the throne: 'conscious that he did not possess the genius, talents and strength necessary. I shall add by this renunciation a new guarantee and a new force to the engagement which I spontaneously and solemnly contracted on the occasion of my divorce from my first wife.'

The muddle over the succession was a sign for some of the liberal nobles to call for a Constitution, while Prince Troubetskoi and some of his troops came out on the side of a federative republic. Nicholas, the younger brother, then took on the role of legitimate Tsar, and – in the usual way of legitimate Tsars – put down the revolt with great ruthlessness.

The Lievens then promptly and tactfully acclaimed Nicholas as their true and beloved Emperor and they were rewarded by being elevated to the rank of Prince and Princess Lieven. The grief and despair they had suffered over the late Tsar Alexander was soon forgotten in the pure joy of acclaiming his successor.

By the beginning of January Darja was in ecstasies over the fact

175

9 Nicholas I. When Mme Lieven became Her Serene Highness Princess Lieven she said: 'With Nicholas one knows upon what to count'

that the Duke of Wellington had been chosen to congratulate the Tsar on his accession. 'I am writing you a line, dear Alexander, which the Duke of Wellington will bring personally. I am overjoyed that the Duke is going to see our beloved country, and I am sure that his arrival will be greeted with the greatest pleasure by the Tsar and the Russian public. I rejoice in advance at his success, and of the impressions which he will bring back from our homeland. The Duke has the best and noblest character in the world, and he is acclaimed as much for his noble feelings as for his high military reputation.'

She added that the Duke was overjoyed at the idea of going to Russia. This was not true. Greville wrote that Wellington had been overcome with melancholy at the long journey he had to undertake, being deeply affected 'as if he had some presentiment that he would never return'.

Princess Lieven's feelings about the Duke had now taken on an affectionate, admiring and enthusiastic note. 'England could not have sent an ambassador who was more worthy of the solemn occasion. The Duke himself is full of admiration for the superb conduct of the Tsar.'

She was referring to the promptitude with which the Tsar had put down the revolt against him. The Duke always preferred action to words. 'Dear Alexander, what great events! What a character our Tsar has shown himself to have! What respect, and what admiration everyone in the world displays towards him! What a magnificent race of Princes ours is! Poor Princes of the rest of Europe! How meagre they seem at the side of our own! If you saw me Russian to the very depths of my soul during my stay in Russia, you can imagine how I feel at this moment!... I have no other thought except *for* Russia.'

Then she referred in oblique terms to the Palace revolution which had been suppressed. 'We are awaiting with impatience the end of the work of the Military Commission ... I should say, with Wellington, where Kings know how to rule, and to punish, no revolution is possible ... I am content.'

She was particularly pleased to see her brother Alexander's name referred to in so many 'honourable and flattering terms'. He had, of course, helped the Tsar to put down the revolt. The Lievens and the Benckendorffs were still on the winning side.

It is unnecessary to underline that these letters must have been written either with the thought in mind that the spies of the Tsar would open them, or that if couched in sufficiently flattering terms brother Alexander would be able to show them to the Tsar.

By the middle of the year 1826 her brother Count Alexander

Benckendorff had been appointed head of the Imperial Gendarmes. He had also been made Chief of the Department of Justice, a euphemism for the Secret Police, and was attached to the Tsar's private household, and thus became inseparable from the Tsar himself. It was prudent to have men about who were quick at spotting insurrections, and as quick to quell them. The Tsar Paul had been murdered because his Secret Service chief was on the side of the conspirators.

The Tsar had expressed a desire to see 'dear Bonsi' – this was a command. Darja expressed herself in fulsome terms at this pleasing thought on the part of the dear Emperor. Nothing was going on in England, and the moment could hardly have been better chosen. The only sorrow in her heart was that she would be vegetating on the banks of the Thames while Bonsi would be enjoying all the delights of Petersburg. 'I have no thoughts but for Russia, the Imperial family, and the Tsar, whose greatness I have long foreseen.'

The only request she did make of dear Alexander was that he should write to her all the details of everything her husband did, and the people he saw. Bonsi was a wretched correspondent and she knew she could hardly count on hearing anything from him. Perhaps she did not trust Bonsi's tact, and yet he was, if anything, more subservient than herself where the Imperial family was concerned. The whole rise of his tribe in the history of Russia was based on treading the Imperial tight-rope, and it was hardly likely that he was going to fall off because of any lack of tact on his part.

Prince Lieven was being sent to Russia at the same time as Wellington. For Wellington, apart from his official duty of congratulating Nicholas on his happy accession to the throne, had another role – that of special envoy to the Tsar. In the Protocol signed on 4 April 1826, the way was being prepared, as the Princess wrote, 'for the emancipation of Greece'. The idea was to bring pressure to bear on Turkey to give the Greeks some semblance of self-government. England had now become the ally of Russia in the Middle East, and this was partly as a result of Darja's mission from Petersburg. She could congratulate herself.

While Bonsi was away in Russia, she herself had spent some profitable days cultivating the friendship of Canning. The King had attempted to conquer his dislike of Canning, and he was agreeably surprised that Princess Lieven was becoming one of Canning's intimates. As a result of this new friendship, the King invited both the Princess and Canning down to the 'Cottage'. As she wrote to

Metternich (with whom she was still keeping up a tenuous relationship), Mr. Canning came to talk to her regularly every Sunday and gave her a summary of the week's politics.

The Court, domestic politics, we touch on everything. That man is an extraordinary character. One might suppose from the vivacity of his impressions and the rapidity of his mind, that he would take things up and then drop them, that his opinions would be changeable, but this is not so. He proceeds by leaps and bounds, but always along the same road. He will do foolish things, but they will never make him turn aside from the path he has marked out for himself. In everything, he will always get what he wants. I fancy that even opposition pleases him; it strengthens him in his purpose.

In some ways Darja could have been writing about herself, and her new-found admiration of Canning possibly stemmed from the fact that she had found in him some characteristics of her own manner of behaving. Added to which they had the same sense of humour, and of the ridiculous, and down at the Cottage, there was a great deal to be laughed at.

The King found the Princess's new friendship for Canning useful. 'I give the King thousands of opportunities for showing his Minister a politeness which is not due to his rank in Society.'

But Darja's close intimacy with the King had its disadvantages. After one of his usual heavy luncheons the King was out for a little sport. The Princess' description of what followed reads like a scene out of a Restoration comedy. Her suite was on the ground floor with long windows looking out on to a walk which was shaded by trees. When she was getting ready for the afternoon drive, she looked in the mirror, and saw the King slipping behind a hornbeam which shaded the walk. She opened the French windows and called to ask him if the company were awaiting her. He gestured to her to keep silence and made it quite plain that his intention was to slip into her room – and her affections. She restrained her laughter and, always resourceful, called to her maid to bring her hat. When the King saw the maid coming into the bedroom, he turned on his heel and slipped back into the bushes. In his hurry and his flight he nearly tripped over, and Darja was left smiling to herself at the ludicrous incident.

A few minutes later she walked into the drawing-room and when the King saw her, he bowed low in the manner of the *ancien régime* and for the rest of the day, as if to overcome his discomfiture, treated her with the most exaggerated respect.

By August, Bonsi was back in England, and the Princess took up her correspondence with her brother. Her husband had come back infatuated with the Tsar, 'and delighted with you. I rather take credit to myself for having discovered in the Grand Duke Nicholas *le grand homme*; I had the foresight, others will enjoy the experience. I do not, as you see, forget my own perceptiveness, in which, I admit your right to share, as I remember how often our talk turned upon him. He had already a great reputation abroad, which will increase and be strengthened as time goes on. My husband, who is sober minded in most things, is, I can well see, most enthusiastic.'

It took the flattering attentions of the Tsar to rouse Bonsi to any enthusiasm. 'On his return to London, Bonsi was received with marked attention, and, as you may well imagine, was urged to talk by everyone – the King, the Ministers.... I have given him little peace, as I am not wholly devoid of curiosity. At the present moment he is very busily engaged with Mr. Canning, and this may go on for several weeks, after which "Foreign Affairs" will change to Paris, and we shall enjoy a respite here.'

She had found Bonsi decidedly thinner after his travels, and she herself was no fatter. They were both in need of a rest.

Other benefits had flowed from Bonsi's mission to Petersburg. Her son Alexander was impatiently awaiting his appointment to the United States mission which Bonsi's closeness to the Tsar had secured.

Referring to her brother's appointment as head of the Secret Police she admitted in a letter: 'Your position is a difficult one, but I can well understand that one gives one's self entirely to such a master, and when one's heart is in one's work – difficulties disappear.'

She added a postscript. 'We have this instant received the judgement of the Tribunal, the sentences and the noble proclamation of the Tsar on this affair. It is an admirable manifesto, and now, thank God, the curtain falls on this tragedy, and will not again be raised.'

This fulsome paragraph referred to the putting down of the revolt against Nicholas and the whole concept of autocracy. The Military Tribunal had sat behind closed doors. It was true that – for Russia – the sentences were lenient. Three hundred and twenty one persons were accused, they were all members of the nobility, and only five were executed. The investigations, in which presumably brother Alexander as Chief of the Secret police was concerned, unearthed three secret organisations: the Northern Society based in St. Petersburg which desired a Constitution, and a government based on a Constitution; the Central Society, recruited in the garrisons of Lesser Russia which favoured a Republic, and the United Slavs from the Southern Provinces who tended towards the idea of a Federation. One of the leaders, Prince Sergius Troubetskoi had the idea of making himself Tsar, should the revolt succeed. He was disappointed, and condemned to death, but subsequently the sentence was lessened to penal servitude for life.

The beloved and noble-hearted Tsar had made sure that no one should think that revolts could be taken lightly. On the other hand he had made few enemies, except possibly in the families of the men who were executed. As Princess Lieven wrote: 'With Nicholas, one knows upon what to count.'

With the rise of Canning, the Duke of Wellington began to be of less importance. Metternich and the Duke were part of former Congresses. Their ideas stemmed from the past; she looked towards the future.

Canning, it seemed to her, was a man of great talent, an honest man, not at all a Jacobin, and was the sole member of the Cabinet who was well and truly a friend of Russia. As for the King, he was in good health, enjoying his beautiful bizarre Pavilion, his good cuisine, his loud orchestra, and his fat Marchioness, Lady Conyngham. It seemed to the Princess that the reign of the favourite was in the decline. Was the King perhaps becoming bored with her?

As for Wellington the Princess, who was, as always, a partisan for her own country, was no longer his friend. 'The Duke pursued his career of hostilities against us; his reputation has suffered a great set-back. His conduct is bad, perfidious, and his sole intention – which is openly avowed – to embarrass and upset his rival, Canning, in spite of any ill he might do to his own country. Canning will remain. The King seems resolute in supporting him, and it is on these occasions that the King counts for much in England.' Canning, became – if briefly – Prime Minister in 1827.

Metternich also suffered the lash of her pen. 'M. Canning is on our side. The Austrian complications have taken M. de Metternich far away. Le voilà joliment planté. Tant mieux!'

It is hard not to feel that it was Dorothée who had been 'joliment plantée', and she resented it.

'I believe myself, that Metternich, the man of wit and intelligence is dead, because there is not the slightest hint of this in his conduct. He is a usurper who persists in all the political errors into which his vanity has led him.'

181

But in the month of August 1827, Canning died after a long and painful illness. Darja felt it as a great personal loss. It must be admitted that it was unfortunate that she had eliminated the Duke of Wellington from her friendship. She kept up a bold front, and wrote of him as the sincere friend and ally of Russia. 'The Duke of Wellington is still cold towards me. He has not pardoned me for having preferred the Minister who was friendly towards Greece to the Minister who was a friend of the Turks.' But now the death of Canning had brought Wellington to power again. 'The King has given the Duke back his post, but hardly taken him back into favour.'

This unfortunate turn of events posed problems for the busy Ambassadress. 'The Duke of Wellington is restored to the chief command of the Army. The Duke of Wellington is Austrian, he prefers the rogueries and double dealing of Prince Metternich to the loyalty of the Emperor Nicholas.'

It was not a sensible move. Charles Greville in June 1828 remarked that the Princess was acting with the greatest impertinence and had used her influence with the King to undermine the Duke and his Ministry. She had done nothing but attack the Duke since she had become attached to Canning, on his rise to power. She had acted dishonestly with the Duke.

There were those who considered that her interference and her meddling were beginning to exceed the bounds of prudence. She may have thought that she knew everything about the undercurrents of feeling in England. She prided herself on knowing all the ripples on the surface of the political lake. There was one thing which she had forgotten – she was a foreigner. And to foreigners there were things which were not forgiven – and sometimes not forgotten.

CHAPTER THIRTEEN

La Chute

In October of 1827 at the battle of Navarino, Admiral Sir William Codrington (with the help of some few French and Russian ships) blew the Turkish fleet up in the harbour of Pylos. It was the physical expression of years of haggling and diplomacy with Greeks, Turks, Russians, Emperors, Prime Ministers, Kings and on a lesser level, diplomats.

The Princess Lieven was overjoyed. It seemed to her as if the guns of the British Navy had blown up all the enemies of Russia – Metternich, Wellington, and all the superannuated collaborators of the old regime. She seized her pen and wrote to her brother:

Dear Alexander, Why don't you write to me? The couriers arrive, the fire-ships arrive, but your letters do not arrive. Well, well, vive Navarino! There is a treaty which has *not* been stillborn – as M. de Metternich predicted – quite the contrary, the child is remarkably lively. We are delighted, the English Government a little frightened, and the French the reverse of satisfied, except for the fact that it distracts public attention. As for the Austrians it goes without saying that they are furious and greatly disturbed. The English public is full of proud boasting, there has been burning and sinking of ships, and much massacring – that is to their taste. The masses do not stop to ask the cause; the Opposition is squabbling, and asks by what right these things have been done.

Her joy was short lived. A nonentity, Lord Goderich, had taken over the Ministry on the death of Canning, but after the battle of Navarino his government fell, and the Duke of Wellington became Prime Minister.

It was not a good omen for Darja. In racing parlance she had put her money on a horse which had dropped dead at the winning post, been replaced by a bad runner, and finally beaten by Wellington. But this extraordinary and determined woman was undeterred. She continued to attack Wellington, even when he had returned to power.

Since her success as intermediary of the Tsar, her pride and pleasure at her own astuteness had become more and more apparent. Now she hardly disguised her feelings, and her open belligerency was made clear in her letters.

'Wellington has managed to impose on the English nation.' She could not understand the hold which he had on the public at large, for to hear what people said one would have thought that the Government could not have held on for another two days. 'Wellington paid no attention to all the clamour, he took on an air of defiance, and everyone else was afraid. In spite of his mediocrity, he is wily, he flatters the ultras and the liberals equally, and both are his dupes. People are very easy to deceive; and this is a thought which comes naturally to the mind when one sees this nation, which is supposedly so wise and thoughtful, becoming the dupe of a Minister who is so mediocre.'

The Duke of Wellington at first regarded the Princess as a gadfly. Possibly he would have felt himself humiliated had he paid too much attention to her activities. He knew that he had it in his power to get the Lievens recalled had he a mind to do so, but he refrained. In the meantime he behaved in a civilised manner which earned only the contempt of the Princess. 'The Duke of Wellington continues to pursue a polite and conciliatory attitude. Perhaps he will go as far on this way as he has gone in the opposite direction. I don't trouble myself to decide if he does this from compulsion or by conviction; in spite of his mediocrity, he has trickiness in his soul and he has been so little on our side that it will be a long time before his charm seduces me into another point of view.' Down at Windsor, when visiting the King, he had laid himself out to be especially charming to her. He had complained to her that she treated him badly, that she did not invite him to her house as she had done formerly. In effect, she thought, he had been stung into courting her. But it had had no effect; she was not going to be taken in by his wise air, or his social graces. Those were the only assets which he had.

A short while later she was writing that Wellington had resumed his former malevolence (presumably against Russia). If it had not been for the troubles in Ireland, she believed that he would have drawn the sword against Russia on the day he heard that the Tsar had blockaded the Dardanelles. But the Princess had to admit that public opinion was not on the side of the Russians. She remarked sarcastically on the total ineptitude of the British Government. They had made such a fuss that summer over the Russian renunciation of belligerent rights in the Mediterranean that they did not know what to say to the public in general. It was possible that these blunders could serve the interests of Russia. 'That is to say, if we starved Constantinople and forced the Sultan into suing for peace.'

Her letters give the impression of a woman with a high shrill voice putting forward her opinions and prejudices without a great deal of reflection. She had once written to Metternich that she was above all a woman, and in spite of her years of political intrigues, a woman she remained. A woman with all a woman's facility to see only the point of view of her Tsar and her country, with no balancing factors. To Darja the landscape was black or white. The noble Tsar with his golden sword was up against the machinations of these tricky Europeans. Time and chance were to teach her harder lessons. But now she was in the full sunshine glare of the high noon of her influence. She could flatter the King, toy with the Opposition, write a précis of Bonsi's despatches to save the Foreign Minister of his Imperial Highness from boredom, and despise the Duke of Wellington.

It does not seem that Prince Lieven took any part in these vendettas of his wife. It was to her brother that her missives were directed. In her letters the name of her husband was seldom mentioned as the years went on. She bombarded General Alexander Benckendorff with her opinions, prejudices, half-truths and political gossip. She knew that everything would be passed on to the Tsar, and that perhaps her letters themselves would be shown to him, which explains the fulsome terms in which she always referred to the Imperial family. Some echoes came back to her in London which proved to her that her work was well appreciated. She was the ear of Russia in a possible enemy camp.

'I have to thank you from the bottom of my heart, dear Alexander, for the Emperor's message which you have conveyed to me – so attentive, in such good taste, and showing such friendship! I am happy and touched that he should think of me for a moment. This is a feeling which comes from my heart and from my vanity!'

Some few months later her mother-in-law, old Baroness Lieven, Governess, and Trainer of Tsars died. This produced another orgy of sadness, mitigated with renewed feelings of gratitude to the Tsar.

How can I express to you, dear Alexander, all the sentiments which flooded into my heart on reading your letter of March. The touching respect with which the Tsar has honoured the memory of my excellent mother-in-law on the occasion of her obsequies, the pious tears which he has shed on her remains, the fund of gratitude which he has expressed down even to her humble servants, all these details only serve to underline the greatness of his soul, and are reasons for drawing down upon him the blessings of God – and of his grateful subjects. A man who shows such sentiments in his heart merits every prosperity which will come to him. I shed tears when I heard the news which touched me so closely – tears of thankfulness, tears of remembrance for that virtuous and incomparable woman from whom the Tsar has allowed me to inherit such marks of honour. The favour is so great, and the manner of graciously according it makes it only the more priceless. Never has an equal honour been received with greater emotion, and I cannot forgo the need to express this myself to the Tsar.

All this overflowing gratitude stemmed from the simple fact that she had been made Lady of the Bedchamber on the death of her mother-in-law.

If Darja had taken one iota of the trouble and used the flattery which she used towards the all-powerful Tsar with her English friends and acquaintances, the sequence of events would have had a different dénouement for her. But the Tsar was like Jove, he held the lightning in his hand, and it could strike with death and terror. English politicians were little men engaged in running about in their own small rabbit warrens. A Russian ferret could easily frighten them, with no fear of recriminations.

Political life in England was not as simple as Darja saw it, nor were the English quite the dupes she took them to be. She wrote with great self-satisfaction of her quarrels with the Duke, but had little idea of the real opinions of the people who surrounded her.

Lord Palmerston wrote to his brother the Hon. William Temple who was Chargé d'Affaires at St. Petersburg in April of 1828: 'The Duke is very anxious to break with Russia. He has a strong personal dislike to Russia. He has had violent quarrels with the Lievens. A great many little things have contributed to set him against the Lievens. Mrs. Arbuthnot and Lady Jersey (who both have influence over him) hate Princess Lieven … she was foolish last year when Canning came in, and too openly expressed her joy at the Duke's retirement, and was too, to a certain degree, uncivil to him.'

A month later Darja was rejoicing in the bad humour of

Wellington, and recounting a conversation she had had with Lord Palmerston: 'After all,' he said, 'whether for those who, like me, trust, eyes open or eyes shut, in your Tsar, or for those who distrust him, or pretend to do so, there is one and the same course – and that is to show confidence in him, and to act upon this principle.'

Her spirits rose. She remarked triumphantly: 'These intriguers have been very clever. They emerge from their well-spun web covered with glory! A single word of the Tsar has scattered them to the winds! How imposing to Europe must be the sight of this Tsar at the head of his army assembled for a great and noble purpose!'

In April of 1828 Russia declared war on Turkey, a move unpopular with Wellington whom she had described as being 'obstinate as a mule'. Scarcely had she finished her letter than they were quarrelling again 'so seriously that I at once put the scene on paper, and if I can find it I will enclose it with this letter'. She added that the King was well disposed towards Russia, and would do something if he could.

But Croker puts the other side of the coin. 'They say that Princess Lieven did really say something to the King about the change of his Ministry, and that His Majesty answered her that if his Ambassador at St. Petersburg should presume to criticise the conduct of the Tsar in the internal affairs of his Empire, His Imperial Highness would instantly recall him.'

Had the Princess heard this remark it might have given her pause for thought. It was a warning shot across the bows of the triumphant argosy of the Lievens in London. But all unheeding the Princess glided on, her sails billowing in the sunset, proud of herself, proud of her achievements, and proud of the Russian armies forging ahead to scatter the Turks. The Princess rejoiced in the military victories announcing various surrenders, and rejoiced almost as much in the discomfiture of Wellington. 'This England is too insolent – she needs to have troubles, and she will have plenty. This is for your ear alone, and so I am going to put this letter under lock and key until I hand it to the courier.'

In August of 1828 she reported that the Duke had gone to Cheltenham – looking very ill, adding hopefully: 'Prime Ministers don't live long; his relations with the King are very uncomfortable and a little embittered. He wishes to be master, and the Master is obliged to hold his tongue for the nonce; for Wellington is strong from the fact that there is no one to take his place – but his autocratic ways irritate the King. Pray tell Count Nesselrode the remark attributed to the King concerning the Prime Minister: "King Arthur must go to the devil, or King George to Hanover".

Neither the one nor the other has yet started on his journey.'

It is unlikely that the King would have said this for the Princess had reported to Lord Aberdeen how very much the King had disliked Hanover on his visit with her to his German kingdom.

But her triumph in the Russian victories had its dark conclusion. Costa, her second brother, died of fever during the campaign in the Crimea. He was commander-in-chief. Out of the army numbering 120,000 men, the hospital entries exceeded 210,000 in the nine months from May 1828 to February 1829. Owing to the primitive conditions of the time death from disease was a potent factor in war and the number of reinforcements needed indicated a disregard of human life on the part of the noble and excellent Tsar.

The news of Costa's death reached Darja via Count Nesselrode on 28 August 1828 and she was prostrated with grief.

My dear Alexander, from now on my *only* brother, it was only yesterday evening that I learned in a letter from Count Nesselrode to my husband of the shattering news that our angelic Constantine has been snatched away. What a tragedy for us! How I loved him! He was so good and tender towards me! Dear Alexander, love me more than you have ever done before – I have need of consolation, of tenderness. Nothing, except you can replace the tie of nature of which my heart feels such a deep need. Constantine, so dear, so good! What will become of his poor children? Tell me everything, every detail which has to go with our tragedy. Tell me the day when we should weep the most. Has anyone thought of sending a lock of his hair? If so, please *share* it with me. This is a grief which has overwhelmed me, and will never be effaced in my heart.

She was overcome and appalled at her loss – Costa dead in the midst of strangers! It was out of the order of nature. She realised that in the sequence of life, on would lose one's parents. When she thought back her mother was taken from her at a young age, and the Empress had taken her, a motherless girl, under her wing. But to lose a brother – why should he be taken so early?

'How little we know that we wish, or why we wish it – I who was so eager for this war, had I but known what it would cost me! This is a regret which time will never efface.'

Her letters reflected only too well her deep sorrow and melancholy. Her husband wrote: 'She is plunged into the most profound sorrow. Each day seems to increase rather than diminish her grief.'

Unfortunately her grief did not serve to curb her activities. The

188

Turco-Russian conflict rumbled on and had its repercussions, poisoning the relations between the Russians and the Cabinet in London. The Tory Ministry of Wellington had to contend against both Whigs and Radicals. The Princess profited from all these cabals. She felt herself in an impregnable position, for she knew that she was the prime object of their attention, and even if they had it in their hearts to disguise the hostility which they felt against the policy of Russia, they could not ignore her. She realised that she was feared, and continued to multiply her intrigues against those Ministers whom she considered to be the enemies of her country.

Her letters reflect her indefatigable pursuit of her ends, and give an idea of how intricate were the webs of the complicated intrigues of this volatile woman, who was so untiring in her role as a zealous, well-placed and patriotic agent of her Tsars. Ironic indeed that such an arch schemer and manipulator as Darja did not seem to realise that she herself was being manipulated and that her popularity rose and fell in proportion to her successes. Sometimes she was properly regarded as an irreplaceable agent of influence, and a well of delicate information, then ignored and nearly abandoned, then in favour again. Able to report what she heard to her brother – she was supremely confident, over-confident. She felt she knew exactly how to make difficulties for the English politicians, and yet on the surface give an impression of total frankness, discussing policies, and personalities in an open way, criticising, defying, and teasing the men in government and out of it, without giving a thought to their feelings, or their irritation. In retrospect, it is clear that she was set on a disaster course, but because the English were deceptively polite she did not realise it.

Rumours did filter back to her that Wellington was beginning to feel that he was being pushed to the limit by her bravado. It might be, she was told, that the Duke would ask the Russian government to recall the Lievens.

She replied: 'He would not dare!'

But the Duke did not follow his wishes by deeds. It was not that he did not dare, as the Princess had said so disdainfully, but perhaps because he remembered their old friendship. Although he had referred to the Lievens as 'wretches', he had added, 'I am *above* making them my victims.' It was a magnanimous and sensible attitude from which Darja could have learned much.

Then, when the power of Wellington was beginning to decline, the Princess, according to her usual process, became more and more intimate with Earl Grey, his potential successor. There were those who thought she was his mistress, but it seems to have been more an *amitié amoureuse*. Grey was accustomed to write to her every morning, perfuming his letters with musk. And again Bonsi, perhaps in the interests of Holy Mother Russia, seems to have turned a usefully blind eye to the new situation, either because he was personally indifferent, or on instructions from St. Petersburg. But when eventually Grey became Prime Minister, he in his turn disappointed her, and was not disposed to be less anti-Russian than his predecessor.

Darja was angry with him. 'You would do well to become the Grand Turk – then I should be afraid of the rope, and I would always be of the same opinion as yourself.'

Had she been disposed to think more deeply she might have realised that the thought partly reflected her relations with the Tsar. But she did not have to fear Lord Grey. She had betrayed her intense displeasure with him for his way of voting over the independence of Greece, and had told him that she would never see him again.

He had replied with firm dignity that she was threatening him, and although it was a threat which he must take seriously, he followed his duty: 'If our friendship breaks on these grounds – it will never be renewed'. It was a clear warning about her behaviour. She retreated and became at once all good sense and charm. She did not want to lose a friend, or a political connection, nor did St. Petersburg.

'I only wish you, once for all, to take the firm resolution to remain friends with me. Think – I have good sense, a little wit, and above all a deep friendship for you.' The words were the words of Darja; the unseen voice was the voice of Brother Alexander, head of the Russian Secret Police, anxious to keep her on target.

But in spite of her triumphs, there were undercurrents running against her. Already, in 1829, it had been rumoured that the Lievens were to be recalled. Lord Heytesbury wrote from St. Petersburg: 'With respect to the Lievens, I shall take no steps for obtaining their recall, but at the same time shall do nothing to prevent the adoption of such a resolution.'

Darja may now have had some slight misgivings about her husband's situation in London. Count Matuscevitz, who was Nesselrode's First Secretary in the Russian Foreign Office, was sent to 'assist' Prince Lieven in conducting negotiations arising out of the Russo-Turkish war. It would seem that the real purpose of his visit was to examine the situation of the Lievens in London, and report back to St. Petersburg. It is a method which has not been abandoned over the centuries by Russian governments. Subsequently Bonsi was asked to return to Russia to replace Count Nesselrode as Foreign Minister while the Count was on leave.

Darja had been nervous about Matuscevitz from the beginning. He had spent ten months in England and they had done everything to be helpful to him. English people had flattered him, which had perhaps turned his head. 'I should have liked him to have resisted the excessive devotion to England by which he seems to be carried away,' she wrote to Alexander. 'He leaves us at a moment when the Ministry seems inclined to show in their relations with Russia a more polished *surface*, and a more becoming attitude. As for their real disposition – it is as thoroughly hostile to us as it has ever been; and however much they may make of the velvet paw, we must not lose sight of the cat and its claws.'

The visiting Russian had made other friends, much to Darja's dismay. King George was convinced that Matuscevitz would come back as Ambassador, and had said as much to the Count himself. The Count had bowed, and replied: 'Sire, j'accepte l'augure!'

It was not an augury which boded good to the Lievens. Apart from other considerations, the temporary Ambassador had entered into many English pursuits which Darja herself did not enjoy. He had hunted with gusto in the Shires, flirted with the ladies, dancing and dining, and making himself thoroughly popular with everyone. It did not seem to Darja that this was in the best interests of herself – or of Bonsi.

When Matuscevitz came back to replace Bonsi on the planned return to Russia, Darja was very uneasy. She wrote to Lord Grey about Matuscevitz saying that he was not her friend. 'He is enchanted at my departure because he wishes to be everything with the Ministers. This is a disagreeable discovery for I had believed him to be really attached to me.' Deceivers are always disagreeably surprised and outraged at being deceived.

Bonsi and Darja set out for Russia in May of 1829. It was not a journey which she had been anxious to make – in fact she had written to Alexander that once the partition of the estates had been made (presumably after the death of Constantine) there did not seem to her to be any need for Bonsi to go to Russia that year. She betrayed her nervousness at their situation. Supposing a few weeks in Russia should turn into months? Things changed so quickly.

But circumstances forced them to set out, and Bonsi was perhaps anxious to protect his properties which were to accrue from his wife's inheritance.

The Prince Lieven left his wife in Warsaw. The Tsar was to arrive shortly, and here the Princess met again her erstwhile lover, the Grand Duke Constantine, dissolute elder brother of the Tsar, who was still acting as Governor of Poland.

Warsaw was buzzing with Highnesses and nobilities of all shapes and distinctions which she noted with satisfaction: 'All Russia is assembled here. Old friends to see again – long conversations – my brother and Nesselrode permanently established in my drawing-room.' All the usual fatigues of Court and social life, but there were compensations: the Tsar was all kindness, and her pleasure at the audience with him was great: 'I almost forgot the respect due to him in the delight at seeing him once more.'

It was as well to remember to leave one's English manners behind when encountering the Tsar. Her enchantment with Nicholas I was not always shared by the English themselves. Some years later Lord Aberdeen drew a quick sketch of him: 'The visit of the Tsar was most successful. All ranks were equally charmed with him. He is, as you say, a remarkable man'.

But to English eyes undazzled by his power, there were reservations. 'He is not quite what I expected. He speaks well, and his speech carries conviction. But in spite of his commanding presence, and manner and power, there is something about him which always inspired me with a sense of melancholy. I believe it is the expression of his eye [sic] which is very peculiar.'

This little vignette gives the feeling of thoughts about a noble dog of uncertain temper. But to Darja he was the All-Highest. She was with her own people again, and able to take up her inherited post as lady-in-waiting to the Tsarina when the Diet assembled in Warsaw. It was the usual impressive Russian scene, the ladies in their Court dresses glittering with jewels, and the men in their impressive uniforms. What the Poles were feeling at all this display of wealth and power was never mentioned. A year later they were to make their feelings only too clear.

'No one could have looked more thoroughly Imperial than did my master. Still, it was a curious sight – he on his throne, and the Grand Duke Constantine at the other end of the hall – among the deputies. The cordial relations existing between the two brothers are really admirable, and very touching.' It was certainly an admirable thing – in a country where heirs to the throne were occasionally obliged to engineer the murder of their fathers.

After a fortnight of junketing in the Polish capital, Darja took the overland journey to London, and Bonsi went on to St. Petersburg. But things were changing. In Berlin, she learned with great regret of the death of George IV. It was not a shock, for she had already noted that he had become enormous 'like a feather bed, while his legs, also swollen, are as hard as stone'.

The British, who had never liked the extravagant, and, in their view, dissolute, monarch regarded his passing with little regret. But the Princess mourned him. She had forgotten the boredom at the Pavilion and the Cottage, and remembered only his affection for her, and what a pleasant host he had always been. She was highly critical of the popular attitude towards him. 'He is completely forgotten, and, if remembered, it is only to criticise his morals. It is in the middle and lower classes especially that this side of his character has left a very unfavourable impression – an impression which overshadows much that was striking and brilliant in his reign.'

Victorian morality had begun to cast its shadow before it, but Darja regretted the late King – as a friend.

On the international front, the Russians, after some setbacks, finally defeated the Turks and the Princess made no secret of her triumphant feelings. 'Glory to the Tsar, and to Russia! What a splendid triumphal war, what a splendid triumphant peace! We should all of us indeed be happy, dear Alexander. I wonder whether at Petersburg you are able to enjoy this twofold success as I do here.'

For some time Darja had tried to influence Lord Aberdeen, while despising him as a 'wretched diplomat, merely, the chief clerk of Wellington'. When peace was signed between Turkey and Russia, it was Lord Aberdeen who received the full brunt of her triumph, and her spite.

'I could not have imagined anything more delightful than the propositions which Lord Aberdeen put before me – especially as they were accompanied by his tragic expression: "Well," he said, "your glory is complete. Russia dominates the Universe today – in spite of your modest language, you are all powerful. As for us, we appear to have been your dupes, and are humiliated and disgraced."

She did not hesitate to rub salt in the wound: 'So much the worse for you. But we did not deceive you, you deceived yourself. Your own illusions, or rather those which inspired your patron, the Prince Metternich, those were your real enemies.' So much for any residual memories of the adored Metternich, the man she had seen as the other half of herself.

She reported to her brother that, after continuing with his sad complaints, Lord Aberdeen had concluded that it was only in allying themselves with Russia that England could find a guarantee of peace and safety in the world.

'Thank God, my Lord, you are at last coming to admit as a truth what we have all along felt, and have endeavoured to impress upon you. But in order that this truth may bear fruit you must deal frankly in the matter, and loyally with my Emperor – that is the rub.'

She saw her beloved Tsar as having driven back the forces of Turkish barbarism with 'his glory increased by his clemency'. As for the Duke of Wellington, when he threatened, she wrote to her brother: it was then he was at his weakest, and one had only to stand firm, and he would bend. He knew that she herself, and the Russians, were aware of his character, and knew it inside out. That was precisely why he detested Russia: 'He would prefer a little innocence which he could lead, according to his own ideas, as he does the rest of the *corps diplomatique*.' She was convinced that she had his measure. After all a year or two earlier he had tried to patch up the rupture with her.

'Wellington had a long tête-à-tête with me – all sweetness and friendship. He spoke to me about his own position, and said that it was the strongest which any Prime Minister had ever held in England. I made a little quiet fun on the subject of his colleagues and Ministers; he laughed and had to admit that he had only chosen fools. What a curious kind of vanity!'

She foresaw the end of Wellington's power, and when his Ministry eventually fell, her deep friendship with Lord Grey would prove useful. He became Prime Minister, with Lord Palmerston as Foreign Minister. That last appointment she felt she had every reason to congratulate herself upon.

Her account of the appointment of Palmerston was that Earl Grey had suggested Lord Lansdowne, but she had objected on the grounds that Lansdowne was a Whig. 'When I named Lord Palmerston to him, he recoiled and hesitated very much.'

On the other hand she had a very clear recollection of Lord Palmerston's concern and agitation that he should get the post. 'I was living at Richmond at this time, though I came into town every day, and he galloped from one to the other of my residences. His obsession was keen, and my desire to serve him was very great. Finally I ended by doing so.' This was not true. The Foreign Office had already been offered to Lord Lansdowne who had refused it. Lord Palmerston, like the Princess Lieven, took an equally inaccurate view: 'As soon as Lord Grey was commissioned to form a Government – he sent for me.'

Full of self-congratulation, Darja was unaware of the storm clouds. Once upon a time, in the dawn of her love for Metternich, she had dreamed of leaving London for good, and settling down in Vienna. Now she felt London to be her home. She was constantly and fervently referring in her letters to her brother to her loyal Russian heart; but nearly twenty years in England had disoriented her, and many of her habits and her tastes had become English. But in spite of that she continued to support every action of Russia with blind faith.

In 1830 the Poles rose up against the Russians, and the Russians put down the insurrection with some ferocity. They took Warsaw, and the Tsar, as a simple solution to the Polish problem, made himself King of Poland. This was not to the taste of the British, or of Earl Grey. He had invited one of the chief Polish insurgents Count Czartoryski to London for a conference with himself, and the Foreign Secretary, Lord Palmerston.

This invitation infuriated Princess Lieven, and she sent her subservient husband to Lord Grey to protest, following up this official protest with a furious private letter to Lord Grey. Earl Grey replied with dignity: 'To anyone except yourself my reply would be short,' and he addressed her as 'dear Princess', instead of 'dearest Princess', ending his letter 'your sincere friend', instead of 'your affectionate friend'. Yet again the Princess was obliged to recoil at being in his ill graces.

There were others who did not value the friendship of the Princess, and these included Lord Palmerston. At the beginning of 1833 a quarrel broke out between London and St. Petersburg about the replacement of the British Ambassador, Lord Heytesbury, who was anxious to return to London. According to Greville, Nesselrode had written to the Princess Lieven asking that Heytesbury might be left in Petersburg. She had replied to the Russian Foreign Minister telling him that the rumours were that either Adair or Canning would succeed him. It was alleged that Petersburg had objected to Sir Stratford Canning on the grounds that he had been uncivil to the Tsar when he had been Grand Duke. But according to the story which the Princess told, the Russians had remarked that Canning was suspicious, spiky and distrustful.

This was the tenor of the message which Darja was deputed to take to Lord Palmerston. Palmerston received the Princess and her message with seeming compliance and promised that Stratford Canning should not be named as Ambassador. But then perhaps Palmerston saw the circumstances as his opportunity. He named Canning as Ambassador to St. Petersburg in the *London Gazette*.

The Tsar at St. Petersburg was duly affronted. Lord Durham, Earl Grey's son-in-law, was in Petersburg at this time, on a mission to try to get Russia to join in a treaty with France and England. At the same time he had been primed by Princess Lieven to send a message back to London reaffirming the Tsar's total opposition to Stratford Canning as Ambassador.

Lady Cowper, later to become Lady Palmerston, told

that Palmerston was provoked by the Princess's interference, that her temper had got the better of her, and she had thought to carry it with a high hand, having been used to having her own way, and that he had thought both *she* and her *Court* wanted to be taken down a peg; that the Princess had told Nesselrode she could prevent this appointment, and, what had done more harm than anything, she had appealed to Grey against Palmerston, and employed Durham in St. Petersburg to make a great clamour about it. All this had made Palmerston angry, and determined him to punish her who he thought had meddled more than she ought, and had made the matter personally embarrassing and disagreeable to him.

She had been forgiven many times, by the Duke, by Earl Grey, and by many others. Her defiant cry about the Duke of Wellington: 'He would not dare!' now had a hollower ring. Rumours of the opposition to her reached her ears, and for once she was thoroughly alarmed. The Tsar sent for her, and she hurried back to Petersburg to try to remedy the imbroglio. She had heard that the Tsar was threatening to recall his Ambassador to the Court of St. James's. But she came back to England totally reassured, radiant from the memories of the reception which the Tsar had accorded her. He had met her in his imperial yacht, and, according to Greville, took her on board, and 'when they landed drove her to the Palace and escorted her to the Empress, who was *en chemise*.'

She was quite certain that the peril to herself – and Bonsi – had been averted. 'Dear, dear Alexander, how can I come to terms with my happiness both with Russia and with England,' she wrote in fulsome terms, 'I am very content to find myself back here with my husband and my old ways, and with good friends. On the other hand, as you know, my heart remains over there; how much I admire and love our dear Emperor.'

Once back in England the memory of him was even more dear to her. She remembered every one of his words, his gestures, and she was overcome with emotion at having to leave all that. She had never felt her heart so full.

'Make sure that he does not forget me. Tell him of all the respect, fervour and devotion I have for him.' Then, thinking possibly that she was writing too warmly to be believed, she added: 'But be brief about my love for him, it would perhaps suffice if he learned once and for all, that my fidelity, my gratitude, and my passion for him can never be equalled.'

But in spite of her efforts, the conflict between the Cabinet in London, and the Tsar in St. Petersburg grew, and became more embittered. The Tsar flatly refused to receive Sir Stratford Canning. Canning was *persona non grata* even before he had arrived. Canning's opinion was quite succinct: 'It remains to be seen whether the Lievens will have to make a back somersault over the Baltic.'

The Tsar made his pronouncement: Sir Stratford Canning would never pass his frontier as Ambassador.

Palmerston, in a strong position, as having no imperial *amour propre* to wound, and not being touchy like an absolute monarch, took on an insouciant air. He would appoint no one else. The Embassy in St. Petersburg, the most important Embassy in the whole of Europe, according to the Tsar, remained in the sole charge of the Secretary. The pride of the absolute monarch was wounded and affronted. Something must be done.

In May of 1834, the blow fell. The Tsar recalled the Lievens.

The long reign of the Princess in London was over.

When the letter arrived at the Russian Embassy, Bonsi raised his hands in joy, and Darja let hers fall in desperation. She, at last, realised that the end was in sight – she had to leave England. The realisation came to her that Lord Palmerston was the reason of the recall. To leave England! The England that she had learned to love so much. The England she must leave now not for a few weeks, but for ever. She had forgotten one thing which Talleyrand was to underline for her: 'It is always in the power of the Foreign Minister, however mediocre he may seem, to send away an Ambassador.'

Lord Palmerston had willed it, and that was what had happened.

The Tsar threw the Lievens a small *douceur* – Prince Lieven, like his mother before him, was appointed to oversee the education of the Tsarevitch, and Darja to take on her duties as lady-in-waiting to the Tsarina.

Darja was sunk into depression. For so long she had sparkled and intrigued her way through English society, and now at last she was brought face to face with the fact that all along she had been merely 'a foreigner'.

The Times reflected the growing Radical opinion of the country: 'The recall of Prince Lieven (or rather Mme. La Princesse) is an event.' The 'Thunderer' then went on to dismiss her activities as mere meddling. She had given abundant reasons for the recall for more than twenty years. 'There never figured on the courtly stage a

197

female intriguer more restless, more arrogant, more mischievous ... She fancied herself 'a power', she was, however, more frequently, a dupe, the dupe of her own artifices reacted upon by those of others. Her Serene Highness would have put down this journal – would she not? She would have flung us bodily into the Thames, as a certain ex-Minister, no doubt could testify. But, alas! the Thames is not the Neva.'

The Times assumed that Count Matuscevitz had been sent to London to remove the Lievens, and the writer at Printing House Square tendered to the Count his sincere congratulations on 'having after a long struggle well executed his *delicate* task.' Darja wept bitter tears when she read this leading article. So many triumphs, so many social graces, so much love and affection lavished on the country she regarded as her home-from-home, to end in this shabby way.

No doubt *The Times* had a shrewd idea that she was more of a secret agent of the Tsar than a friendly Ambassador, and had no compunction in thundering forth its opinions.

Her friends and acquaintances were divided in their opinions about her recall. Some regretted the passing of a witty, amusing, colourful figure, others were glad to see the back of a gossiping intriguer. Her female friends were equally divided in their ideas about her. But the Duchess of Sutherland felt that some amends should be made, and decided that a suitable presentation ought to take place to commemorate her departure. After all she had amused and entertained so many of them for so many years.

Metternich had given her a bracelet when he was contemplating retiring from being her lover, and the social ladies of London decided on the same tribute. A large number of them had originally decided to subscribe to the gift, but when it was bruited that the bracelet was to be jewelled many of them withdrew. It was one thing to be upset at her departure, but quite another to dip into one's reticule too deeply. Thirty names remained on the list.

There was the usual difficulty over the inscription. The Duchesse de Dino recalled: 'Twenty ways of putting the inscription were tried.' Eventually the Duchesse herself was consulted, and she thought of a simple French sentence which was translated: 'Testimony of regard, regret and affection presented to the Princess Lieven on her departure by some English ladies of her particular acquaintance.'

The Princess chose the jewel – it was a single large pearl. It was appropriate – pearls are for tears.

She told her great friend, Harriet, Lady Granville, 'I carry on my arm everything that I regret, and everything that has given me so much pleasure in the past.'

To her brother she wrote: 'You can have foreseen, dear Alexander, the effect which the news brought by the Consul-General Buckhausen would have upon me. A total change of career after twenty-four years of becoming accustomed to totally different moral and material standards is a grave change in one's life. They say that one can regret a prison when one has passed many years there. On this count, I must regret a beautiful climate, a wonderful social position, and habits of luxury and comfort which I can find nowhere else, and – many friends who had nothing to do with politics.'

It was a heart-felt sigh from a woman who had made a fundamental error of judgement.

Harriet Granville drew a word picture of the England which the Princess was shedding tears at leaving:

No words can say how I enjoy the beauty of the place, the charm of the country in England. I rushed to the vegetable garden and walked up and down between spinach and dahlias in ecstasy. The tenu, the neatness, the training up of flower and fruit trees, gates, enclosures, hedges are what in no other country is dreamt of; and then there is a repose, a *laisser aller*, a freedom and a security in the life of a country house as no other destiny offers one. I feel when I set out to walk as if alone in the world – nothing but trees and birds; but then comes the enormous satisfaction of always finding a man dressing a hedge, or a woman in a gingham and black bonnet, on her knees, picking weeds, the natural *gendarmerie* of the country, and the most comfortable well-organised country. Then at home, if the people are there whom one loves, the whole day is passing from one enjoyment to another....

There was so much for Darja to weep for, and to regret. The Duchesse de Dino felt sympathetic for the great sorrow which she knew the Princess was experiencing. The knife was turned in the wound by the numberless dinners and receptions which she had to attend. Lord Palmerston, as if to savour his triumph, gave a splendid dinner of farewell to the Lievens. Everyone suffered from the embarrassment of this ironical gesture, and the Duchesse had the feeling that the Princess, in spite of her iron social discipline, was about to faint under the strain. 'She is really very unhappy, and I am very sorry for her ... she weeps to leave England, and she fears St. Petersburg.'

Then the Duchesse pinpointed the weakness of her diplomatic

friend – she had no resources within herself, and always needed pleasant surroundings, and the stir of news and conversation to make her feel alive.

Earl Grey made his sad adieux, speaking of the sorrow he felt which was 'so impossible to express ... Never will I forget the happiness which I have found in your company, and I will never cease to regret its loss.'

She herself realised that things which she had taken so much for granted were slipping away. 'I must repeat that it is the respect, the affection, the esteem and the unanimous expression of regret of which my husband is the object.' She had perhaps never realised it until now. 'I am not exaggerating when I say that the Government, the Tories, even the Radicals, look on his going as a catastrophe. He is touched by these signs of regard, and it would be impossible for him not to be.'

Amongst the emotions, there were all the troubles and upsets of packing. Twenty-four years of memories to be packed, or rejected. They were in a dilemma: 'We are taking all our household things, and leaving everything of luxury and value, because I am sure that we shall be given a house which is already furnished.'

The British Government had been very polite and had offered them a ship for either Hamburg or Petersburg. Happily the offer had been made by the First Lord of the Admiralty: 'Had it been made by Lord Palmerston I believe I should have said "no" straight away.'

She was overwhelmed and wearied by visits, packages, and sighs: 'my own as well as those of others: I shall get no rest until the day of our departure'. She had one other worry which she confided to her brother: 'You know we are without hearth or home, and how very important it is for us to know whether we are to live at Court or not ... Henceforward my country will be the house which I shall inhabit.'

But in spite of her brave words, on each stage of her journey she wrote back to England, to her friends, and the country which she had lost. On reaching Hamburg she wrote to Earl Grey:

My dear Lord ... the crossing was execrable, everybody was ill, and I almost died of it. I have eaten nothing since I left London, and have arrived here so weak that I cannot stand, with my back all broken, and not an idea left. Pity me, for I deserve it. How am I ever going to live away from my dearly-beloved England, and without ever seeing you? I start on my journey tomorrow. Give Lady Grey many tender messages from me. Tell her how much her name on the famous bracelet touched and flattered me, and how this bracelet is in my eyes the greatest honour that has ever been paid me. How proud I am of it, and how happy, and yet how sad ... What between weakness, fatigue and sorrow, I am almost dead. Adieu, and again adieu.

From Lübeck, the next stage of her journey, where she embarked to sail up the Baltic to Kronstadt, she wrote to Lady Cowper. 'I am sleeping here, and shall embark tomorrow. I want to send you my love once more while I am still in Europe. That is a terrible thing to say, I implore you not to repeat my remark.'

The suggestion was that Russia was hardly Europe. Already the shades of the Tsar's authority were closing round her. 'I feel a little better today, but tomorrow I shall feel more miserable than ever because I am about to travel over that enormous expanse which will separate me from everything I love. Oh God! How I love everything that I have left behind! I think of nothing except London.'

But as the ship slipped away into the mists of the Baltic towards Russia, the old life was slipping over the horizon, and before her lay a land she had almost forgotten, and had visited only twice in twenty years.

CHAPTER FOURTEEN

A return home – to exile

The Princess had been filled with dark forebodings about her return to Russia. It was as if the vast landscape had stretched out to draw her back into its grasp. She tried to keep up her spirits when writing to her English friends. There was nothing so tiresome as a gloomy correspondent. But she pined for news from England. To Lady Cowper she wrote imploring to be kept *au courant*. But, in spite of herself, and her resolutions, she could not forbear a great sigh of regret for the past, which had been so happy in retrospect: 'Not a day passes but I regret my separation from England, all the more when I realise that it is for ever.' This was the saddest thought of all – for ever.

As for herself it was difficult to give an idea of her life – it was so different from England, so very different. She had been a few days at Tsarskoe Selo with the Court, and now was back in St. Petersburg for Court celebrations. She was finding life at Court terribly tiring, very seldom was she invited to the small intimate gossipy dinner parties which she loved, generally it was a question of a hundred, or even two hundred sitting down to a banquet. This happened every evening, and then it was necessary to join in games and dancing. The evening would be concluded with a formal supper. Every day they had to dine in the open air in full evening dress, and it was terribly hot, so hot that even a light chiffon wrap was unnecessary.

But soon the weather changed and the cold hand of the Russian winter advanced. 'Dearest,' she wrote to Lady Cowper, 'this climate is frightful, it makes me weep.'

She occasionally reproached her English friends – they did not understand her situation. If only Lady Cowper would come to visit her. What a pleasure it would be to show her the apartments at Tsarskoe Selo. Her suite was at the end of a colonnade facing the hanging garden of the Empress Catherine. It was built entirely of glass with pillars of assorted colours – the bedroom, the colour of

202

amethyst, the ante-room sapphire. 'There is a large reception room with walls entirely of amber with Florentine mosaics inlaid with the amber.' She herself had a complete suite of rooms – drawing-room, and four ante-rooms with walls and pillars of agate. The magnificence was amazing, but the Tsar (in whose gift all this richness lay) was away.

There were ambiguities in her situation, and she wrote a worried letter to her brother: 'Write me a few lines and tell me above all what you think that my husband and I can do to fall in with the thoughts of the Emperor in his absence. Does he wish his children to be treated with a little latitude, or not? Is it true that it is only a case of having a visit of an hour on Sundays with the Tsarevitch? That is what his professors have said. But were the professors *correct* in their thinking? Please enlighten me.'

From the tenor of her letters it would seem that the appointment of Bonsi as *gouverneur* to the Grand Dukes and Duchesses was merely a Court appointment, more or less a sinecure. The Princess went every day to pay a ceremonial visit to 'Mesdames les grandes-duchesses'.

Every evening she received the ladies-in-waiting. She had executed to the *letter* the wishes of the Tsarina, but had nothing on which to base her actions. She had at last seen the Tsarevitch (*Monseigneur Le Grand-Duc Héritier*). It had been a difficult encounter, as if he at sixteen had great difficulty in bridging the gulf which lay between them. Sixteen and fifty. There were other points which she found it more difficult to express tactfully. But she did tell her brother (quite frankly) that the Grand Duke seemed to have some difficulty in expressing himself. He was charming and tactful, and seemed to wish to appear well socially, but she was sure that if he came more often he would find it easier to gain social poise and aplomb. She had tried her very best not to bore him, and little by little he seemed to be coming out of his shell, sometimes she even felt that he took pleasure in her society. It was not an easy task. From her description one gathers the impression of a tongue-tied young man who had led a very restricted life. Yet she was doing her best, and wrote in glowing terms of admiration about him. He had a charming face, and expression, it was such a pity that he found it so difficult to talk. But progress was being made. It was easier when she had someone else there who could ask questions. She was trying to bring him out, to give him an idea of the rest of Europe beyond Russia, occasionally telling a few anecdotes about the history of her times, sometimes a joke or two, a stupid remark in the middle of a serious talk. She assured her brother that Monseigneur, the Grand Duke, seemed to follow all this with his eyes and his ears, and occasionally she had even made him speak a little about his own life. Sometimes he had managed to express a few charming sentiments, but at the moment he lacked the energy, clarity and the elegance of language which his father the Tsar had in such abundance. 'I wish that the Tsarevitch could imitate him – but it will come.'

When writing to her brother she did not express her 'horror' at the Russian climate, but merely said that to greet her back in her native land it seemed as if it were going to be as freezing in winter as it had been baking in summer. She was thinking of going back to town so that she did not succumb completely to the cold. But to Lady Cowper she exclaimed, 'Why is my native land so cold, and so distant?'

The Tsar came and went like some bright comet. It was November in St. Petersburg, it was snowing and she had pains in her head and chest. The Tsar had only stayed four days and had immediately taken himself off in his sledge with his son. It was high time she pulled herself together and arranged her new house, so that when the Tsar did return, she could receive the Court. She had been told that the house which had been allotted to her was the most beautiful in St. Petersburg – how could she tell? She had seen no others.

The narrow Court life she had known as a very young girl was closing in upon her. When at Tsarskoe Selo she gave little balls for the Grand Dukes and Duchesses, and she put a brave face on the monotony of her life. The Imperial family were so charming and so amiable that she ought to have been happy. But occasionally there were reminders of her old life. Two young men, the Marquis of Douro, son of the Duke of Wellington, and Canning, son of her dead friend, came to see her. She received them with the utmost happiness, and took them all round her apartments, and showed them as much of the Palace as she dared. But she could not present them to the Tsarevitch. 'It would not have been etiquette to let him see foreigners who had not yet been presented to the Tsar himself. Above all we wish to be correct.' When the Tsar came back she hoped that the Tsarevitch would be able to receive them.

Lord Douro was a striking copy of his father, so much so that it made her laugh. He was already a lieutenant-colonel, and Canning was proposing to go into Parliament, although he was only just old enough. It was a breath of her old life to see and chat to the two young men. For although she made the best of it, the iron discipline of the Court irked her. There was always the necessity, the total necessity to obey, and she felt deprived both of news, and of society. She realised that, to her correspondents, her letters might

204

seem stupid as a consequence of this, but the only topic was: 'Is the thermometer above or below zero?'

To Lord Aberdeen she wrote: 'Our life here is brilliant and *respected*. I would like it well enough if only I could forget England, and if I were not living in a climate made for bears. I feel so far from Europe in this beautiful château... There are agreeable acquaintances, but the ideas and conversation are so far from what made my daily nourishment for twenty-two years. It is very sad, my lord, to have to leave habits which I had followed for so long, and habits which were so dear to me.'

This letter was written only five weeks after her return to Russia, but as winter approached her spirits and her health began to deteriorate. In January she wrote: 'I have been ill and my sufferings were so great that it had been decided to send me post haste to Italy. The cold is attacking my lungs. The day was actually fixed for my departure, but my courage failed me at the idea of separating myself from my son, George, and I asked a few days grace to nerve myself for the ordeal.'

She remembered it was the Christmas season at Panshanger, and her next remark seems to indicate that apart from the waltz she had introduced the Christmas tree to her friends. 'Fanny will have remembered my lighted trees.' She wept to think that there would be none for her this year, but when she looked at her dear bracelet she remembered her English friends, and 'whenever a package comes for me I am careful to preserve the paper in which it is wrapped – it has the lovely smell of England'.

It was kind of her friends to worry about her, but she did not see how she could visit them before the month of May. She saw no one. Night began at three o'clock in the afternoon. She was not allowed to leave her room. They were trying to preserve her 'in an artificial atmosphere as near as possible to the English climate, by means of casks of hot water, constantly replenished, which they press against my body on either side. In this way they hope to preserve me until spring.'

It had been decided by the doctors that she must spend at least two winters out of Russia. This upset her. Was she supposed to wander about Europe without her husband and without George, her beloved son? She had begun to realise that in Russia only healthy people prospered, and she was far from healthy. She was in a state of despair, the sky was always grey and overcast, and the whole landscape a wilderness of snow and ice. It came to her that she lived in a prison, a beautiful prison, but still a prison. It was only too apparent that Bonsi was hardly prepared to sacrifice his way of life for her. Once back in Russia, the Prince had speedily settled down to the way of life which suited him admirably, that of a subservient courtier. 'Vraiment' was thoroughly at home, and his favourite phrase was probably all that was needed in the familiar and monotonous pattern of Court life. All Bonsi was prepared to do with regard to her health was to accompany her as far as the frontier. He was not going to leave his comfortable post, nor his duties to his Tsar and the Imperial family for longer than was necessary.

Then in March of 1835, like hammer blows from a frozen country, Darja was further stricken. Arthur, her youngest son, named after the Duke of Wellington, his godfather, fell ill with scarlet fever. After eighteen days at his bedside, the child still hovered between life and death. He was only nine.

The King's godson George, who had been so admired and petted, at the English Court, had already died of the same disease. 'Poor darling George! He, alas, is gone for ever. Never will I see that dear child's face again.'

In spite of her efforts Arthur followed George to the grave.

In April of 1835 the Princess wrote to Lady Cowper from Königsberg: 'Dearest, kindest friend, can you believe that I still live after all my cruel misfortunes?' How could she go on without George, and without Arthur? They, at least, were at rest, while she suffered still. It was as if everything she had loved and cherished of England had been taken from her – both boys had been born in England, christened in England and begun to grow up in England. England had given her the joy of these two sons, and Russia had taken them away. Aged fifteen and nine, they were only at the threshold of life. Why did she herself go on living?

From her frantic letters to her brother it would seem that she had not been at the funerals of her sons, but later references seem to contradict this idea. But she gives no details of what had happened, there are only sharp cries of grief. 'Make sure that a policeman stands guard over the precious child, and that he does not lose sight of him. Great God! A policeman instead of his mother... I have death in my heart. Why am I still alive, why have I ever lived?'

Bonsi, as he had said he would, accompanied her as far as Königsberg, and then he was called back urgently to the Court. He was quite prepared for his wife to go to Berlin to get medical advice, or Italy to recover her health, but in no way was he prepared to jeopardise his snug situation as friend and adviser to the Imperial family.

It would seem as if the death of the 'English' sons of Darja and

Bonsi, brought on the death of their marriage. On 5 April, she had already written to her brother in terms which showed she felt the marriage to be at an end. They had only arrived that morning; she had been resting. Bonsi was a little indisposed. But he was being very kind to her. It was a strange moment to separate from him: 'But it will be for ever, my dear brother; I can no longer live a life without either interest or occupation', a life which could only be made up of the sum of her unhappiness, and the souvenir of the death of her sons. Her spirit was dead, her heart was dead, it was impossible for her to go back. As for Alexander she loved him with all the forces which still remained within her for loving.

Bonsi did journey with her to the gates of Berlin, and there he left her. He did not want to lose any time in getting back to St. Petersburg. As for herself her mortal sorrow grew with every day. Despite everything her separation from her husband had been cruel in the extreme – cruel for both of them. Life for her was over. Or so it seemed.

Darja and Bonsi had six children. The little girl who had died in the first years of their marriage, then their three sons, Constantine, Alexander and Paul, all now grown up. She had been separated from them for some time, as they had been sent away to make their way in the world, in the Army or the Diplomatic Service. Constantine had been a worry to his parents as he led a dissipated life, and they had hoped that in the disciplines of the University of Dorpat he would pull himself up. The two boys who had remained by her side were George and Arthur, her 'English' children, living proofs of the twenty-two years she had spent in happiness in England. They had been destroyed by the climate of Russia.

She had made it quite clear to Bonsi that their parting was to be for ever. It seems possible that Bonsi did not take her words seriously, and that he expected that, after a few months mourning, she would come to her senses. Darja had always suffered from extremes of elation and depression, and the loss of her two favourite children was obviously a very heavy blow, but life would go on for Darja and Bonsi once they had taken up the threads of Court life again, he thought.

But they were never to see one another again. There was no remedy and no going back. She would journey on alone.

Her letters from Berlin, from Baden-Baden, or wherever she journeyed gave the impression that she could get no rest or peace from her crushing sorrows. One thing she was quite determined about: she would never return to Russia. Bonsi, and her brother Alexander bombarded her with letters demanding her return. Her cure at Baden was completed, there was now no reason for her not to return. But she was thinking of England, and had written to Lady Cowper saying that she thought of spending part of the autumn and winter in England. It was the season of country-house visiting, and she wondered whether her friend could arrange a series of visits for her. There was a slightly ominous silence from her correspondent at this suggestion. Some weeks later her dear friend wrote; she had been discussing the matter with one of the Princess's sons who happened to be in England, and they both felt that it were better that she should go either to Naples – or possibly to Paris. England would be much too full of unhappy memories for her, it was much too *soon* since she had left. Darja did not reply to these effusions and excuses, so Lady Cowper wrote again – could it be that the Princess was offended at her advising the postponement of a visit to England? Darja was not deceived. To Lord Grey she wrote: 'Would you believe it, my Lord, Lady Cowper has written me a letter filled with what she deems good reasons for preventing my coming to England! And she cites, as the most cogent of these – Lord Palmerston!'

This was not the only brush which she had had with erstwhile devoted friends. The Countess Nesselrode, wife of the Chancellor of Russia was also in Baden taking the cure, and had presumably given the Princess a sharp talking to about returning to Russia. Darja wrote to her brother in bitter terms: up to now she had always found that she kept her friends, and now at the moment when she needed them more than ever, and her unhappiness might have seemed to give her extra rights to understanding, she found that she was mistaken. She had suffered another cruel wound, due to the weakness of human character: 'All the Russians in Baden turn towards the source of favours – and follow Madame de Nesselrode, avoiding me completely. This will spoil the rest of my stay here.... You have forgotten, in mentioning Tsarkoe Selo to me, that my health can no longer stand the climate of Russia, and I must stay away for at least a year and a half...'

Her doctors had advised Paris, and it was there she was thinking of going to pass the winter. 'I believe, dear brother, that I have very hardly earned the right to seek some relief from my terrible grief anywhere I can find it. But, if it is necessary to obtain the permission of the Tsar for this, I am counting on the fact that he will not refuse it to me.'

She was wrong.

But for the moment even if the Tsar had not yet issued his Imperial *ukase* demanding her return, Darja was adamant against setting foot in Russia again. It was an appalling country. It had taken from her everything which she loved, and needed.

In the middle of September she arrived in Paris, accompanied by a beautiful niece, Marie Benckendorff, daughter of her dead brother Costa. She had acquired a companion and a new place to live. It remained to be seen how Paris would suit her. At least she was now in Europe and although she still wrote despairing letters to her brother, the air of Paris seemed to revive her. There was only one thing which she asked – that her brother should treat her with tenderness, and that the humanity of the Tsar would accord her the only thing which could help her – permission to stay abroad. The idea of displeasing her beloved Tsar would poison the few poor enjoyments which she might have left to her. 'Tell him that I only seek his good wishes in trying to assuage my pain.'

No permission came.

But the Princess Lieven settled down in Paris for the winter. She had begun to take up the threads of life again. Her friend Lady Granville was now installed as British Ambassadress in Paris, and she reported on the progress of the Princess. 'She stays at home, drives out with her beautiful niece who is living with her; she "receives" from eight to ten, avid for news. She cries: "Chat – amuse me!"'

But those who had decided that Darja was a spent force were seriously in error. Despite her teutonic/slav moods of despair and her ill-health Darja, ever interested in those around her, was possessed of one of the greatest of assets, an indomitable, if often hidden, will-power, and zest for life.

Harriet Granville, who was a sharp observer, drew a picture of a woman determined to distract herself, and to try to get back into her old world. But Lady Granville had an official position; she was not going to be embroiled any deeper than was necessary. 'I will try to be useful to her, on the other hand I am quite decided not to let her become more demanding than would suit me.'

By the end of 1835, her letters began to show the revival of her spirits, and she wrote to Lady Cowper: 'I watch everything with great interest, and I listen; there is a great deal to learn, and to laugh at.' She relayed such gossip as she had been able to gather. Talleyrand was so much *better* since the death of his wife, and she had often dined with him *en famille*, although he was still in mourning. She had already begun to gather some political figures into her orbit. M. Thiers she had met at one of these intimate dinners. She wrote of her life to Lord Aberdeen: 'I live in an intimate little circle – they come together at my house every evening. Diplomats make up most of the company but I see the French people most often, Monsieur Molé more than anyone.' She was sorry he found himself out of office. Others whom she entertained were the duc de Broglie, Guizot and Thiers. Thiers she found to be the most lively, although M. Guizot was a remarkable man, but more serious and reserved.

On 21 January 1836 the Princess wrote to M. Guizot (Ministre de l'Instruction Publique) tendering her regrets for his invitation, and saying that her mourning did not permit her to go out into society. But she was living at the Hôtel de la Terrasse in the Rue de Rivoli, and little by little, in spite of her mourning, during the winter and spring of 1835/1836 she began further to establish herself in Paris, and to lay the foundations of the large acquaintance which was to be hers for the rest of her life.

She had not yet received permission of the Tsar to stay abroad, but she was beginning to feel that Paris suited her health, and her spirits. The autumn of 1836 found her at Baden again – her fate still not decided.

Bonsi and her brother Alexander were writing to one another about Darja in convoluted and guarded language. On the one hand the Tsar had said that he did not forbid anything – and left her free. On the other hand, he was displeased that anyone, particularly a woman whose family had been so favoured by the Imperial family, should choose to take herself off abroad, and out of the orbit of her Tsar. Bonsi wrote that she was at liberty to live anywhere – except Paris. The rope was being tightened.

Bonsi was doing his best to act as an honest broker, but in his position, it was not easy. Alexander had written a sharp reply to his errant sister, and Bonsi was very thankful that he had received permission *not* to send it. He could very well see that it might upset his wife. He understood Alexander's point of view, that although the letter might displease Darja at first sight, it was only the strict truth, and she ought to have no cause for complaint. He ended by saying that he himself had made it *quite* clear to his wife that she could live anywhere – except Paris. No doubt the lack of letters from him had induced in her a different state of mind. But he had very good hopes that his strictures would succeed in changing her conduct. The two Russians writing from St. Petersburg and Nijni-Novgorod were quite firm – Darja would obey them.

She did not.

She was not at all well at Baden, and had already sent off letters about her frail health from various learned doctors. They were unanimous in recommending *Paris* for her total return to good health. She hoped that Bonsi would have the good sense to show the letters to the Tsar. Meanwhile she was extremely upset at the idea of Paris being forbidden to her, and wrote to the Countess Apponyi in Paris. The weather was appalling – cold and rainy. She had heard nothing from her husband for two months. Her position was the cause of great suffering for her and she could make no plans for the future. She had a persistent cough and rheumatism; nothing seemed to be right for her in Baden. The most important thing for her was the doctors' advice: 'Do you know that they very strongly recommend my return to Paris? I was well there. Here I am in a pitiable state, much worse than last year.' All sorts of remedies had been tried, and now there was nothing else to try. It seemed to her doctors better that she should go to the country which suited her. She would wait for definite news from her husband, and whether he could join her, and if he gave her no hope, then she believed she would take the road to Paris.

This she did. Cholera was raging in Italy, and Germany did not suit her at all. She wrote to Lord Aberdeen that very pressing reasons had been given to her for returning to Russia, but it was impossible. 'M. Lieven knows that.' In Paris she had found a temperate climate, some friends, and distraction of the spirit, which was the sole remedy for her unhappiness. Perhaps Bonsi would come to join her at the end of next summer, and then her future could be decided.

She was soon being drawn more and more into French politics and into admiration of M. Guizot. He was becoming acknowledged as the greatest talent in the government. 'He is a man who is respected for his gifts and his integrity is unusual amongst the new men. He has an intelligence which is deep, straight, very ambitious, and proud. He is a man who has fanatical followers, forty members of Parliament who are devoted to him, and who is disliked by all the rest. That is his position in the Chamber, and in the Ministry. With the exception of two or three *doctrinaires* who come to power with him, all the rest find him insupportable. The King does not like him, and M. Molé actually dislikes him – because of his arrogance.'

It was a quick pen portrait of a politician whose actions and thoughts she had been observing. She had met him from time to time at various receptions, and they had not always been in agreement with one another. Guizot himself had written to his confidante Laure de Gasparin: 'I have made my peace with Mme. de Lieven'. As Guizot became more friendly to the Princess he wrote that he had in fact asked her to dine from time to time – intimate dinners – just the Princess, himself and two other people.

10 François Guizot: 'He has an intelligence which is deep, straight, very ambitious and proud'

Some gossip did ensue about these intimate little dinners, but Guizot dismissed it – people were quite wrong about his dinners with Princess Lieven; no one found them at all strange, they had achieved nothing except to surprise and worry his political opponents.

The Princess was gradually once more becoming a political force, and her influence was spreading from her apartments in the Hôtel de la Terrasse.

But a sudden tragedy struck Guizot and the Princess wrote to him in great distress: 'It is just this moment, Monsieur, that I have learned of your frightful tragedy.'

The son of Guizot by his first wife, Pauline de Meulan, had died suddenly from tuberculosis. It was a bitter blow. Guizot had put all his hopes for the future in his son, a young man of exceptional ability. They had everything in common, and to Guizot it was a blow from which he was never totally to recover or able to overcome.

Darja wrote to him:

Amongst all the messages of sympathy which you will have received, in the midst of so great a misfortune will you allow me the vanity of believing that my thoughts might be of help to you? I have the right more than anyone else to feel for you in your sorrow – a right which I have bought very dearly. I sought out people who were unhappy when I was so cruelly struck. If your heart is looking for someone unhappy – think of me, more unhappy at the end of two years than I was on the first day. Today I regret not having anything to offer you – simply the right to tender the knowledge of my strong, tender compassion, and if you will allow me to add – my very sincere friendship.

A few days later she wrote to say that his reply had touched her. She would be very glad to see him – all she wanted to know was the day and the hour when he could come to her. She would make sure that she was *chez elle* – and alone. Her whole morning would be reserved for him. 'Our unhappiness, Monsieur, seems to forge a link between us, a strong link. Learn to find strength in my own heart.' Should he do this it would be a charity which he would be according her. All the words of his message were engraved into her thoughts. They had done her good. At last there was someone who understood her sorrows.

It was the beginning of a long-lasting love and friendship, which endured over twenty years, and to which more than 5,000 letters bore loving witness.

CHAPTER FIFTEEN

Vous n'êtes plus seule

On 15 June 1837 François Guizot and the Princess Lieven sat next to one another at a dinner party given by the duc de Broglie. Suddenly they were drawn together, and saw one another in a different light. Their mutual unhappiness had forged the beginning of the bond, and an equally mutual attraction strengthened it, and made it into something which was to give both of them solace and encouragement through many trials. They constantly referred, in their long intimate correspondence, to 15 June as the day which had changed and altered their lives.

A few days after this meeting, Guizot was writing to her saying that he would never rest content until he had lifted the veil of sadness from her eyes, and been able to overcome the grief in her soul. He likened his feelings towards her as being similar to Raleigh's cloak, but for him the cloak would always have to be under her feet protecting her from hurt. He wanted to pour into her soul a refreshing perfume, and to revive her spirit.

It is easy to laugh at the love letters of others. The spectacle of a widower of fifty writing in highfaluting terms to a sad lady of the same age is comical to some. Lytton Strachey found it extremely funny, and remarked in his sketch of the Princess Lieven that 'on reading these letters one did not know whether to laugh or to cry'. For obvious reasons, the childless and wifeless Lytton Strachey could not feel for two people who had lost their best-loved children, their stake in the future. They were both worldly people: Guizot had his political and literary ambitions, and Darja was determined to get back the social status and influence which she had previously enjoyed. Yet at the heart's core they were themselves unhappy children seeking comfort, and knowing that each had the need to speak truthfully to someone without the necessity to hide their true feelings of discomfort, unhappiness – and perhaps simplicity.

214

Only ten days after their meeting at the dinner party, they were again together, this time at the house of the Countess de Boigne at Chatenay. After dinner they had walked in the Park, and had exchanged vows of love and fidelity, a promise to remain together for all eternity and to pledge to one another *un éternel adieu* – a farewell that would live forever. And with this eternal adieu they were to sign their letters and hurried notes for over more than twenty years.

The following month the Princess left for England. She had planned this visit before her momentous meeting with Guizot, but his letters comforted her on the journey. From Abbeville she had written him a happy incoherent letter and in reply he had expressed his sentiments about true love, the love which he felt himself to have found in her. He despised so-called romances. True love, true admiration, and true devotion were very rare; 'that is why people who know nothing about it call it romantic'. He felt that when real devotion exists it was quite simple, quite positive, and quite practical. But one must not deceive oneself and take fantasies for love. These are mere marsh lights which fly through the air giving the impression of being stars, but the stars themselves are not less strong and distant because other comets appear and disappear briefly in the sky below them.

They wrote to one another, impatiently, almost frenetically, like two young people in love for the first time. If the post was late he was frantic, if he had neglected to write or missed the post she was overcome with grief, and yet when they received the letters the pair were full of such profound joy, they could hardly express themselves.

She wrote from London that although she was happy to be there, she could not sleep.

I heard the clock of St. James's chiming all the half-hours. My soul was so agitated, I got up and I came to you – to write to you. I wrote you a very boring letter about my doings yesterday. I did not dare to let my feelings get the better of me, and to have the pleasure of describing my real sensations ... I would say too little, I might say too much. Before I got on to the boat yesterday, I threw myself on my knees, I prayed to God. I had so often asked him to let me die. Yesterday I asked him to let me live, to let me live, to let me keep the love which I had found. There was such confusion, such passion, such sadness – and yet such sweetness in my prayer.

215

From the boat she had gazed at the retreating coast of France, the France that was now her whole horizon.

On 29 July Guizot wrote from Val-Richer, his country house in Normandy, that it was his turn to wait, and to be cast down in waiting, for a letter. A few months ago he had not felt like this. They had met and now everything was different. In a day, in an hour, they had learned more about one another than many people do in a whole lifetime. Yet everything which they had not known, they had immediately *felt*, and when they had expressed their feelings it was something they had always known, and had always felt.

In a long letter he went on to describe his ambitions, and then, suddenly, he managed to convey the truth about their relationship as it would be. She was of the same nature as himself, politics were her passion but like him there was something else she needed. She had different feelings underneath, as he had himself. A deep need to be understood.

In fact you seemed to me to be a person who would understand and pluck out of my soul both the surface, and that which is hidden, that which is for the whole world, and that which is for one person only in the world. That is why, Madame, you have such a strong attraction for me, that is why by instinct as by choice so quickly and suddenly I felt this. I cannot be deceived – I am *not* deceived am I? I am firm, absolutely firm in this belief. With each action, and with each word you reveal yourself to me just as you are, just as I know you to be. Each step I take along this pleasant and enchanting path, I am overcome with joy, as if I had discovered my one great treasure. Let your letters arrive soon. I have only had one to add to my rapture and my faith....

He was overjoyed at being linked to so noble a being, both overjoyed and proud.

Again it is easy to smile, but both Darja and François Guizot himself were children of the romantic movement, their sentiments were of necessity expressed in terms of heightened emotion. Yet it is an emotion which still springs from the page with love and with truth. When she had been to church, she wrote afterwards to Guizot saying that it seemed to her that she had prayed – in some sort of fashion, and the image of God and François had fused, so that when she came out of church she felt she was leaving 'your house, but without leaving you. I shall never leave you, Monsieur!

I feel that I can tell you everything because you alone are capable of understanding my soul.'

Even when she was having an audience with Queen Victoria she wrote that she was still thinking of him. She had found the Queen very charming, pretty, really, pretty with a childlike air. She seemed to have a countenance which was at one and the same time intelligent and sweet, yet with an open expression. It was a miracle that such a young girl, only eighteen, had so much aplomb, curiosity, and interest in affairs. From the day she had ascended the throne she had cast aside all her habits, and childish affections, and had made herself into a *man* in the space of a single hour. She understood everything, was engaged in everything, and seemed to have a real spirit of command, and even to instil fear 'which the old Kings who went before her never did'. It was a shrewd assessment of character, of a young woman who had seized the reins of power with pleasure and avidity, from a woman who had long been conversant with men and affairs.

Towards herself, the Princess admitted, the Queen seemed somewhat reserved, and chatted of nothing in particular. This was not surprising. Uncle Leopold, the former friend and intimate of Princess Lieven, had been bombarding his niece with letters warning Queen Victoria against the Princess. She was an intriguer, a dangerous woman: 'a rule which I cannot sufficiently recommend is never to permit people to speak on subjects concerning yourself or your affairs; should such a thing occur change the conversation, and make the individual feel he has made a mistake.'

This was precisely what the Queen did when the Princess attempted to chat on topics which ranged beyond small talk. It was a different reign, and a different dynasty, the old easy chats at the 'Cottage', with the King, happy with his fat mistress, had gone. Darja waxed lyrical about the Queen. She had charming shoulders, a little waist encircled with the Garter, and the motto of the Order round her arm, and such an air of dignity! 'This Court is so different from those I knew for twenty-two years.'

But although the Princess was away, some of her troubles pursued her. Suddenly, while she was in London, Bonsi wrote to her saying that he was going to take the cure in Baden, and from there he proposed to spend the winter in Italy. She could not, of course, go with him on the journey, but he was quite willing to meet her as he wished to see her, and no doubt she could decide on a town where she could join him. He gave this letter to Count Orloff, who happened to be going to London, charging him to impress on the Princess the absolute necessity of their meeting. But as soon as the Count met Darja, she was able to make her husband's messenger feel that she was incapable of undertaking such a journey. Even journeying from Paris to London had adversely affected her health.

The Count was quite firmly and convincingly on her side: 'It is for him to come to *you*,' he said, 'and not for you to go to meet him. Give him a rendezvous either at Le Havre or Dieppe.'

Darja took the Count's advice, and wrote to her husband to this effect. She then set out for Paris, but on the way, fell ill and suffered a violent haemorrhage. For some days she hovered between life and death. After a week, she managed to take the road again, but when she reached Paris, she was in a state of total exhaustion. This was not improved by a letter from Bonsi ordering her to leave Paris at once, and adding a vague threat: 'I demand a firm answer, because I myself am obliged to take any delay into account when I consider steps which I will have to take as a consequence of a refusal on your part.'

The Tsar was speaking, and his mouthpiece, Bonsi, was echoing the thoughts of the all-powerful Tsar. Darja wrote again, quoting the opinion not only of her doctors, but also the advice of Count Orloff which she had taken. But she was whispering in a storm. Bonsi now had the courage of the Tsar's convictions.

'My letters have left you with no doubts, I hope, that I *insist* on your rejoining me. I have made it quite clear that in the case of your refusal I will be obliged to take measures which are repugnant to me. I declare quite categorically today that if you do not come, I shall take away your income. I must also make it clear to you that if I do not receive a reply in three weeks, I shall be obliged to act, as if you *had* given me your refusal.'

What he did not say was that the Tsar had refused him permission to see his wife. But Darja, in spite of being ill and alarmed, did not lose hope. It was quite clear that she was unable to leave Paris because of her health, and she consulted her friends as to how she should proceed: she spoke to de Medem, the Russian Ambassador to France, Lady Granville, the English Ambassadress, and of course, to Guizot. As a result of all these consultations, she wrote to Count Nesselrode, and to Count Orloff, imploring them to mitigate the harshness of the decisions of which she felt herself to be the victim.

To Count Orloff, she expressed her anger. Her husband had threatened to leave her without a sou, and not only that, he had made it quite clear that, living or dead, she must return to Russia:

My dear Count, it is impossible, and I will never believe it, that the Emperor wills or sanctions this. A vague word on his part

218

would seem to M. Lieven an absolute order, and his total obedience would make him liable – by an error of judgement – to try to force me to do his will: this is not only a blunder, but it is unworthy of him, and certainly unworthy of the Tsar. No, the Tsar would never stoop to prescribe to my husband such conduct towards his wife; and the Tsar, that model husband, would never be the cause of dispute in a household united by thirty-seven years of habit.

In the same letter, she added that she was not, after all, an obscure person, she still lived in the great world, and this way of behaving on the part of her husband was hardly to be regarded by herself, or anyone else, as the action of a gentleman.

She wrote frantically to her brother, recalling the past, when they had been of one mind. 'Do you remember when we were driving in your drojki in '33 at Peterhof, when you spoke to me of my husband, you said: "If ever your husband threatens you, refer him to me; I am there to protect you." The moment has come! Protect me!'

She went on to emphasise that she would not yield; to go back to Russia would mean her death. 'I am not going to give my husband the shameful satisfaction of being able to go to the Tsar to say, "Sire, I have obeyed you. My wife is dead!"'

The letter ended with another threat to appeal to public opinion. People would be on her side, they would help her. Everyone could see the injustice to which she was being subjected. She would not suffer a persecution which she had in no way merited.

In the middle of these dramatic exchanges, her son Alexander arrived in Paris, with messages from Bonsi to impress on his mother that it was indeed the will of the Tsar which Bonsi had expressed. Young Alexander had further orders to bring his mother back with him; but when he saw her, and had consulted her doctor, he realised that what she had written was the truth. She was very ill. Seeing the state she was in, Alexander immediately changed his views, and counselled his mother to resist.

Darja wrote another despairing letter to her husband. She pleaded that her views should be put to the Tsar. The Tsar must be made to realise that it was not possible to fulfil his wishes to the letter, as Bonsi was trying to do. She demanded justice! Her courage would not fail, and her spirit would not flinch even in a situation which had never happened before to a woman like herself. Only her heart was full of misgivings because she was forced to doubt his feelings. 'Leave me at least your affection.' In her heart the long years of her marriage had left some residue of love – six children, and all those years. She had been faithful, in her fashion. She did not deserve such cruelty.

But no reply came from Bonsi, and her brother Alexander, those affectionate drives in his drojki forgotten, sent an unsatisfactory answer. The Tsar suspected her of beginning a political salon. Perhaps the All-Highest and his faithful Chief of Secret Police, brother Alexander, suspected that the salon could be the base of anti-Russian propaganda?

Again she wrote a frantic denial reiterating all her old arguments about her health, her doctors, the retired life she led, and she became very indignant at the idea of a political salon.

Political salon? She occasionally received outstanding men of all political colours, and all parties, and only five Frenchmen who were her friends, her intimates. What had she to do with politics? She was absolutely cut off from all that. With M. Guizot for example, it was of religion they spoke. 'He has gone through similiar tragedies to my own, even greater. He is Lutheran, like myself, a man of the highest morality, and his friendship with me, and our conversations have helped me more than any distractions could have done.' Who did she see – their own Russian Ambassador, some few English people, a few Austrians who happened to be in Paris. Was this a political salon? Was she to be denied the solace of a few friends?

But the crux of the matter was not the exercise of the Imperial will on the craven heart of Bonsi: it came in a chilling letter from brother Alexander to Darja. 'You should not be surprised, after so many years of superiority over him, that he should not seek to revenge himself.' It was there in the open, clearly stated – revenge.

The worm Bonsi had turned at last.

Darja wrote again, more in sorrow than in anger. What, she asked her brother, was this superiority which she had exercised over her husband? 'This superiority – I did in fact exercise for many long years to his *own* use and service, and now that he can no longer make use of it, he wishes to punish me.'

She was affronted. This was a new excess of injustice. 'To end, my dear brother,' she wrote, 'I have nothing to reproach myself with as far as my husband is concerned. However harsh the storms of our life have raged, our unhappiness has always brought us together.' Had her letters to Bonsi not always been tender and affectionate? It is her husband who is guilty of a grave wrong, showing no heart and no pity for her, his wife.

'You, you have always been to me exactly what I expressed when we walked down the staircase of that sad Hotel Ostermann for the last time, in that crushing moment when I got into the carriage to follow the coffin of one of my children, and to precede the other. You have been for me a father, a brother, a husband. You always will be, won't you?'

It was a sentence which breathed gratitude and family affection. Bonsi was the choice of the Court and her family, a suitable husband, and she had brought him a suitable marriage portion. To her brother she had given not only the affection of her girl's heart, but the long years of devotion of a woman. That surely could not fail her.

But Bonsi had not given up ingratiating himself with the Tsar. The Prince Lieven was *en voyage* and had reached Naples from where he wrote to the All-Highest.

It is very painful to me, Sire, not to be able to announce to Your Majesty an equally satisfactory result on the second point which She [presumably the Tsarina] confided to my care. Nevertheless, I beg you, Sire, to believe that I have neglected no means of persuasion which I could use on my wife; that my entreaties have been repeated, and even followed up by harsher measures to which our thirty-seven years of marriage have never before been subjected. She was anxious that your Imperial Majesty should be made aware of the reasons why she could not comply with the orders which had been transmitted through me. Relying on her upright character as much as on her constant attachment, I am reluctant to doubt her protestations, or to believe that she has not done everything she possibly can to obey two wills which are so sacred in her eyes.

Two wills – the will of her faltering husband, and the will of her implacable Tsar. She defied them both. She stayed in Paris.

Bonsi's letters had been written at the end of 1837. But unknown to him, there were other thoughts in Darja's mind and other reasons besides her health which made her so resolute in her defiance.

On 6 August she had arrived at Boulogne and had immediately written to Guizot. Her health was a little better, but she had slept badly because she wanted to express to him the thousands of thoughts in her heart. 'My meeting with my husband! You cannot begin to understand how that idea upsets me.' For two years she had never ceased asking Bonsi to come to her. She had pressed on him that the most earnest desire of her soul was to see him, and when she had written urging him to rejoin her, she had indeed *felt* this tenderness towards him. 'I thought it, and I felt it, because I never say anything unless I feel it.'

221

And now what kind of welcome could she give him – her husband? These were the thoughts which were wounding her to the heart. All she could think of now was one thing – to get back to France, the source of her happiness. 'I have dared everything to come back. I am here today and my situation vis-à-vis M. Lieven comes before my eyes in all its horror. Horror – yes, Monsieur, horror that is the word.' Guizot had lifted her up and cured her, and for the very same reason she was more unhappy. Did he understand what she was trying to say, but of course he did, he could penetrate into every feeling of her heart. 'That is my joy and my triumph! My thoughts stifle me. How can I continue to live in the state in which I am? I tremble from head to foot. I have terrible moments – and yet it is so sweet – so sweet!'

But there were other less agreeable moments. A month after this *cri de coeur* came a letter from Guizot. Had she seen the article in *Le Temps*?

Under its political chronicles *Le Temps* of 18 September 1837 regaled its readers with some interesting chat. Headed *An Amorous Doctrinaire*, the paragraph ran:

Do you know which path the severe Calvinist is taking to gain power? Do you know what the great orator of what M. Royer Collard has been pleased to call – austere politics – has been doing – guess! I will give you a thousand guesses. He is in love! In love with whom? In love with a very seductive person, clever, witty, and very well-known, a lady of rank, who is a princess, something more than a princess – a real power in the diplomatic field. But in spite of the charms of the object of his love which could have attracted him, the love of a puritan doctrinaire – I hesitate to destroy an illusion – seems more like a political calculation. But in spite of everything he seems to be enjoying his role of *cicisbeo* to his Chancery Goddess. She had some little illness, and he passed all his days seated at the bedside of the beautiful convalescent; reading improving books, and even being so tactful as not to read her a certain history of England. It is true that this love affair has entirely changed the political views of the suitor.

Guizot was incensed. Had Darja ever heard such infamy put about? In spite of all their precautions, he had not dared to hope that her name would never appear in the newspapers, but he had never thought it would be from the source from which it came. He mentioned Madame Emile de Girardin who had been spending an evening with the Duke and Duchess of Sutherland. Some people steal purses, and some people steal names and anecdotes, whether true or false. Darja herself was equally indignant, she could not sleep. Was this the beginning of a new persecution? Could it be that M. Molé wanted to force her to leave France? There were other aspects of the affair which upset her. Did Guizot believe that the Tsar would permit her name to be mixed up with petty French political intrigues? Would she expose herself to such things? What would it look like in the great world to which she belonged?

'In my country, Monsieur, I am a very great lady, by virtue of my standing in the Palace, and even more because I am the only lady in the Empire who can be counted as living in familiarity with the Imperial family. I *belong* to the family, that is my social position at St. Petersburg and why the anger of the Tsar is so great to see a revolutionary country (like France) *honoured* by my presence. Monsieur, don't laugh, I have a great desire to laugh myself, but it is in deadly earnest. With the Tsar's ideas imagine what he will say when such gossip from a petty journalist reaches his ears?'

She had begun to realise that whatever sweet and charming thoughts her relationship with Guizot gave to her soul, it had its disadvantages, and, at the centre of her being, in spite of everything that had happened to her, she remained a Russian aristocrat, and a Russian patriot. Those two things at least she could never forget.

It was not only the French political gossips who suspected her. Her old friend and lover Prince Metternich had not forgotten her either. He wrote to his Ambassador in Paris: 'I am surprised that you never mention the Prince de Talleyrand nor the Count Pozzo di Borgo, nor the Princess de Lieven in your despatches... She will be stirring in some direction or another, because it is not in her nature to rest quiet.' Charles Greville noted that the Princess seemed to have settled herself into an agreeable social position. It seemed to him that the presence of the Princess in Paris in the conditions in which she found herself could not fail to be useful to her Court; 'a woman like herself could always glean information which could prove useful and interesting to her country'.

No one was willing to believe that she had broken with her Tsar.

Lady Granville saw the Princess almost every day and she wrote to her sister, Lady Carlisle, that Princess Lieven was looking beautiful, and in great spirits. She always had company, and she was able to defend herself against bores – she simply crushed them. Harriet Granville assured her sister that the Princess was more interesting, amusing and agreeable than she could possibly describe. She was full of chat about those people whom she liked, and gossip about those whom she disliked. 'This revives Paris in a dead and desert season.'

It was a quick appraisal of the reasons for the Princess's charm – worldly and amusing, she was amused by everything in her world – politics, love affairs, relations, Court affairs, anything and everything was interesting to her. 'I am amused by people as much as by the things which are going on', she remarked about herself.

Two years after her retreat from Russia she was rehabilitated. There was only one disadvantage – nobody trusted her. The Tsar turned to her a face of stone. To the English she was a Russian spy. To the French she seemed to be a symbol of reaction. To the Austrian Chancellor a mere Russian spy who was of no further use. To her husband a business partner who had broken her contract. To the world she showed a smiling elegant face, only to Guizot was she able to express her real feelings. In July of 1838 she wrote to him after a brief separation. 'How time will hang heavy on my hands. I am cast down even before we have separated, and I feel like weeping twenty times a day. I am utterly forlorn – it seems as if it were a year since I saw you. Give me strength!'

She contrasted her situation with that of her friend and lover – he had his work, his family, his country house at Val-Richer, his interests, his political ambitions – she was alone!

He wrote in reply, soothingly: 'Remember that the first words which united us, truly united us were "You are no longer alone".' He tried to make her believe it, and it was the sole consolation of her inner life.

She had moved out of her apartments in the Hôtel de la Terrasse into the Hôtel de Talleyrand in the rue Saint-Florentin where she had rented a whole floor. Her bedroom was the one in which Talleyrand had died. The Duchesse de Dino, his niece, was extremely indignant. 'Unless the Princess becomes ill I shall never go into a room in which I have suffered so much.' But Darja was happy, she was engaged with upholsterers; she was arranging everything so that she could have a permanent 'home' as she called it – and a background for Guizot to receive his political friends, for it was as much for him, as for her, that the habitués called at the rue Saint-Florentin.

Bonsi was still interfering in her life, even so far as his sons were concerned. Guizot wrote: 'Make sure that Alexander does not yield on the subject of the religions of the sons – if the idea of his marriage is renewed. The future of your sons worries me. Their situation is very delicate. Their father will do nothing for them, but they must not themselves give him any *reason* for refusing to help them. What a country where well-born capable young men have the sole idea – at thirty years old – to *leave* the public service!' He contrasted Russia with Europe. He himself would always prefer the West!

Darja was still unsure of her own situation. She had spoken to Medem, the Russian Ambassador, who had recently seen her son. There was now absolutely no doubt that the silence of her husband was on the express orders of the Tsar, and yet she did not think that her brother was in the Tsar's confidence. What could she do? Her sole comfort was the fact that Guizot loved her, and she would always need his *douces paroles*.

Although he loved her, he could see her imperfections, which only made him love her more. Her greatest fault was to take pleasure only in something which was totally perfect. 'When I see you proudly and disdainfully reject anything or anyone who is mediocre, or slow, or cold, insufficient, or muddled, everything which bears witness to the imperfections of this world, I love you ten times more. And then when I see you sad and bored, I wish that you were easier in your relationships, and less difficult. No, I am lying, stay as you are, even if you have to suffer. I would infinitely prefer it.'

There was only one thing which he would wish for her – if she could develop leanings to reading or writing, and exercising a taste for solitary and reflective thought, she would perhaps lose nothing, and perhaps even feel better: 'But you only like *people*.'

It was as if she could only live when she was in the presence of others, solitude was a cause of alarm, and a descent into despondency. But she still had many causes for her despondency. In 1839 her son Constantine who had always given her so many causes for anxiety went to America. She wrote to him, and some months later, the letter came back with one word on the back: 'Mort.'

Bonsi had remained firm to his promise to the Tsar to make his wife return to Russia or reject her entirely – he had never even informed his wife of the death of their son.

On 17 November she wrote to Lord Aberdeen. 'I would have replied to your letter earlier but this sad note announces to you that I have been struck by a new misfortune – I have learned, without being prepared for it, and in the most barbarous manner, that my third son, Constantine, is no longer on this earth. Merely by the return of a letter which I wrote to him and which has been sent back to me by my banker in Petersburg, I learn that he died in the month of June, and that his father knew of it in July, deliberately leaving his brothers, and myself in total ignorance of his fate! Milord, it is a barbarous country which forces a husband and father to treat his wife and children in such a fashion.'

To Guizot she wrote: 'What a country! What a master! What a father! I tremble when I look ahead and think of the future of my children.'

Her husband had been going out in society, he had been seeing people who knew them both, and yet he had never given the slightest sign of mourning, and Bonsi had not written to tell her of the boy's death – merely because she was out of favour with the Tsar. The dear and cherished Emperor had now shown an entirely different face. What was to become of her sons in such a country?

In the autumn of 1838, Bonsi himself was ill and had gone to Italy to recuperate in a warmer climate. Mutual English acquaintances spoke to him about his treatment of his wife. Lady Granville wrote to her brother in Rome that she considered 'Vraiment' to have behaved shamefully. It was fairly certain that Harriet Granville must have known of the true reasons for Darja's refusal to return to Russia, but she also knew that the climate and the sharp, tragic memory of the death of her sons were also reasons why Princess Lieven refused to go back. In the aristocratic circles in which the Princess moved, infidelities were accepted, but not acknowledged, and differences were condoned even if they were not forgiven. 'Vraiment' had shown himself to be more a Russian than a gentleman.

Whether as a result of these representations, or because he had again fallen ill, Bonsi did at last write to his wife. The letter only reached her after his death. Written in December of 1838, it showed that his true feelings had returned to him, and, as Darja wrote to Lord Aberdeen: 'I thank God that his last thoughts were tender towards me. I mourn him with less bitterness, and can weep sincerely for his loss. We passed our life together, I only knew life with him – married at fourteen, thirty-eight years together – the joys and griefs of life, we shared them all. Everything is finished, there is nothing but destruction around me.'

Her English friends in Paris gave her sympathy and solace. Harriet Granville invited her to the British Embassy. There was no doubt, she wrote to her sister Lady Carlisle, that the Princess felt her husband's death really sincerely. 'Much more than those who do not see her in these moments, when all is laid open, would ever believe her to be capable of. Tenderness for whatever called for it in the past, forgetfulness of every cloud, on her knees in torrents of tears, hoping that she had not often given offence, or failed in kindness. . . .'

Then the shrewd Lady Granville noticed that the Princess's mood would suddenly change and she could be diverted by some piece of news or gossip. She was indeed a creature of swift changes of feeling as she showed herself in all her spiritual *déshabille* with Guizot. She gives the impression of a changeable day in spring which promises sunshine, and suddenly black clouds shroud the sun, and the day ends with claps of thunder and lightning. It is a character of volatility carried to its ultimate. If only, as Guizot had said, she had some reflective occupation.

From the Tsar and Tsarina came no word of condolence. Her brother Alexander, Counsellor of the Tsar, was as unforgiving as his master and controller.

'I had a letter from my brother,' Darja wrote to Guizot on 2 March 1839. 'He had received my two letters. A reproachful one, and the other one which I wrote *after* the death of my husband. His letter to me, alas, contains nothing but reproaches that I will not return to Russia.' She had written a reply, but she wanted to show it to Guizot before she sent it off. Alexander, however much she thought of him as her brother, was no longer the man she had known in the past. He had merely carried out the Imperial orders. He had even censored Pushkin's drama *Boris Godunov* and advised him to turn it into something more along the lines of the romances of Walter Scott! Darja could no longer look to her brother for protection.

Perhaps in living so long in Europe, away from the atmosphere of Russia, and the steel hand of the Tsar, she had forgotten the lack of freedom of action, or even freedom of thought.

Meanwhile she set off for a cure at Baden. She re-read Guizot's letter, sitting near an old castle, on a beautiful mountain, in the middle of ruins, of rocks and magnificent pines – she stopped drinking asses' milk and began her course of baths again. She had seen Madame Nesselrode, and they had talked about Bonsi's will, which was apparently missing. She hoped that there would be no difficulties with Paul, but the atmosphere in St. Petersburg seemed to have poisoned her son's spirits. Her sons had been received by the Tsar and Tsarina, they had even passed a whole evening *en famille* with them. The Tsar had behaved towards Paul and Alexander as if they were close relations. He had assured them that they were close to him, and that these feelings would always exist between them. 'In short it is as it should be, but as I never dared to hope. But Alexander contrives to slip in a sentence to let me know that the Emperor continues to be displeased with me. You can see that there will be no question of a pension.'

There were other difficulties about money, which bore out the old saying that it is impossible to know anyone until you share an inheritance with them.

Darja wrote to her brother complaining that she had been asked to sign an official paper which had the effect of handing over the property which Bonsi had left in England to Alexander. She complained that she had signed it in a hurry not being able totally to understand what its implications were in English law. The upshot of her letter was that she was being cheated of property which should legally have been hers. Again Alexander wrote a chilling reply. 'You should not be surprised – Paul has exactly the same attitude to money as you have yourself.'

Admittedly the Princess had always been extravagant which had often annoyed Bonsi, who no doubt had the same careful attitude towards money as he had towards kowtowing to the Tsar, but there is no evidence that she was mean or grasping. Alexander, unable to force his sister into complying with the Tsar's commands, was perhaps wielding the financial knout as Bonsi had tried to do. It was all to no avail.

She did have a letter from the Tsarevitch, the *Prince Héritier*, who wrote (very tactfully) from London, where his letters were not under surveillance. He expressed his sincere sorrow at the 'circumstances' which prevented their meeting. It was, commented Darja, a poor letter, but it was a souvenir, and all that he dared to do. The eyes and ears of the Tsar, like the modern Russian communist party, were everywhere.

The *Prince Héritier* formally thanked 'the widow of the Prince de Lieven' for all the friendship which her dead husband had always shown him, and which he sincerely appreciated. The Princess swallowed her pride and wrote a reply couched in the grovelling language suitable for an *Altesse* adding that 'his were the first and most precious words which she had received for many years'.

It did not make any difference. To Darja her native land had turned a face carved from ice.

She was never to go back to Russia, nor to see the adored Tsar again. She settled into her apartments in the rue Saint-Florentin and, with a few breaks for cures or holidays, there she was to stay for the rest of her life.

Paris, as so often, had welcomed an exile and made much of her.

CHAPTER SIXTEEN

Twenty years of love and happiness

Bonsi died in January 1839. Darja managed to obtain a small income from the remains of his estate. She was not treated with generosity, but at least she had saved something from the wreck of the past, and she was making a new life for herself, and spinning a web of new interests. She was not *tranquille*, as Metternich suspected, but she had friends, interests, and a faithful lover.

A good deal of quiet fun has been drawn from the relationship of the pedagogue François Guizot and the great Russian aristocrat, but if their letters to one another are read with attention one cannot fail to feel a deep well of sympathy and real humanity which flows from these sometimes exaggerated effusions. The sentiments may seem to the modern reader to be over-expressed and perhaps over-written, but the real feelings shine through the mists of the past.

They kept their anniversaries, 15 June, the day they had met, a very special day for them. They sent one another gifts, carefully thought-out gifts on each New Year's Day. In 1841 he sent her a comedy, a flower, and a bible. She wrote thanking him for his little letter, and the gifts – the camellia was especially superb. There was so much she wanted to say to him, she had dreamed, and she had thought about him, but it was hard to put down her feelings. He wrote more clearly, more expressively – there were two charming things in this world, the pleasures which stemmed from old habits, these were steady and reassuring, and there were the unexpected pleasures – he wanted to give her both of these. He longed to see her happy, always happy.

Every now and again they sprinkled their letters with odd English phrases. Something was a 'God send', they would be together 'till death do us part'. She was his 'dearest, ever dearest'. It was as if the sincerity of their feelings had to be expressed and sealed in two languages. These letters were their interior life – something which was necessary to both of them, necessary for survival. On the surface they lived a worldly and political life, but underneath it ran the comforting love which gave them a hold on life which had struck both of them with so many bitter blows.

Guizot was right, their love for one another was not a marsh light, it was a fixed and steady thing in both their lives.

Captain Gronow, the ex-military dandy with a dyed moustache and club-man's manners who had made his home in Paris for many years, drew a quick sketch of Guizot in his public capacity both as a lecturer and a politician.

M. Guizot, when he commenced his lectures on public history at the Sorbonne, appeared like a luminous meteor on the political horizon. The expression of his views of ancient literature, the energy and the dignity with which he explained to his admiring audience, the philosophy and the religion of Rome and Greece ... the crowded hall was filled with impatient students awaiting the presence of their much loved professor, who with difficulty threaded his way, amid immense applause, with a slow and solemn step, to the chair of the professor. He poured forth, at first slowly, in a continued flow of elegant language, eulogiums upon the great writers in his own language, and then, with an impetuosity that seemed to convey an electric impetus – his face at first sombre and inexpressive, lighted up with supernatural animation; and as he gazed around, he inspired each of his auditors with the conviction that he was listening to a being of a superior order.

It is a description which gives a faint reflection of the attraction which Guizot had for the Princess Lieven. Like an actress who senses the changing feelings of her audience, and finds a playwright to express them, so Darja had sensed the changed feelings in the world around her, and had found a man who expressed those feelings.

Captain Gronow also partially explained why Guizot was not universally popular in the Chamber. 'In the Assembly M. Guizot spoke in a different style from how he did at the Sorbonne; and it was somewhat difficult to define the emotion that predominated in him; no sense either of triumph or defeat was apparent. Cold, sombre, meditative, he spoke with authority, and it was only at rare intervals that any great animation was visible in his countenance.'

But when the Princess first became close to Guizot, he was one of the coming men, and she had chosen correctly.

Balzac has drawn a joint portrait of Guizot and the Princess in his short novella *Les Secrets de la Princesse de Cadignan*. He describes her apartments on the ground floor of an hotel where she lived, modestly surrounded by portraits of her old, illustrious, princely and aristocratic lovers. He draws a picture of her modest retired way of life, and with a novelist's *legerdemain* he carefully makes her nearly twenty years younger than she was at the time of her meeting with Guizot. Guizot becomes the distinguished Daniel d'Arthez, 'one of those rare souls who joins a noble character with an outstanding talent'. A poor man who had made his way up in the world of politics without changing the ancient simplicity of his way of life. Yet the circumstances of the meeting of the fictional Guizot with the fictional Princess are superimposed on a plot about one worldly woman amusing herself by deliberately choosing a lover for another. The Princess in the story is a woman who has had many lovers, but has never loved anyone, and the Daniel who is thrown into the lioness's den is the noble character who is going to unlock the heart of the Snow Princess. 'She managed to regain a little-girl innocence and yet at the same time retain a feeling which was at one and the same time, august, noble, and with a queenly air. It is impossible to describe the effect of this strategy on the open and frank character of d'Arthez.'

Although Balzac touched on the fringe of truth, he left aside the real tug of tragedy which had brought two such dissimilar souls together.

After Bonsi's death the idea of marriage hovered in the air. To carry on a long running *affaire de coeur* was second nature to Darja: she had been born and bred to intrigues both political and amatory. To the Calvinist-bred Guizot, it was all new and strange. There is some evidence to suggest that he had suggested marriage, and that the Princess had recoiled from the idea. A friend once said to her: 'There is a rumour that you are going to marry M. Guizot', but the Princess merely laughed. 'Could you see me', she is supposed to have replied, 'being announced as Madame Guizot?' As she had written to Guizot himself: 'In Russia I am a great lady and received as one of the Tsar's family.' The Tsar might have totally rejected her, but her ideas of being a *grande dame* remained, and much as she was drawn into the net of the soothing love of Monsieur Guizot she would never have become Madame Guizot.

But some time in 1840 she acquired a little house at Passy which she called Beauséjour, and here she would pass the summer months, and Guizot would visit her. Here she would wait for him, longing for his coming, and here they would enjoy some hours of quiet happiness. She wrote that she longed for 'la paix du cottage', for tranquillity, and for his love. Marriage for her, as for many

231

Russians, was not a matter of love, it was a matter of family politics. Her experience of marriage had not been happy, and perhaps at the back of her mind she had the good sense to see that the little everyday difficulties of living would spoil something which still kept the freshness of that first day, 15 June. Beauséjour was their 'home' as they called it. Why spoil an idyll by trying to capture it? The idyll was the butterfly in the sun, to net it and pin it in a case would be to destroy its essence. Far better to sigh, to dream, and to await one's *bien aimé* at Beauséjour.

There were, naturally, rumours of their relationship. Guizot always remained after the last guests had left. On one occasion a forgetful guest went back to retrieve something he had left behind and found that Guizot had already doffed the *Grand Cordon* of the *Légion d'Honneur*, which was hanging on a chair. Another anecdote makes the *femme de chambre* find it in Darja's bed. To read the three volumes of their letters makes it clear that theirs was a deeply passionate love which gradually became an equally deep and passionate friendship; like the best of marriages, it did not dwindle but increased in its necessity to the two partners.

So the Princess settled down, and, as she told Lord Aberdeen, lived as she used to do, 'receiving' every evening. Diplomats, English people, birds of passage, and French politicians – all were only too happy to meet on the common ground of her salon. The ups-and-downs of politics were made easier under her aegis. Even the path of political opponents was smoothed under her penetrating eye. Thiers and Guizot met in her drawing-room after four and a half years of political animosity. She wrote to Harriet Granville: 'They looked at one another – there was a moment of stupefaction. I burst out laughing, they decided to laugh with me, and they remained together chatting comfortably for an hour and a half, touching on all subjects; the ministerial situation, the parliamentary situation, the present, the future, and deciding that for France there is either Thiers, or Guizot, or Guizot or Thiers; all this with total freedom and independence, and no spirit of rancour. It was obviously a pleasure for both of them, and I was happily amused.'

This little sketch gives a feeling of the spirit of her salon, and why she drew so many men and women of different countries and parties to her. Nor did she lose her friends. She met her old friends in England from time to time, and when she did not see them she was in constant correspondence with them. She had correspondents everywhere in the country houses in England, in the châteaux of France, and when she took the waters at Baden-Baden she met Russians bringing back memories of her youth.

232

They were able to remain friendly once they were away from the inhibiting influences of their native soil, and the sharp eye of the Tsar's police. Whatever her faults, the Princess was a woman who made and kept friends.

As she grew older her *toilette* became more stereotyped. She no longer followed the fashion. Much to the distress of her friend Lady Palmerston, she had been forced to sell her diamonds. Now as she got older she no longer attracted by her youth, her beauty, or her wealth, yet she was still treated like a queen. She now wore a close bonnet of white lace, an almost nun-like *coiffe*, a dress of black velvet, her sole decoration was the cypher of the *Demoiselles d'Honneur* of the Tsarina of Russia.

There were occasional small squalls which ruffled the lake of her salon. At one point when Guizot resigned his office, and was suspected of organising a cabal against his erstwhile colleagues, the diplomatic corps became embarrassed that they should be seen in the company of a man known to be intriguing against the government. It is to be suspected that in some senses the Princess was gradually being lured back into the net of the Russians. Count Pahlen, the Russian Ambassador, who had succeeded Pozzo di Borgo in Paris, was deputed to tell the Princess that he could hardly frequent the Princess's salon in the rue Saint-Florentin if the offending and offensive Guizot were to be seen in his company. This message was duly conveyed to her. In her turn she explained the contretemps to Guizot who was angry. But he did agree to see the Princess at such times as would not embarrass the diplomatic corps.

But he had decided he would teach 'Messieurs les Ambassadeurs' a lesson. Up to that point in his career he had never been interested in foreign affairs, but now under the stress of the insult, he changed his stance. When, as is inevitable in politics, the government of M. Molé fell, and Marshal Soult became First Minister, Guizot was appointed to be French Ambassador in London. He had his revenge.

In late February of 1840 M. Guizot arrived at Calais *en route* for his appointment in London. He had, not unnaturally, been bombarded with advice from his Princess (and she continued to shower him with letters, weighted with her deep knowledge of England and the English during his ambassadorship). He took it all in good part. Her first letter had arrived at Calais and was awaiting him on the mantelpiece. 'An unhoped for pleasure, and yet a pleasure which had been hoped for!' Tomorrow he would be in the places she had loved, and where she had lived. That will be his consolation. She must not fall into imaginary terrors, it was enough

233

11 Princess Lieven in 1856 by G. F. Watts. She now wore a nun-like bonnet of white lace and a dress of black velvet

to have to combat tangible ills and existent fears They *will* be together again – in London – and together again, sitting on the green sofa in Paris. She must have courage.

In 1862 François Guizot published the story of his Embassy in London and conveyed his first feelings about the capital. As he approached the cold clear sun was extinguished by the vast fog which lay over the city. It was still day, but a day without light. 'London conveys the idea of unlimited space filled with men incessantly and silently displaying their activity and their power. And in the midst of this general greatness, the external neatness of the houses, the wide footpaths, the effect of the large panes of glass, of the iron balustrades and of the knockers on the doors impart to the city an air of careful attention and an attractive appearance which almost counterbalances the absence of good taste.'

The house in Manchester Square occupied by the Embassy in the time of François Guizot has now become the home of the Wallace Collection of French paintings and *objets d'art*. He found the city quiet, no one bothered him, he wrote: 'I am surrounded by a hive of bees who work without humming.'

But soon the buzzing commenced. He saw Lord Palmerston, the man who had effectively dismissed the Lievens. The son of Count Nesselrode had arrived from Moscow with instructions for the Russian Ambassador, Baron de Brünow. The past of his adored Darja was all around him. He was anxious to make a good impression on the Queen – Talleyrand had made a long harangue to William IV, on the other hand his successor Sebastiani had said nothing. What was he to do? Lord Palmerston was quite clear on this point: the Queen did not want to have to reply to *speeches*. His first interview with her had been somewhat marred by the fact that he had had only an hour's notice. Horses were called for hurriedly, and he had set off for 'Buckingham' and had to apologise to the Queen for the lateness of his arrival.

Guizot displayed touches of humour in his letters to Darja – the boredom of a dinner at the Palace, the long monotony of a levée with the English dressing up with robes, wigs and what he described as purses (which no one, not even in England, wore any more), and all this with a great air of seriousness. The Russian Ambassador had not called on him – the official explanation was that he had not yet presented his credentials to the Queen, and it was not *en règle* for him to call. Again it is to be suspected that the bad odour in which the Princess Lieven was held in St. Petersburg had something to do with this. Eventually, when M. de Brünow did call, he was full of excuses, amiable, and fluttering round, all civilities and charm.

Guizot's ambassadorship in London was considered to be a success. He met everyone, he was invited everywhere, and he was enjoying himself.

He had also had some minor diplomatic coups – in spite of not being a diplomat. The difficulties whirled round – the Eastern question, the Sublime Porte, the Pacha of Egypt – should the Allies get Russia to help them in the Middle East? Or would that do more harm than good? All these questions occupied the minds of both Guizot and Palmerston. Guizot took the view that if Russia once got a foothold she would not be dislodged: 'Who tells you that they will be able to retire promptly? Who tells you that the war, once launched in Syria will not continue longer than you may have foreseen? The Pacha has a considerable army … it is said he is organising an army to cross the desert and get into Palestine. They speak of five thousand camels engaged in this project …'

Whether it's tanks or camels, the Eastern question seems a fixed and ever present difficulty.

Guizot wrote that Palmerston acted and spoke sometimes lightly and sometimes rashly, which is possibly a fair judgement. The feelings of the French towards Palmerston's adventures were expressed by Guizot in a letter referring to English difficulties in China, and a possible small war in Sicily. 'It seems more than enough for this country, and at this time to have two wars on hand, one in China for Pills [the Opium war] and another at Naples for matches [a possible war over the sulphur monopoly].'

François Guizot had some knowledge of English, but very often as he admitted, he spoke French to people who were speaking English to him, which is a very comfortable way of carrying on a conversation with people who are conversant with both languages. He told Darja that, in spite of everything, he was making some progress in English – a duologue had few difficulties; he managed to follow in a trio or a quartet, and even in general conversation he could follow, but the accent! That he would never achieve.

He had made a few blunders and been soundly scolded for them by Darja. What did he mean going to dinner with Madame Maberly? She had an extremely bad reputation. 'Your position', wrote the Princess, 'demands more prudence.' Her husband would never have dreamed of demeaning himself by dining in such company. In fact, if anyone had said to *her* that he was dining chez Madame Maberly she would have immediately have known where to place *him*. It was possible that the Duke of Wellington might have done such a thing, but after all *he* had figured in the memoirs of Harriette Wilson! Guizot was all apologies and all innocence. How was he to know? He had seen Colonel Maberly in London.

'Remember,' she wrote, 'you are in a glass-house. Everything will be remarked upon. The English are infinitely more subtle than one imagines, and singularly observant and curious, while all the time having an air of seeing nothing.'

It was a shrewd remark which had been garnered by long years of making her own mistakes.

But as his social success increased her long-distance jealousy pursued him. He had mentioned some pretty young ladies he had seen at the Queen's ball, and this had upset her. He was all lover-like apologies. What a frightful thing it was – to be away from the loved one! 'What mad agitations, what absurd hurts we inflict on another!' In Paris, she was crying, she would be ashamed to tell him what she felt, how she walked across her terrace, and her tears were falling so that the passersby were looking at her.

He reassured her. They were together 'for better and for worse'. He remembered a charming quotation from his favourite puritan writer, John Newton: 'Since the Lord gave me the desire of my heart in my dearest Mary, the rest of the sex are no more to me than the tulips in the garden.' She had not the slightest cause for her fears.

But Thiers had been consulted. He had asked if Guizot was bored in London. She replied that on the contrary he seemed to be enjoying himself a great deal. 'Eh bien, you had better go over there – otherwise he will be unfaithful to you.'

This she decided to do. Love was a frail flower however strong it might seem. On 27 May she wrote for the first time without the formal 'vous'. 'Mon bien aimé, I have such a need to tell you again that I love you, and to hear your words of love in exchange! There I have written it ... but I will try to rein in my feelings and to tell you in person.'

By July she was in London, and they were together, and all thoughts of jealousy forgotten, they were reconciled. But London had so many sad memories for her. She remembered her lost sons and she was not happy there. Even in August the fog came down and she felt as sad as the weather. Guizot had gone to France to spend a holiday with his children at Trouville. 'I arrived in Trouville yesterday. The pleasure of my children is charming to see, I wish I could send one half of this happiness to you...'

There were successes and failures during Guizot's mission to London. The success of persuading the British government to allow the ceremonial return of Napoleon's ashes to Les Invalides, and the failure of the Eastern question.

A short while after Princess Lieven arrived in London, Palmerston had acted against the French. He signed the

Convention of London in which Great Britain, Russia, Austria and Prussia undertook to protect the Sultan against Egypt. France had benefited from the hostilities between the Sultan and Mehemet Ali, and had managed to possess herself of a few colonies in North Africa at the expense of the Ottoman Empire. Palmerston's counter-coup had annoyed the French. There was a serious risk of a war between England and France. Louis Philippe, whose position was far from secure, did not want a war. He dismissed Thiers in October of 1840, and recalled Guizot from London. Darja's *bien aimé* became Foreign Minister in the government of Marshal Soult. They were together again in Paris.

If Darja had not been happy in London, there were good reasons for this as she was afterwards to discover. In October of 1840 she wrote angrily to her brother that she had complied with his wishes when she was in London, and had told him that her letters from there would have some interest for him, which they had. Imagine her surprise when her two friends Lady Palmerston and Lady Clanricarde told her that M. de Brünow, the Russian Ambassador had said to their respective husbands: 'Be careful of Mme. de Lieven. Mme. de Lieven is *not* a Russian, she is an emissary of France, the slightest word which is said to her will go straight to the French Embassy.'

She had nothing to hide, she told her brother. M. Guizot was an eminent man of probity, and her relations with him were well known. She had noticed when she arrived in London that the *corps diplomatique* were acting very coldly towards her. Her indignation boiled over in a long letter. After so many years of devotion, so many proofs of her love for her Tsar – to be denounced and slandered by two old friends, two Cabinet Ministers of a foreign government! Did her brother know what she had said to Lady Palmerston and to Lady Clanricarde: 'The *Tsar* does not believe it, the Tsar will never believe it, because he knows *me*.' She had had a kind word from the Tsarina which had comforted her heart, but if her heart was appeased, her honour was outraged, de Brünow had stained the noble name which she bore, and had dishonoured her as a loyal subject of the Tsar. Whatever happened, however she was treated, and however badly the Tsar managed to get his loyal helots to behave, she went on believing in his nobility, and she went on giving her loyalty to him. Tsar (or Party) the Russian heart remained forever loyal and forever credulous. She added that a *dame d'honneur* of the Tsarina could not remain under the threat of such a calumny. It was on this count, and not on her own, that she demanded that Monsieur de Brünow retract what he had said, she must insist that he do this, or else she must have some action (presumably a letter) which would rehabilitate her reputation in the eyes of others. Something which would make it clear that she had never deserved odious suspicions to be cast on her name. 'I ask you sincerely to bring this letter to the attention of the Tsar himself,' she wrote.

There does not seem to exist any answer to this angry plea. But in spite of all the sufferings which the Tsar had inflicted on his loyal subject Darja, she believed in *him*, and she continued to write to the Tsarina. She chose the same way of corresponding which she had used with Metternich, the diplomatic bag under the cover of writing to the Countess de Nesselrode. These letters were received regularly by the Tsarina, and at breakfast time she would read them to the Tsar. After having heard the contents the Tsar would take the letters to his study, to re-read them, and use the information they conveyed. Darja did not conceal the fact that she was in constant correspondence with the Tsar, her Tsar, and his Court. Everyone in the *corps diplomatique* knew it. In fact she talked about it openly to prove that she was not a spy in the employ of the Russians as many of her ill-wishers held that she was. The Duc de Broglie remarked that she wished that her salon, where Guizot naturally held first place, should be open to either French or foreign politicians, either those who lived in Paris, or who were passing through, and could bring her news from countries beyond her salon. Her fascination was with news, gossip, and high politics, and she could not keep her nose out of what he called 'this manure heap of affairs'. The Duc de Broglie added, 'in spite of the benevolence which she showed me, my conversation seemed to be much more interesting to her on the day when my relations with the Minister of Foreign Affairs allowed me to bring information which she could not come by in any other way.'

This perhaps explained her influence over Guizot which operated sometimes to the profit of France. During the whole of the time that the July monarchy endured, Darja worked towards the strengthening of the Franco-British alliance.

In 1843 Guizot managed to persuade Queen Victoria to visit France. This was the crowning achievement of the Guizot Ministry, an attempt to calm the squalls which had blown up over the Eastern question in 1840 during his Embassy in London. Louis Philippe was generally looked down upon by the crowned heads of Europe. The Tsar considered him a usurper (odd considering how he had obtained his own Imperial crown); the King of Prussia, when travelling anywhere, managed to avoid Paris, and Metternich's sovereign of Austria considered him an intruder in the comity of crowned heads. Only the bourgeoise Queen Victoria

239

seemed to have things in common with the Citizen King. It was therefore planned in the summer of 1843 that the *entente cordiale* should be cemented by a visit by the English royal family to the French royal family at the Château d'Eu.

When the news of this visit reached Princess Lieven she was wild with joy. The diplomats in residence in Paris were decidedly put out at this piece of intelligence. The Austrian Ambassador, Apponyi, was openly contemptuous, calling the journey 'a little girl's fantasy'. Darja countered by saying that it was a fantasy that was accepted by the Foreign Ministers of both countries, and she added, with some point: 'I have been told that the diplomatic corps would be angry at this piece of news.' Count Apponyi reddened and denied that he was at all put out by it.

The Princess was living down at her small house Beauséjour in Passy, enjoying her lover's triumph and her peaceful 'vie du cottage'.

It was a far cry from Beauséjour – to the 'cottage' and the 'Cottage' at Windsor, the boating parties at Virginia Water, the two fat Princes and the bejewelled Marchioness. Times had not only changed, but the whole horizon had been transformed. The Princess was afraid that the Russians might act in a stupid way, and before she left for her holiday she spoke to one of them. 'Kisseleff came to see me yesterday before I left.' She told him quite bluntly that the whole of the diplomatic corps were behaving very foolishly, and it would be sensible on his part to see that the Russians behaved better. He admitted to the Princess that he had made a bet that the Queen would not come, but he now regretted it. In a schoolmistressy manner worthy of her knowledge and her past, the Princess advised him to 'regulate his language'. He decided to follow the line laid down by the Princess. When someone said to him that Queen Victoria was simply a 'petite fille en voyage', he replied, 'But a little girl who is a queen, and who arrives escorted by a strong fleet, and accompanied by her Foreign Minister. It is not a little girl, it is the government of England.' The next time the Princess met Kisseleff she congratulated him on his change of heart and expression. 'I praised him and told him to continue. When one has a little brain and influence this is how one should behave. I seriously wished to help Kisseleff.' In pointing out to him that his colleagues were fools, she had not only helped him, but her country.

She was avid for news of the visit, and demanded all the details from Guizot, which were duly conveyed. An English bed for the Queen; no carpets, as the parquet was so beautiful, far better than anything Her Majesty would see in in England. Porcelain, silver, furniture all being augmented from Paris. A beautiful carriage in the best possible taste to bring the Queen from Tréport, fortunately large enough to fit all the royal family. The only question mark was the weather. But at the last moment the mist lifted, and the sun shone on Eu with great brilliance. Everything was prepared. The bands had studied 'God Save the Queen', and a Saxon march for Prince Albert.

The details for the three-day entertainment caused a few headaches – should the two monarchs be allowed to take a little boat trip? Supposing a keen wind blew up, and they were unable to land on the shore again? That could be a cause for laughter. What kind of theatre entertainment did the Queen prefer? Something on the lines of a light opera, but not too light, it was better to be cautious. They finally decided on opera comique 'et le vaudeville *Jean de Paris, et les Deux Voleurs*'.

At last the great day arrived. The cannons announced that the Queen was in sight. The French King with his train of followers embarked to go by water, solemnly escorting the Queen of England into Tréport. Calm sea, blue sky, cries of the population, shouts from the sailors. Everyone full of emotion, and the Queen saying to Guizot: 'I am charmed to see you again.'

Then the solemn procession in the King's barge to the shore. Cheers, more emotion, 'les shake hands', and the journey *en calèche* to the château where the troops were drawn up to salute the royal arrivals.

Lord Aberdeen, who accompanied the Queen, was as disposed to be friendly as the Queen was to be amused. He chatted to Guizot and both men were assured and reassuring: the talks would be, as diplomatic talks are always alleged to be, open and frank. Guizot was pleased to hear that Lord Aberdeen had been nettled at being lectured by the Russian Ambassador in London, de Brünow, and the Princess's other old friend, Neumann, the Austrian Chargé d'Affaires, on the total folly of this royal visit. If an English Queen wished to visit a French King that was an Anglo-French affair, and had nothing whatever to do with Austria – or Russia, said Lord Aberdeen.

The *voyage en mer* took place after all (the weather being pleasant and calm). Guizot assured Darja by his daily letter that she had no cause for alarm. 'It was charming, eighteen rowers, all handsome young men in white shirts, white trousers, and such a cheerful air in spite of the sweat which poured from their bronzed foreheads.' The sea so calm, the sky so blue, what a pleasure it had been! 'At that moment I was thinking of you,' Guizot wrote to his own Princess. 'I saw you in the Royal barge, and I helped you to climb on board the Royal yacht. You were a little afraid, but I was not afraid, I held you by the arm, and I was so happy. How little external things matter when they are set against what matters to the soul, and fills it.' She may have been absent but she was always in his heart.

After the trip by sea, there was luncheon in the forest: the Duc de Monpensier made the Queen roar with laughter. There were presents to be exchanged – two Gobelin tapestries for the Queen, and a large Sèvres *coffret* showing *la toilette des femmes* of every country. He assured Darja that the *coffret* was quite 'convenable', which presupposes that the ladies had completed their *toilette*.

There was evidence that Kings and Queens were human people; coming back into the Park they went through the orchard. 'We stopped to eat peaches. The Queen bit into hers like a child, but the King took a knife out of his pocket, remarking "when one has been a poor devil like myself, one always keeps a knife in one's pocket".' They also sampled the pears, and the hazel nuts. The narrative does not say whether the King produced a pair of nutcrackers for the hazels. The Queen was cheerful and happy, Lord Liverpool roaring with laughter, Lord Aberdeen smiling shyly. Everyone went back to the château in high good humour. Which all goes to prove that simplicity was the key note of the whole successful visit.

Prince Albert was given the *Grand Cordon* of the *Legion d'honneur* – in a friendly and intimate ceremony. He pressed Guizot's hand saying: 'Now we are colleagues.' 'This pleased me', wrote Guizot, and Prince Albert added that the Order of the Garter for the King would follow next year – when he made an official visit to Windsor.

It was all very pleasant, and civilities and farewells having been exchanged, the royal yacht set off at a smart pace for Brighton on a rising tide. The visit was over. It did not achieve everything which was hoped, nor did it avoid the revolution of 1848 which brought about the downfall of Louis Philippe – and of Guizot himself.

Captain Gronow draws a clear picture of Guizot in office, and attributes the downfall of the King partially to the unpopularity of his Ministers.

M. Guizot, the austere intrigant as he has been cleverly designated, was himself of Spartan probity and proud of his comparative poverty; but at the same time he permitted, or at all events did not prevent, the peculations and speculations on the Bourse, founded on official news ... I can never forget his attitude in the Chamber of Deputies during the period immediately preceding the fall of Louis Philippe. He seemed, with his fine head thrown proudly back, his eagle glance, his hard flashing eyes, his biting sarcasm, and disdainful eloquence to hurl defiance at his adversaries, and to dare them to the combat; just as a matador strives to irritate the bull he is going to fight by dashing a scarlet flag in his face.

The gallant Captain exclaimed: 'Heaven knows, the French need no egging on *or* stirring up!'

He admitted that Guizot was totally honest and totally free from any taint of monetary peculations, but he had covered up for others. As the rest of the politicians were only in it for the money, they would not have sacrificed a thousand franc note to keep Louis Philippe on the throne. They bleated about the fact that the King had not called the Army to his aid; but they would not have helped him in any case. They had watched the mob bring about his downfall, and then, when all was quiet, crept back to become an official opposition, and to start enjoying their money all over again. Captain Gronow paints an insouciant picture of revolution as he saw it: 'I remember walking down the Boulevards which were crowded with people. It has been remarked that revolutionary movements in France never take place during very cold weather, and the last week of February 1848 was singularly mild and warm.... I felt quite certain that the persons assembled at various points were combining their plans, and that we might look out for squalls.'

The Municipal Guards did not behave well, the troops were not called out early enough, and after hanging about all day they began fraternising with the mob.

When he got to his Club, Gronow found the clubmen rejoicing at the downfall of the Ministry and deciding that it was all a storm in a teacup. Their ideas were soon shattered when a cart full of dead and dying people was dragged by with the mob shouting 'Aux Armes! Revenge our brothers!'

The usual single shot had been fired by an agent, Lagrange, at an officer who was attempting to disperse the crowd, the officer was killed instantly, and the soldiers replied by mowing down the peaceful crowd with their muskets – the revolution had started.

On his way to the Chamber of Deputies Captain Gronow met a member of his Club, one Emmanuel Arago. He was a Republican and was radiant with joy. He placed himself at the head of sixty or seventy of the armed mob, forced his way into the Chamber, and with some friends made his way to the tribune where they levelled their muskets at the heads of the President and the Deputies. The President – and the Deputies – not unnaturally fled. Arago and his friends raised an immense shout of 'Vive La Republique'. 'In this extraordinary manner, and almost I may say by chance, the Orleans dynasty ceased to reign over the French people, and Louis Philippe was driven from his throne, as he exclaimed during his flight: "Absolument comme Charles X – absolument comme Charles X!"'

The Princess and Guizot were not the only people to be swept out of the Continent by the fire of revolution. When they finally settled down for a long stay in Brighton they were joined by the Prince Metternich and his third wife.

Even a revolution did not cause the aristocratic old man to lose his sang-froid or his dignity. In the middle of the tumult at the Chancellery which preceded his fall, the man whom Canning had called the Grand Inquisitor of Europe retained his calm approach to wars and revolutions. As he walked through the buzzing throng his high forehead and carefully arranged white hair seemed to have been frozen by time. His lined face and aquiline nose expressed an air of total disdain. Thin, and elegant he wore a green tailcoat, with pale grey trousers, and round his neck a carefully arranged black silk cravat. As he walked for the last time through his Chancellery, leaning lightly on his gold-knobbed walking stick he looked on the agitated mob present as if they did not exist. No one dared to speak to him.

So now the two old lovers met again. The Princess Lieven was sixty-three and her erstwhile fascinating lover was seventy-five. When they looked at one another did either of them remember the letter he had once written to her? 'If by a cruel destiny I should not see you again for a very long time, if our next meeting was destined only to take place at an advanced age, our souls would still be as one. Two essences which have mingled as ours have done can never be sundered, they are so strongly linked as to be beyond the bounds of the merely physical. It is for us to seek that this essential joining does not fall away when we are apart.'

Thirty years on, the goal was very different. Two old aristocrats, representatives of régimes which had lost their sway in many kingdoms, met by the seaside in the cheerful atmosphere which had been created by the Regent and his fat mistress. Prince Metternich must have looked with some amusement at the bourgeois *doctrinaire* with whom the Princess had passed so many years. On her side the Princess regarded Metternich's third wife with some scepticism: 'She is fat, vulgar, good-tempered, and has easy manners; he serene, and full of self-satisfaction, and interminable chat, long, slow, and heavy, very metaphysical and boring when he is speaking of himself and his infallibility, but charming when he talks about the past, and most of all about the Emperor Napoleon.'

Ah, the past had been charming when he had sat at her feet metaphorically unravelling silk, or changing carriages to be beside her. And the glory of Napoleon? Just some ashes which had added a certain political stature to M. Guizot when they were returned to Paris.

The old lovers, Metternich and the Princess, were to meet once again in Brussels where the Metternichs finished their three years exile before returning once again in 1851 to his estates at Johannisberg: 'The Rhine runs in my veins', he wrote, 'and to look at it is an enchantment.'

For Metternich to look at the Princess was not perhaps such an enchantment: to him she seemed like an ancestor who had come down from a framed portrait on the wall. Always dressed in black, she wore a huge hat with a green veil and constantly clutched a fan in her hand. She was at one and the same time, solemn, imposing, and yet, as in her youth, always avid and agitating for news.

After her exile in England, the Princess was able to go back to Paris, and she began to appreciate the charms of the Prince Louis Napoleon, once he had been elected President of the Republic. It was as well to keep one's gaze fixed on the rising star. There was no chance of Guizot returning to office, but he came to her salon always the first, and left always the last. She took up her old habits at the rue Saint-Florentin, and renewed the lease. With the rise of Louis Napoleon she set herself the task of a *rapprochement* between France and Russia. When Eugénie, afterwards to be Louis Napoleon's wife and Empress, was engaged to him in secret, she was told that she must visit the Princess. The Princess was a power to be reckoned with, and it was as well to be regarded as her friend. The young woman saw in front of her 'an old woman, thin, dry and hard'.

This was not the woman whom Guizot visited every day. Underneath the exterior and the wrinkled face there was still the eager heart of the girl who had left the Smolny Institute when the nineteenth century was beginning, and everything seemed to be possible.

But the interview between Mlle. de Montijo and the Princess gave the assembled company food for thought. The duc de Broglie, who was present, wrote, 'I cannot forget that it was in the Princess's salon that it was the last time that I greeted the beautiful foreigner whom I had known previously as a young secretary at the Embassy and who was to be called to be Empress in a few days. The news was already circulating and all eyes were fixed on the girl.'

There was an indication of the attitude which her guests had towards the Princess Lieven. They realised that she was still a political indicator, a barometer of what was to happen. The duc added: 'As soon as I saw the hostess seat the young beauty on a high sofa while she herself sat on a low chair at her feet, I understood the choice had been made, and I had no time to lose in paying my respects, if I did not want to be mixed up with the great crowd of potentially hopeful courtiers, who no doubt had drawn the same conclusions as myself.'

The Princess had made the right decisions, but in the long run she was to draw the wrong conclusions. There is always a tendency for the party in Opposition to take the view that the country is not behind the people in power. It is a comforting thought. In this case it led Darja to write to the Tsar by way of his Foreign Minister and the Tsarina, reassuring him that there was no fear of war with the French. All the gossip and rumours which she heard round her echoed the same thing; the régime was far too fragile to sustain a prolonged foreign war, and the new French President, later to be Emperor, would yield rather than take up arms. 'Napoleon will not draw his sword', she reassured the Tsar.

The Russian Ambassador in Paris, Count de Kisseleff, had an entirely different opinion and wrote urgently to his sovereign urging caution. But the idea of winning a victory without the necessity of fighting flattered the vanity of the Tsar. He dismissed the opinions of his Ambassador and sent him a lofty reproof. The Russians became more and more hostile and arrogant. The Crimean War broke out.

The Empress Eugénie said: 'It is an embassy of women who have made war!'

The Princess Lieven, the loyal Russian had made a grave error. It was an error which was to strike hard against herself. She had often been designated a Russian spy by those who did not like her, and while she had made no secret of her correspondence with her homeland, there were also those who considered that this could be a double deception. The cleverest deceivers were those who appeared to be open and frank. The Princess had to leave her apartments, her salon, her friends, and what she continually referred to as 'mes habitudes'.

In February 1854 she found herself ostracised in Brussels with other suspect Russians. She was very sad. The country of her adoption was at war with the country of her blood. Her salon had been the last resource for civilised political conversation. Would it ever exist again? From Brussels she followed with anguish the progress of the war. The appalling casualties, and the deaths from disease. Her beloved brother Costa had died in the same way, and in the same place.

But in 1856 she was able to go back to Paris. The Tsar in whom she had believed and who had treated her with such harshness was dead. Peace was made, and she was back in her salon, one of the greatest social and political survivors of her time.

'Her salon is becoming important again in diplomatic circles. I am sure that after the mothers whose sons have come safely back from the Army, no one is happier or more jubilant at the idea of peace than Madame de Lieven ... there are not too many people *chez elle* so far, but enough to keep ennui at bay.'

She was nearly seventy-two and her health had never been good, but now she seemed to decline a little, although she never lost her interest in the things around her, or her power to comment on them. Once she had been afraid of death, but when it approached she faced it with calm and with confidence.

She became reconciled with her son Paul, and when she saw him crying beside her bed, she said gently to Guizot: 'He has a tender heart. You must always regard him as your friend, I ask that of you.'

She had heard that an old friend of hers had just arrived in Paris, and sent a message: 'You are arriving, and I am going so far away, come quickly before it is too late.'

The Pastor Cuvier came to give her the sacrament which she received simply, serenely, and with sad dignity. To the last she remained conscious of the social niceties, planning the menu for her Benckendorff nephew and niece who had arrived from Stuttgart. To her doctor she said: 'If I do not die this time, it will be a pity, I am ready.'

Feeling herself choking she asked for her fan. They tried to relieve her pain with a plaster, and she wrote quite clearly in English: 'How long must it remain?' And then a few moments later she said to Guizot: 'Leave me, leave me, I wish to sleep.'

Between living and dying the shadows came out of the past – she was peering into the snowy street – no one except the sentry – what was that carriage speeding so swiftly along? She could not see the faces. There was danger. Danger for Bonsi. England, the green fields – the country houses – the Prince Regent peering from the shrubbery into her bedroom – the Duke smiling as he leaned over the piano – Neumann singing – Spa in the sparkling autumn sunshine, she was in the carriage with Metternich, he took her hand, vowing eternal love – but poor Bonsi, she had her duty! Marital rights, his two 'English children', George and Arthur, the terror of her return to Russia – 'it will kill me' – the little coffins, she could not go back to Petersburg, they must understand. 15 June

247

– Guizot understood her sorrows – 'C'était pour toujours' –
Guizot, 'mon bien aimé' – 'merci pour vingt années'...

When Paul, her son and Guizot had left the room, she died quietly.
She had not wished that they should see her in her last agony. It was
a triumph of good manners over death.

An hour after her death Paul gave Guizot a letter which she had
written and sealed the evening before. 'I thank you for twenty
years of affection and happiness. Do not forget me. Adieu, adieu.
And do not refuse the carriage.' She had always been disturbed that
Guizot had no carriage and had often repeated, 'I do not mind that
you are not rich, that pleases me. But I shall never resign myself to
the fact that you have no carriage.' She left him her carriage and
8,000 francs to pay for its upkeep. She was practical to the last.

She wished for no funeral service, just a few prayers in her room
and then her body to be put immediately on the train for Courland.
She wished to lie beside George and Arthur in their family vault in
the Castle at Mitau.

Her friends sincerely mourned her passing. 'This is a death
which touched me very deeply and a void which will never be
filled. Without being one of the intimates of the Princess,' wrote
the historian Barante, 'I had much pleasure in her society; c'était
une personne d'une haute raison and d'un caractère noble et sur.'

It is a good epitaph for an aristocrat.

Select Bibliography

Aberdeen, Lord, *Correspondence of Lord Aberdeen and Princess Lieven 1832–1854*, ed. E. Jones Parry, London 1938.

Alison, Sir A., *Lives of Lord Castlereagh and Sir Charles Stewart*, 3 vols., Edinburgh & London, 1861.

Almedingham, E. M., *So Dark a Stream*, London 1959.

Askwith, B., *Piety and Wit: A Biography of Harriet Granville*, London 1982.

Balzac, H. de, *La Princesse de Cadignan*, Paris 1869.

Boigne, Mme de, *Recits d'une Tante* (Mémoires de la Comtesse de Boigne née d'Osmond), 3 vols., Paris 1907.

Bryant, A., *Years of Endurance 1793–1802*, London 1942.
Years of Victory 1802–1812, London 1944.

Byron, Lord, *Poetical Works of Lord Byron*, Vols. 5 & 6, London 1856.

Chambonas, Comte A. de la Garden, *Souvenirs du Congrès de Vienna*, Paris 1901.

Chateaubriand, F. R., Vicomte de, *Mémoirs d'outre Tombe*, édition du centenaire intégrale et critique en partie inédite. Etablie par Maurice Levaillant, 4 vols., Paris 1949.

Cooper, A. Duff, *Talleyrand*, London 1932.

Coughlan, R., *Elizabeth and Catherine*, ed. Jay Bould, Millington 1974.

Creevey, T., *The Creevey Papers*, ed. Sir H. Maxwell, 2 vols., London 1903.

Croker, J. W., *The Croker Papers*, ed. L. J. Jennings, 3 vols. London 1884.

Custine, Marquis, *Journey for our Time* (The Journals of the Marquis of Custine) ed. & trans. P. P. Kohler, London 1953.

Daudet, E., *Une vie d'ambassadrice au siècle dernier, La Princesse de Lieven*, Paris 1903.

Fitzgerald, T. P., *The Political and Private Life of the Marquess of*

Londonderry, Dublin 1822.

Fouché, J., *Memoirs of Joseph Fouché, Duke of Otranto*, London 1892.

Fulford, R. T. B., *George IV*, London 1935.

Grant, Mrs. Colquhoun, *Mother of Czars*, London 1905.

Granville, Harriet Countess, *Letters of Harriet Countess Granville 1810–1845*, ed. The Hon. F. Leveson Gower, 2 vols., London 1894.

Greville, C., *Journal of the Reigns of King George IV and King William IV*, eds. L. Strachey and R. Fulford, London 1937.

Grey, Earl, *Correspondence of Princess Lieven and Earl Grey*, ed. & trans. G. Le Strange, London 1890.

Gronow, R. H., *Reminiscences and Recollections of Captain Gronow 1810–1860*, 2 vols., London 1892.

Grunwald, C. de, *La Vie de Metternich*, Paris 1938.

Guedalla, P., *The Duke*, London 1937.

Guizot, F., *An Embassy to the Court of St. James's in 1840*, London 1862.
   Lettres de François Guizot et de la Princesse de Lieven, Preface de Jean Schlumberger, annotée par Jacques Naville, 3 vols., Paris 1963.

Hanoteau, J., *Lettres du Prince de Metternich à la Comtesse de Lieven 1818–1819*, Paris 1909.

Hassall, A., *Viscount Castlereagh*, London 1908.

Hennings, C. T., *Eastern Europe*, London 1846.

Holme, T., *Prinny's Daughter*, London 1976.
   Caroline, London 1979.

Jackson, J. H., *Estonia*, London 1948.

Lagny, G. de., *The Knout and the Russians or the Muscovite Empire, the Czar and his people*, trans. from the French, London 1854.

Leigh, I., *Castlereagh*, London 1951.

Londonderry, Marchioness, of, *Russian Journal of Lady Londonderry 1836–1837*, ed. W. A. C. Seaman & J. R. Sewell, London 1973.

Lieven, Princess Dorothea, *The Lieven-Palmerston Correspondence*, trans. & ed. Lord Sudeley, London 1943.

Lieven, Princess Dorothea, *The Private Letters of Princess Lieven to Prince Metternich 1820–1826*, ed. P. Quennell, London 1937.

Maurois, A., *Chateaubriand*, Paris 1938.
   History of France, London 1949.
   Byron, 2 vols., Paris 1930.

Metternich, Prince, *Memoirs of Prince Metternich*, Vols. III & IV, London 1881.

Nicolson, H., *The Congress of Vienna*, London 1946.

Plamenetz, J., *Revolutionary Movement in France 1815–1871*, London 1952.

Priestley, J. B., *Prince of Pleasure*, London 1969.

Rappoport, A. *The Curse of the Romanovs*, London 1907.

Réau, L., *St. Petersburg*, Paris 1913.

Reinbeck, G., *Travels from St. Petersburg*, trans. from German, London 1807.

Ridley, J., *Lord Palmerston*, New York 1971.

Robinson, L. ed., *Letters of Princess Lieven during her residence in London 1812–1834*, London 1902.

Sauvigny, G. A. de Bertier de, *Metternich et la France après le Congrès de Vienna*, 2 vols. Paris 1968.

Sorel, A., *L'Europe et la Revolution Française*, Paris 1904.

Stapleton, A. G., *The Political Life of the Rt. Hon. George Canning*, 3 vols., London 1831.

Strachey, L., *Portraits in Miniature* (Queen Victoria), London 1931.

Temperley, H., *Unpublished Diary and Political Sketches of Princess Lieven together with some of her letters*, London 1925.

Tocqueville, A. de, *The Ancient Regime and the French Revolution*, London 1966.

Turgenev, I., *Home of the Gentry*,
Fathers and Sons, London 1955

Wilmot, M. & C., *The Russian Journals of Martha and Catherine Wilmot*, London 1934.

Witt, Mme. de, *Monsieur Guizot dans sa famille et avec ses amies*, Paris 1880.

INDEX

Aberdeen, Lord 188, 192, 193–4, 205,
209, 211, 225, 226, 232
accompanies Queen Victoria to
France 241, 242
Aix-la-Chapelle, Congress of (1818)
80, 87
social life at 87–8
Albert, Prince 241, 242
Alexander I, Grand Duke and Tsar 5,
10, 18, 19, 20, 23, 25, 28, 53, 54,
62, 69, 84, 114, 138, 149, 151, 170,
171
fall from liberalism 171–2
happiness at accession of 30–1
life and reign: part in conspiracy
against father 21, 22; becomes
Tsar 26; hears of father's death
29–30; turns on conspirators 33;
signs treaty of Tilsit with
Napoleon 45; reconciled with
English 51; appoints Count
Lieven ambassador to London
52; visits England 60–1; ignores
Prince Regent's banquet 60–1;
sees England's Whig leaders 61;
wish to intervene in Greece 117,
172; death (1825) 175
portrait 32
Anne, Grand Duchess 16
Apponyi, Count 240
Apponyi, Countess 155, 211
Arago, Emmanuel 243
Arakcheiv, Count 7–8, 23
Arbuthnot, Mrs. 186
Austria
crushes Piedmont and Naples 116

Bagration, Count 86
Bagration, Princess Catherine 85, 86
bears child to Metternich 86
Balzac, Honoré de
portrait of Guizot and Princess
Lieven in *Les Secrets de la
Princesse de Cadignan* 230–1
Bankhead, Dr. 131, 132
Beauséjour, Passy 231, 240
Benckendorff, Baron Christopher
(father) 2, 6, 10, 14
death 143, 145
Benckendorff, Constantine (brother)
14, 36, 37
death 188, 191, 246
death of wife 139
Benckendorff, Count (later General)
Alexander (brother) 14, 139, 190,
207, 208, 210, 220, 224, 228
Darja's letters to 35–6, 40–6 *passim*,
53, 61–8 *passim*, 99, 103, 104–5,
109, 137, 146, 167, 178, 183,
185–6, 188, 191, 196, 199, 220
promoted captain 46
promoted Chief of Secret Police
177–8, 180
rumour of marriage of 66
tool of Tsar 227
Benckendorff, Dorothea von, *see*
Lieven, Princess de
Benckendorff, Maria (sister) 14, 40, 47
Bennigsen, General 21, 25, 26, 30, 44
Bessborough, Lady 63, 77
Boigne, Countess de 76, 215
on Count Lieven 77
on Darja 77

Bonneval, Marquis de 156, 157
Boris Godunov 227
Bouille, Marquis de 86
    on Metternich 86
Branicka, Countess 9
Brighton 64, 73, 98, 117, 118
    Pavilion 74, 142
Broglie, Duc de 210, 214, 239
Broron-Camus, Count 8, 9
Brünow, Count de 235, 238, 241
Buckhausen, Consul-General 199
Byron, Lord 145
    attacks Castlereagh 129, 132
    Cain 146
    Don Juan 132

Canning, George 135, 140. 141, 154,
        159, 160, 163, 168, 173, 174, 180
    death (1827) 182
    discomfited in foreign policy 151
    foils Royal intrigues 148–9
    relations with Darja 178–9, 181
Canning, Sir Stratford 195
    refused entry to Russia as British
        ambassador 197
Canova 102
Capo d'Istria, Count 80, 99, 152
Carlisle, Lady 223, 226
Castlereagh, Lady (later Lady
        Londonderry) 65, 123, 126, 128
    attacked by Russian fleas 50
    on cold in Russia 49–50, 52
    on fête at Russian Court 169
    on Russian furs 50
    quarrels with George IV's mistress
        117–21 *passim*
Castlereagh, Lord (later Lord
        Londonderry) 61, 75, 76, 80, 87,
        107, 112, 153
    breakdown in King's presence
        130–1
    burial 132
    delusions of blackmail 127–8
    domestic problems 117–8, 119, 121,
        123
    improvement of relations with
        Darja 114–16, 118–19
    international problems 116–17
    overloaded with work 128–9
    portrait by Lawrence 120
    suicide 114, 131, 132
    suspicions of Wellington 122–3,

125, 126
    turns against Darja 121–3, 125
    unpopularity 129
Catherine, Grand Duchess 37
    at odds with Prince Regent 57–8, 59
    visits England (1814) 57–8, 60
    visits Whitbread's Brewery 60
Catherine the Great 2, 3, 6, 21, 29
    death 5
    disorderly life 9
    relations with Baroness Lieven 9–10
    steps towards female education 3
    tries to disinherit son 4–5
Cato Street conspiracy 107–8, 114
Caumont, Madame de 85
Charlotte, Princess 57, 59, 66
    death 69
Chateaubriand, Vicomte de 77
    at Congress of Verona 135, 136
    on Darja 135–6
    on Lieven 135
Clancarty, Lord 60, 133
Clanricarde, Lady 238
Clanwilliam, Lord 70, 71
Clarence, Duke of (later William IV)
        74, 235
    encounter with Darja 74–6
Clogher, Bishop of 127, 128, 130
Cobbett, William 132
Codrington, Adm. Sir Williams 183
Coigny, Madame de 164
Condé, Prince de 5
Conygham, Lady 73, 108, 117–27
        passim, 142, 143, 147, 159
Constantine, Grand Duke 19, 23, 29,
        30, 191, 192
    dissolute life 43
    renounces throne 175
Courland, Wilhemina de Biron de 86
Cowper, Lady (later Lady Palmerston)
        65, 127, 195, 201–9 *passim*, 233,
        238
Crimean War 246–7
Croker, J. W. 187
Cuvier, Pastor 247
Czartorsky, Count Adam 29
Czartoryski, Count 195

Decazes, Duc de 106
Decazes, Duchesse de 104
    on Darja 106–7
Devonshire, Duchess of 63, 155

Devonshire, Duke of 64, 151–2
  visit to Russia 68
Dino, Duchesse de 198, 199, 224
Dolgoruki, Prince Petrovic 42–3
  dies after duel 42
Dudley, Lord 155, 156
Durham, Lord 195, 196

Elizabeth, Empress 3
Elizabeth, Tsarina 30, 31, 37, 42, 50,
  168, 238, 239
Enghien, Duke of 41
England
  dowdy fashions 56–7
  Great Frost of 1814 56
  to Darja 55
  weather 145
Esterhazy, Count Joseph 110
Esterhazy, Prince Paul 106, 147
Esterhazy, Princess Paul 65, 71, 76, 77
Eugénie, Empress 245–6

Floret, Chevalier de 90, 91, 95
Fox, Charles James 63, 132
Franz, Emperor 84
Frederick the Great 3
Frederick William III, King of Prussia
  47
  caught between Napoleon and Tsar
  48–9
  visits England 60
Frederick William IV, King of Prussia
  239

Gagarine, Prince 18
Gasparin, Laure de 211
George IV, see Prince Regent
Gloucester, Duke of 39–40
Gortshakov, Prince 67
Granville, Harriet, Lady 63, 69, 77,
  115, 140, 146, 150, 198, 209, 218,
  223, 226, 232
  becomes Darja's friend 63
  bored by Court life 143
  on English countryside 199
  pictures of social life 70–1
  visits Maréchale Moreau 71–2
Granville, Lord 61, 64
Greece, 178, 190
  rises against Turks 116
Greville, Charles 89, 182, 195, 196,
  223

Grey, Lord 61, 127, 134, 159, 174,
  189–90, 191, 195, 200, 208
  becomes Prime Minister 190, 194
Gronow, Captain
  on Guizot 230, 242–3
Guizot, François 210, 211, 218, 240–3
  passim
  correspondence with Darja 215–17,
  221, 224–30 passim
  death of son 213
  life and career: appointed
  ambassador in London 233;
  ambassadorship 235–8; becomes
  Foreign Minister (1840) 238;
  persuades Queen Victoria to visit
  France 239; exiled in 1848 244; at
  Darja's death bed 247, 248
  love for Darja 213, 214–15, 225
  on Palmerston 236
  portrait 212
  relations with Darja after husband's
  death 229–30
  slandered by Le Temps 222–3

Hanover 112–13
  under George IV 147
Hastings, Marquess of 157
Hertford, Lady 73
Heytesbury, Lord 190, 195
Holland, Lord 61,

Ivan the Terrible 1

Jersey, Lady 65, 103, 186
Jordan, Mrs. 74
Junot, Laure 85

Kinnaird, Lord 155
Kisseleff, Count de 240, 246
Knighton, Sir William 147–8
Koutousov, General 23–4
Kutaissov, the barber 15, 18

Lansdowne, Lord 194
Lapouchkin, Prince Peter 175
Laval, Duc de 155, 156
Lebzeltern, Count 171
Lennox, Lord William Pitt 56
Leopold, Prince 66, 67, 217
Leykam, Marie-Antoinette von 163–4
  death 165
Lieven, Alexander de (son) 110, 180

207, 219, 227
Lieven, Arthur de (son) 106, 161,
 248
 death of 206
Lieven, Baroness 92; penury 8;
 offered post of Imperial
 Governess 8–9;
independence as Governess 9–10;
 situation at Court 10; death 185
Lieven, Charles de 10
Lieven, Constantine de (son) 110, 207
 death in America 225
Lieven, Count (later Prince)
 Christopher de 1, 8, 13, 20, 43,
 60, 61, 67, 76, 89, 91, 96, 102, 114,
 115, 127, 132, 139, 147, 158, 159,
 174, 185, 190, 208, 220, 224
life and career: Minister of War 10,
 14; marriage to Darja 11; loses
 favour of Paul I 17–18;
 diplomatic illness 20, 24, 31, 33;
 hears of accession of Alexander I
 27–9; survives in Alexander's
 favour 33–4; travels with Tsar
 37, 38; attendance on Tsar 40, 42;
 happy at birth of daughter 41;
 aide-de-camp to Tsar 44; returns
 to Court (1808) 46; becomes
 ambassador to Prussia 47;
 recalled to Russia (1811) 49;
 appointed ambassador to
 London 52; happy at
 appointment 52–3; sails for
 England (1812) 53; takes house in
 Streatham 54–5; role in England
 55; embassy finance 58;
 nicknamed 'Vraiment' 73; uses
 Darja's help with despatches 79;
 attends Aix-la-Chapelle
 conference 87, 88; minor role
 compared with wife's 109; takes
 boys back to Russia 110, 112;
 believes Castlereagh is mad 122,
 123; at Congress of Verona 138;
 accompanies wife to Dover 151;
 unhappy at wife's absence in
 Italy 152; welcomes wife back at
 Dover 158; elevated to rank of
 Prince 175; recalled to Russia
 (1826) 178; returns to England
 180; rumours of recall 190;
 appointed temporary Foreign

Minister 190; returns to Russia
 (1829) 191, 192; happy at recall to
 Russia (1834) 197, 206; appointed
 governor of Tsarevitch 197, 203;
 parts from wife 207; forbids wife
 to settle in Paris 210; asks to meet
 Darja 217–18; orders her to leave
 Paris 218; writes to Tsar from
 Naples (1837) 221; writes
 tenderly to Darja 226; death 226,
 229
on war with French 44–5
portrait by Lawrence 110
Lieven, George de (son) 110, 140, 205,
 248
 birth and baptism 104–5
 death 206
Lieven, Jean de 10
Lieven, Paul de (son) 67, 70–1, 168,
 227, 228, 247, 248
 fights duel in Rome 156–7
 injures ankle in Rome 157
 sent to Paris 110
Lieven, Princess de
 adoration of Tsar 185, 186, 192, 196
 appearance 77, 79
 character 146
 detractors 106
 dislike of Chateaubriand 136
 homeland 1
 hostess 107
 life: education, 3, 4, 7; plays Blind
 Man's Buff with Paul I 5; comes
 under Empress Maria's wing 6–7;
 first love 7; marriage, 11–12;
 married life in St. Petersburg 14,
 16; hears of accession of Alexander
 I 27–9; happiness at Alexander's
 accession 30–1; chronicles, early
 1800s 35–46; bored by palace
 etiquette 37–8, 39; holidays 1803
 40; aristocratic attitude to serfs
 40–1; gives birth to baby girl 41;
 bears three boys 42; devoted
 mother 42; rumoured lovers 42–
 3; humiliated by Russian defeats
 (1807) 45–6; meets Queen Louise
 of Prussia 47–8; boredom in
 Berlin 48–9; unhappy on return
 to Russia 49, 50–1; impatient to
 go to England 52–3; settles in
 Russian Embassy, London 53;

256

ecstatic at downfall of French 54,
56; first opinions of English 55–6;
initial lack of social success in
London 58–9; hatred of
Napoleon 62; blossoms in
London society 63, 64–5; attends
Prince Regent 64–5; introduces
waltz to London 65; at Almack's
65–6; friend of Princess
Charlotte 66, 67; becoming
anglicised 66–7; visits Paris 69;
social life 70–1; as intelligence
gatherer 73–4; embarassing
encounter with Duke of Clarence
74–6; meets Metternich 80; love
affair with Metternich 87, 89–96;
pregnancy (1818) 97; writes to
father (1819) 98; letter to
Metternich (1819) 103; gives birth
to fourth son 104; on problem of
godfather for son 104–5;
influence with George IV 106;
letters to Tsarina 107; bored with
husband 109; separated from
sons 110; commiserates with
Metternich on daughter's death
112; makes friends with
Castlereagh 115–16, 118–19;
soothes Lady Conynham 119,
121; loses Castlereagh's esteem
121–2; visits King at Windsor
123–4; encounters Castlereagh in
Kensington Gardens 125;
struggles to further King's
Continental journey 123–4, 126–
7; learns of Castlereagh's death
131; consults Wellington 134; at
Congress of Verona (1822) 135,
137, 138; worried about Russian
ill-will 137–8, 140; usefulness in
London to Russians 138–9; ill in
London (1823) 139–40; intimacy
with George IV 140; boredom at
Windsor and Brighton 142–3;
sorrow at father's death 145;
revises husband's despatches 147;
visits Italy in hope of seeing
Metternich 150–8; reaches Milan
via Paris and Geneva 151; dislike
of Milan 152; reaches Florence
153; in Rome 153–7; returns to
London 157–8; becomes

pregnant and loses Russian visit
158–9; resumes London life 159–
60; with King at Windsor 160–1;
delivered of fifth son 161;
frustrated of seeing Metternich
162–3; jealous of Metternich's
new wife 164–5; on position of
her sons in Russia 167–8; visits
Russia (1825) 168–73; meets
Tsar 170, 171; used as agent by
Tsar 172–3, 174; sorrow at
Alexander I's death 175; elevated
to rank of Princess 175; happy at
Nicholas I's accession 177;
relations with Canning and
George IV 178–9, 181; turns
against Wellington 181, 182, 184–
5, 187; turns against Metternich
181; happy at victory of
Navarino 183; sorrow at brother
Constantine's death 188; visits
Warsaw 191–2; mourns death of
George IV 192–3; triumphant at
result of Russo-Turkish war 193–
4; political intrigues (1830–4)
193–7; recalled to Russia (1834)
197; depressed at recall 197;
presented with bracelet as farewell
present 198; says goodbye to
England 198–201; returns to
Court life in Russia 202–5; health
deteriorates 205; saddened by
deaths of younger sons 206;
separates from husband 207;
takes cure at Baden 208, 210–11;
moves to Paris 208–9; drawn into
French politics 209, 211, 213;
visits London (1837) 215;
audience with Queen Victoria
217; ill returning to Paris 218;
refuses to return to Russia 218–
21; suffers from political gossip
222–3; learns of death of son
Constantine 225; learns of
husband's death 226; income
from husband's estate 229;
relations with Guizot after
husband's death 229–30, 231–2;
acquires house at Passy (1840)
231; advises Guizot on
ambassadorship in London 233,
236–7; visits London 237;

257

accused of being French agent
238; corresponds with Tsarina
239; exiled to England (1828) 244;
meets future Empress Eugénie
245–6; driven from France 246;
ostracised in Brussels 246–7;
returns to Paris (1856) 247;
approaching death 247–8; death
248
love for Guizot 213—17 *passim*,
221, 225
on Canning 174
on Count Pahlen 20, 22
on death of Baroness Lieven 185
on death of Castlereagh 132
on death of Princess Charlotte 69
on Lady Conyngham 108
on London riots (1816) 48–9
on Nesselrode 170–1
on Paul I 16, 17
on Peterhof 39
on Tsarevitch 203–4
on Tsarina Elizabeth 31
on Wellington 177
Paris apartments 224
portrait by Lawrence 78
portrait by Watts (1856) 234
reading matter 145–6
salon (1840s) 232–3, 239
thinness 72, 77
toilette 233
wit 66, 72
Liverpool, Lord 83, 122, 131, 159, 242
Livonia 1
German ruling classes 2
Greath Wrath in 2
London
Almack's 65–6, 72, 109
Carlton House 56, 58, 60
French Embassy (later Wallace
Collection) 235
Great Frost of 1814 56
Pulteney's Hotel 57–8, 60
riots of 1816 68–9
Russian Embassy 53
Londonderry, Lady, *see* Castlereagh,
Lady
Louis XVIII 56, 106
Louis Napoleon, Prince 245
Louis Philippe, King 238, 239, 242,
243
driven from France (1848) 244

Louise, Queen of Prussia 47–8
Luttrell, Henry
on Almack's 65

Maintenon, Madame de 3
Maria Feodorovna, Tsarina 4, 5, 11,
15, 18, 23, 92
chooses husband for Darja 7–8
guardian of Benckendorff girls 6–7
hears of husband's murder 26
interest in Smolny Institute 6
wishes to be sole empress 26, 30
Matuscevitz, Count 190, 198
Medem, Count de 218, 225
Metternich, Prince 42, 76, 79, 80, 114–
18 *passim*, 124–8 *passim*, 131, 134,
135, 136, 140, 148, 149, 151–66
passim, 170, 171, 173, 181, 198,
223
appearance 81
Carlsbad Decrees of 117
character according to others 83–4
charm 81
death of daughters 107, 110, 112
family 83
Lawrence portrait 81, 82
life and career: meets Darja 80, 84;
love affair with Darja 87, 89–96;
love letters to Darja 91–6 *passim*,
follows Darja to Brussels 95;
letters to Darja in England 97–102
passim, 107; visits Italy (1919)
101–2; sends family to Paris for
health reasons 112; meets Darja in
Hanover 112–13; at Congress of
Verona 137; with dying wife in
Paris 161–2; marries Mlle von
Leykam 163–4; exiled in 1848
244–5; meets Darja in England
244–5
manipulation of Tsar 172
marriages and love affairs 85–6
on death of second wife 165–6
on Rome 153–4
opposition to Napoleon 83
Metternich, Princess Elenora 85
death 162
Meyendorff, Baron de
on Metternich 81
Montpensier, Duc de 242
Moreau, Maréchale
on Darja 71–2

Münster, Count 147
Murat Caroline 85

Napoleon 41, 51, 57, 61, 62, 83, 89,
   114
   Austrian wife 83
   collapse of 53–4
   in Moscow 52
   on Metternich 84
   signs treaty of Tilsit with Tsar 45
Nesselrode, Count de 58, 84–91
      passim, 103, 137, 138, 139, 143,
      147, 170–1, 174, 187, 190, 195,
      196, 218
   conference with Darja 172–3
   on Metternich 87
Nesselrode, Countess de 169, 208,
      227, 239
Neumann, Baron de 65, 70, 90, 101,
      147, 241
Nicholas I, Grand Duke and Tsar 67,
      180, 204
   English view of 192
   life and reign: visit to England 67–8;
      succeeds as Tsar 175; crushes
      revolts 177, 180–1; becomes King
      of Poland 195; refuses to accept
      British ambassador 197; recalls
      the Lievens from London, 197;
      receives news from Darja via
      Tsarina 239; death 247
   portrait 176

Orloff, Count 217, 218
Osmond, Madame d' 135
Otello, Rossini's 102
Ouvarov, General 29, 37
Ozarovskys, the 160

Pahlen, Count 20, 24, 28, 33
   banished by Alexander I 33
   conspires against Paul I 20–6
      passim
Pahlen, Count Nicholas 70, 233
Palmerston, Lady, see Cowper, Lady
Palmerston, Lord 65, 186, 187, 195,
      197, 200, 208, 235, 236, 238
   becomes Foreign Minister 194
   farewell dinner for Lievens 199
   provoked by Darja 196
Pancratieff, Colonel 67
Panin, Count Nikita

banished by Alexander I 33
plots against Paul I 18, 19, 20, 22
Paul I, Grand Duke and Tsar 3, 10,
   11, 53
   caprices 15
   eccentricities 5, 6
   fear of Jacobins 16–17
   reign: comes to throne 5; turns
      against wife 7–8; builds St.
      Michael's Palace 15–16;
      conspiracy against 16–25;
      institutes reign of terror 24;
      murder 25–6, 52, 70; truth about
      murder hidden 31
Peter the Great 2
Peterhof palace 38–9, 45
Philippe, Prince, of Hombourg 154
Piozzi, Mrs.
   rents house to the Lievens 54–5
Poland
   rising against Russia crushed 195
Portland Duke of 159
Pozzo di Borgo, Count 136, 137, 150,
   151, 159, 223, 233
Prince Regent (later George IV) 18,
   55, 61, 69, 73, 121, 122, 135, 141,
   146, 151, 159, 187, 191
   cartoons of 54
   Gillray cartoon 144
   life and reign: celebrates return of
      Bourbons 56; at odds with Grand
      Duchess Catherine 57–8, 59;
      plans to welcome Tsar spoiled 60;
      snubbed by Tsar 61; receives
      Princess Lieven 64; protects her
      from Duke of Clarence 76;
      becomes King 105; godfather to
      Darja's son 105; Darja's influence
      on 106; admires Lieven's
      coiffure 109; brings Darja and
      Metternich together in Hanover
      112—13; relations with Lady
      Conynham 117–18, 119, 124;
      unwilling to make European
      journey 122–7 passim; final
      audience with Castlereagh 130–1;
      liking for George de Lieven 140;
      life at Windsor and Brighton 142–
      3, 147–8; offers use of yacht to
      Darja 158; entertains Darja at
      Windsor 160–1; reconciled with
      Canning 174; death 192–3

unpopularity 59, 192

Réau, Louis 4, 24
Recamier, Juliette de 135
Reinbeck, G. 7, 11
  on a Court ball supper 12
Richelieu, Duc de 98
Riga 2, 8, 10
  serfs for sale in 2
  University of Dorpat 110, 207
  welcomes Alexander I 38
Rigascher Anzeiger 2
Robinson, Hon. Mrs. 61
Rome 153–4, 155
Rotopshin, Count 23
Russo-Turkish war 187, 188, 189,
  190, 193

St. Cyr, Convent of 3
St. Petersburg 2, 9, 14, 52, 56
  in winter 4
  St. Michael's Palace 15–16, 19, 27,
  29
  Winter Palace 3, 14, 15, 21, 27, 30
Sagan, Princesse de 85, 89
Sardinia, Queen of 136
Saxe, Chevalier de 58
Scherbatov, Prince 38
Schilling, Baroness Charlotte
  (mother) 3
  banished from Court 6
  death 5–6
Scott, Sir Walter 145, 227
Seymour, Lord George 128, 129
Shakespeare 146
Shelley, Percy Bysshe
  attacks Castlereagh 129
Sheridan, R. B. 60, 63
Sidmouth, Lord 129
Smolny Convent (later Institute) 3, 5,
  6
  building's appearance 3–4
Sophia Dorothea, Grand Duchess 3
Soult, Marshal 233, 238
Souvaroff, Marshall 5, 10
Stewart, Lord 123–6 *passim*
Strachey, Lytton 214
Strangways, Lord 172

Talisin, General 37
Talleyrand, Prince de 84, 223, 224,
  235

on Metternich 83–4
Temple, Hon. William 186
Temps, Le 222
Thames
  frozen in 1814 56
Thiers, Adolphe 209, 210, 232, 238
Thrale, Henry 54
Tilsit, treaty of 45, 51
Times, The
  on Lieven's recall to Russia 197–8
Trollope, Mrs.
  on Metternich 81
Troubetskoi, Prince 175
Tsarevitch 203–4, 228
Turks
  defeated at Navarino 183
  massacre Greeks 116–17, 128
  see also Russo-Turkish war

Upel, Pastor 2

Verona, Congress of 114, 121, 127,
  128, 130, 134, 135, 139
Victoria, Queen 217
  visits France 239, 240–2
Voltaire 3

Walmoden, Count 154
Wellesley, Lady Georgina 163
Wellesley, Marquess 160
Wellington, Duke of 56, 61, 70, 90,
  105, 122–6 *passim*, 129, 138, 140,
  142, 151, 159, 163, 173, 181, 189,
  194
  attends Congress of Verona 137
  barred from Almack's 66
  becomes Prime Minister 183–4
  on foreign affairs 135
  patience with Darja 184, 189
  sends for doctor for Castlereagh 131
  sent to Russia to congratulate new
  Tsar Nicholas I 177, 178
Werther, M. de 132
Whitbread, Samuel 60
Whitworth, Sir Charles 23
William IV, *see* Clarence, Duke of
  Windsor
  'Cottage' 64, 73, 106, 123, 124, 141,
  142, 146, 161
  'Cottage Coterie' 147–8, 149, 159
  routine at 142
Wittgenstein, Count 67

260

Worcester, Lord 70
Woronzow, Count Simon
    Romanovich 19
  as Russian ambassador in England
    51
  settles in England 51
Woronzow, Prince Michael
    Semenovitch 68

York, Duke of 151, 160

Zichy, Countess 164
Zubova, Olga 23, 24, 43
Zubovs, the 36
  conspire against Paul I 21, 24–6
    passim
  inform Alexander I of his father's
    death 29, 30